For my mother and father

Wordsworth and the Poetry of Human Suffering

JAMES H. AVERILL

Cornell University Press

ITHACA AND LONDON

Cornell University Press gratefully acknowledges a
grant from the Andrew W. Mellon Foundation
that aided in bringing this book to publication.

First published 1980 by Cornell University Press.
Published in the United Kingdom by Cornell University Press Ltd.,
2-4 Brook Street, London W1Y 1AA.

International Standard Book Number 0-8014-1249-8
Library of Congress Catalog Card Number 79-21783
Printed in the United States of America
*Librarians: Library of Congress cataloging information
appears on the last page of the book.*

H 23 739 868 0

Contents

Preface

This book is a study of the Wordsworthian spectator and the suffering to which he responds. It explores questions of tragic response and sentimental morality, the literary uses of other people's misery, and the pleasures of tragedy. My protagonist is the authorial self of Wordsworth's narrative poems, who hovers over the actions and feelings of the characters, responding at once to them and to the feelings they evoke within him. Such a figure is not uncommon in the self-conscious works of late-eighteenth-century sentimentalism, but the intermediary presence between reader and story particularly characterizes Wordworth's pathos. The interplay of mind and suffering is the subject that engages him most, after the relation of mind and nature.

It is ironic that Wordsworth has become famous as the poet of nature. His wish, the dream of the unfinished *Recluse,* was to be equally the poet of man:

> On Man, on Nature, and on human Life,
> Thinking in solitude, from time to time
> I feel sweet passions traversing my Soul
> Like Music; unto these, where'er I may,
> I would give utterance in numerous verse.[1]

[1]Text from Beth Darlington, ed., *Home at Grasmere* (Ithaca, N.Y.: Cornell University Press, 1977), p. 100.

The poetry of "human passions, human characters, and human incidents"[2] is for Wordsworth inevitably the poetry of suffering. He does not avert his eyes from wretchedness; quite the contrary, he seems fascinated by it. The *Lyrical Ballads* and the narrative poems from *Salisbury Plain* to *The White Doe of Rylstone* brood upon "Sorrow that is not sorrow, but delight, / And miserable love that is not pain / To hear of."[3]

In his poems on human life, Wordsworth appears as the heir to Steele, Richardson, Sterne, and Goldsmith. The depiction of "objects of distress," for the edification and perhaps titillation of the reader, is the central convention of the Age of Sensibility. Even in his mature work, Wordsworth draws more from the sentimental movement than does any other major English Romantic poet. The people he writes about are those who typically interest the "sentimental traveller."[4] Betrayed women, beggars, maniacs, discharged soldiers, and decrepit old men fairly litter the countryside through which a Yorick or a Harley roams. Indeed, Henry MacKenzie's lachrymose man of feeling encounters each of these (as we think them) Wordsworthian figures. Harley finds in them the powerful emotions by which he defines himself. The dry-eyed poet who is the central figure of Wordsworth's poetry seeks also for such "appropriate human centres" to locate himself in a "hurrying world" (*Prel* [1850] IV, 355–360). If the sentimental response is muted in Wordsworth, the situation, emotion, and vocabulary used are similar. In *Prelude* IV (1805), for instance, the poet "peruses" the Discharged Soldier with a "mingled sense of fear and sorrow"; later he feels "astonishment" to behold the "tall and ghastly figure" moving

[2]William Wordsworth, "Advertisement" to *Lyrical Ballads* (1798), in *The Prose Works of William Wordsworth*, ed. W. J. B. Owen and Jane W. Smyser (Oxford: Clarendon, 1974), I, 116. *The Prose Works* are hereafter cited as *Prose*.

[3]*Prelude* [1805], XII, 245–247, in *The Prelude*, ed. Ernest de Selincourt (rev. Helen Darbishire; Oxford: Clarendon, 1959). This edition of *The Prelude* is hereafter cited as *Prel*.

[4]Wordsworth uses this commonplace phrase in reference to himself in a note to *Descriptive Sketches* (1793). R. F. Brissenden, *Virtue in Distress* (London: Macmillan, 1974), pp. 3–10, 218–267, discusses the figure of the traveler in sentimental fiction.

beside him. Harley, as he listens to an insane girl cry like Wordsworth's Mad Mother, "My brain is dry; and it burns, it burns, it burns," feels "astonishment and pity."[5] Harley's final response, inevitably, is to "burst into tears," and Wordsworth's to seek "with quiet heart my distant home," but the essential drama of both encounters lies in the compassionate, benevolent response to human suffering.

Of course, it should hardly be surprising to find in Wordsworth a man of his time; the poet himself admits, in the "Essay, Supplementary to the Preface," that "the predecessors of an original Genius of a high order will have smoothed the way for all that he has in common with them;—and much he will have in common." This statement, like much Wordsworthian modesty, is qualified: "but, for what is peculiarly his own, he will be called upon to clear and often to shape his own road:—he will be in the condition of Hannibal among the Alps" (*Prose*, III, 80). Certainly his contemporaries noted the originality, not to say peculiarity, of his treatment of pathetic materials. They recognized in Wordsworth's writing a reworking and intensification of what sentimentalism conventionally labeled "the pathetic." Thus, in "My First Acquaintance with Poets," William Hazlitt recalls that "in the *Thorn*, the *Mad Mother*, and the *Complaint of a Poor Indian Woman*, I felt that deeper power and pathos which have been since acknowledged, 'In spite of pride, in erring reason's spite,' as the characteristics of this author; and the sense of a new style and a new spirit in poetry came over me." The otherwise hostile Francis Jeffrey felt obliged to acknowledge that the *Lyrical Ballads* "were undoubtedly characterised by a strong spirit of originality, of pathos, and natural feeling."[6]

One might multiply quotations to suggest that his contemporaries, rather more than modern readers, saw Wordsworth as

---

[5]Henry MacKenzie, *The Man of Feeling*, ed. Brian Vickers (London: Oxford University Press, 1967), pp. 34–35.

[6]*The Collected Works of William Hazlitt*, ed. A. R. Waller and Arnold Glover (London: Dent, 1902–1904), XII, 270; review of *Poems in Two Volumes* in *Edinburgh Review* 11 (1807), rpt. in Elsie Smith, ed., *An Estimate of William Wordsworth by His Contemporaries 1793–1822* (Oxford: Blackwell, 1932), p. 76.

a hawker of strikingly original, but recognizably sentimental, wares.[7] It was left to Coleridge, however, to define the nature of this peculiarly Wordsworthian sentimentalism. Fifth in *Biographia Literaria*'s list of Wordsworth's excellences is "a meditative pathos, a union of deep and subtle thought with sensibility; a sympathy with man as man; the sympathy indeed of a contemplator, rather than a fellow-sufferer or co-mate, (spectator, haud particeps) but of a contemplator, from whose view no difference of rank conceals the sameness of the nature; no injuries of wind or weather, or toil, or even of ignorance, wholly disguise the human face divine."[8] Coleridge delights in the mental activity concerning the stuff of suffering which he finds in Wordsworth's poetry. The contemplator is rather more interesting to Coleridge than the suffering contemplated. The aptness and power of his phrase "meditative pathos" is apparent. The union of thought and sensibility is indeed the focus of Wordsworth's poetry of human life.

Like many of Coleridge's phrases, "meditative pathos" does not belong entirely to its author. Coleridge is, in fact, drawing on Wordsworth's discussion of "the pathetic" in "Essay, Supplementary to the Preface." There, two "emotions of the pathetic" are discriminated. One, presumably innate pity or sympathy, is "simple and direct" and "participates of an *animal* sensation"; the second is "complex and revolutionary," in the sense not of being jacobinical but of revolving within the self. The "Essay" continues: "There is also a meditative, as well as a human, pathos; an enthusiastic, as well as an ordinary, sorrow; a sadness that has its seat in the depths of reason, to which the mind cannot sink gently of itself—but to which it must descend by treading the steps of thought" (*Prose*, III, 82–83). In asserting a response to suffering that causes the mind to go into itself, Wordsworth describes his wish for his own poetry. He values,

[7]See, for instance, Smith, ed., *Estimate*, pp. 34–37, 40–41, 48–51, 74, 93, 99–104.
[8]Samuel Taylor Coleridge, *Biographia Literaria*, ed. J. Shawcross (Oxford: Clarendon, 1907; rpt. 1973), II, 122–123.

like Coleridge, a pathos that not only appeals to crude emotion but also dramatizes the power of mind in its engagement with tragic materials. The poetry resulting from this double purpose has a dual focus, presenting not only the tragedy but also the response to it.

This book proceeds in a chronological manner, largely because Wordsworth's meditative pathos is a product of his growth as a poet. His earliest efforts to use tragic materials were imitative and conventional, plainly revealing his roots in the Age of Sensibility. From these beginnings evolved the quite different pathetic mode of the *Lyrical Ballads:* I am as concerned to discover continuities as to remark on the obvious changes in Wordsworth's manner and art.

The early poems no doubt offer a more "direct" pathos than the poems of *Lyrical Ballads.* They are largely concerned with provoking the "animal sensations" of emotive response. Yet, even in such poems as *An Evening Walk, Descriptive Sketches,* and *Salisbury Plain,* Wordsworth is not content merely to describe a pathetic scene or episode; he also suggests a possible, and rather unobvious, response to the suffering. Descriptions of natural tranquillity follow narratives of human suffering throughout Wordsworth's early poetry. The juxtaposition of suffering and calm forms an important pattern of the poet's imagination, one which incorporates a cathartic response in the experience of pathos. Thus, even before he starts to explore the more problematic issues of sentimental literature, Wordsworth needs to describe the revolution within the self caused by the contemplation of human suffering.

In 1798, however, as his interest in psychology comes to bear on his commitment to a poetry delineating human characters, passions, and incidents, Wordsworth begins to analyze various contemporary theories of tragic response. The result is a tenacious and sensitive exploration of the problems of exploiting human misery in literature. Wordsworth becomes aware of the peculiar moral status of sentimental pleasure, and a major effort of *Lyrical Ballads* and *The Prelude* is to create and legitimize a poetry that can depend on suffering for excitement without seeming ghoulish or morbid. This effort is not entirely successful, but the poet neither glosses over troublesome aspects of the issues involved nor surrenders to facile and simplistic explanations. He does not reach any permanent or final conclusions, and, indeed, after 1805, the center of his inquiry shifts to the metaphysical problem of evil, to suffering taken as a theological issue. It is a mark of Wordsworth's firmness of purpose and ambitious honesty, however, that he pursues the vexed question of the imagination's relation to human suffering as long as he does. The poet's struggle to domesticate an important, yet obscure and morally uncomfortable, source of his imaginative power presents an interesting and edifying spectacle. In another age, I should have said, not wrongly, that such a drama instructs and gives pleasure.

I welcome the opportunity to recognize the contributions of others to this work. My first and greatest debt is to Stephen Parrish, in whose seminar the idea that has become this book germinated. His encouragement and enthusiasm gave me the confidence to develop the idea, and his knowledge of Wordsworth and his advice in stylistic matters have served me well through multiple revisions.

I am also grateful to those others who have guided my studies of Wordsworth and the Romantic background: Dennis Huston, Harold Bloom, Geoffrey Hartman, Neil Hertz, Stephen Gill, Susan Morgan, and Reeve Parker. In reading and annotating parts of this work, Lawrence Lipking has given generously of his time and comments; Mark Reed and James Butler have provided useful information about the manuscripts. My debts to many Wordsworthians will be evident throughout, but I owe particular thanks to M. H. Abrams, whose labors as scholar, teacher, and reader have been of inestimable value in this undertaking.

Portions of Chapters 2, 3, and 4 appeared in different form in "Suffering and Calm in Wordsworth's Early Poetry," *Publications of the Modern Language Association* 91 (1976), 223–234. Part of Chapter 5 was used to quite different purpose in "Wordsworth and 'Natural Science': The Poetry of 1798," *Journal of English and Germanic Philology* 77 (1978), 232–246. The editors of those publications have given permission to use these materials here. The Oxford editions of the writings of William Wordsworth, Dorothy Wordsworth, and Samuel Taylor Coleridge are quoted by permission of Oxford University Press. The excerpt from "Esthétique du Mal," from *The Collected Poems of Wallace Stevens* (New York: Knopf, 1954), copyright 1954 by Wallace Stevens, is quoted by permission of Alfred A. Knopf, Inc.

I am grateful to the Trustees of Dove Cottage for the opportunity to examine Cornell University Library's microfilms of their Wordsworth manuscripts and for permission to use relevant material from them. The staffs of the rare book departments of the Cornell and Princeton university libraries have been genial and helpful, and Marilyn Walden has patiently helped with the final typescript. Financial support has been provided at various stages by the Cornell University Graduate School and the Princeton University Committee on Research in the Humanities and Social Sciences.

JAMES H. AVERILL

Princeton, New Jersey

Abbreviations

BL   Samuel Taylor Coleridge, *Biographia Literaria,* ed. J. Shawcross, 2 vols. (Oxford: Clarendon Press, 1907; rpt. 1973).

BWS   *Bicentenary Wordsworth Studies in Memory of John Alban Finch,* ed. Jonathan Wordsworth (Ithaca, N.Y.: Cornell University Press, 1970).

Chalmers   Alexander Chalmers, ed., *The Works of the English Poets,* 21 vols. (London: J. Johnson et al., 1810).

DC MS.   Dove Cottage Manuscript.

DWJ   *Journals of Dorothy Wordsworth,* ed. Mary Moorman (London: Oxford University Press, 1971).

EL   *The Letters of William and Dorothy Wordsworth: The Early Years, 1787–1805,* ed. Ernest de Selincourt (2d ed., rev. Chester L. Shaver; Oxford: Clarendon Press, 1967).

ML   *The Letters of William and Dorothy Wordsworth: The Middle Years, 1806–1820,* ed. Ernest de Selincourt (2d ed., rev. Mary Moorman and Alan G. Hill, 2 vols.; Oxford: Clarendon Press, 1969, 1970).

Moorman   Mary Moorman, *William Wordsworth: A Biography,* 2 vols. (Oxford: Clarendon Press, 1957, 1965).

Prel   *The Prelude,* ed. Ernest de Selincourt (rev. Helen Darbishire; Oxford: Clarendon Press, 1959). Unless otherwise noted, the 1805 text is cited.

Prose   *The Prose Works of William Wordsworth,* ed. W. J. B. Owen and Jane W. Smyser, 3 vols. (Oxford: Clarendon Press, 1974).

PW   *The Poetical Works of William Wordsworth,* ed. Ernest de Selincourt (rev. Helen Darbishire, 5 vols.; Oxford: Clarendon Press, 1952–1959).

RC & P   "The Ruined Cottage" and "The Pedlar," ed. James Butler (Ithaca, N.Y.: Cornell University Press, 1979).

Reed EY   Mark L. Reed, *Wordsworth: The Chronology of the Early Years, 1770–1799* (Cambridge: Harvard University Press, 1967).

Reed MY   Mark L. Reed, *Wordsworth: The Chronology of the Middle Years, 1800–1815* (Cambridge: Harvard University Press, 1975).

SPP   *The Salisbury Plain Poems of William Wordsworth,* ed. Stephen Gill (Ithaca, N.Y.: Cornell University Press, 1975).

STCL   *Collected Letters of Samuel Taylor Coleridge,* ed. Earl Leslie Griggs, 6 vols. (Oxford: Clarendon Press, 1956–1971).

STCNB   *The Notebooks of Samuel Taylor Coleridge,* ed. Kathleen Coburn, 3 vols. to date (New York: Pantheon Books and Princeton, N.J.: Princeton University Press, 1957—).

Note on Quotations from Wordsworth

The de Selincourt–Darbishire *Poetical Works* and *Prelude* and the Owen-Smyser *Prose Works* are the primary texts used in this book. In the case of poems from *Lyrical Ballads,* however, I have drawn quotations from the earliest published versions: 1798 for the first volume, and 1800 for the second.

Wordsworth and the
Poetry of Human Suffering

1 The Sentimental Background

Los wept obscur'd with mourning,
His bosom earthquak'd with sighs;
He saw Urizen deadly black,
In his chains bound, & Pity began,

In anguish dividing & dividing,
For pity divides the soul
In pangs, eternity on eternity,
Life in cataracts pour'd down his cliffs.
The void shrunk the lymph into Nerves
Wand'ring wide on the bosom of night
And left a round globe of blood
Trembling upon the Void.

—Blake, *The First Book of Urizen*

I

We are apt to forget the closeness of Wordsworth's links to late-eighteenth-century sentimentalism. His restrained, delicately mannered pathos enables us to respond to his stories of little girls lost and bereaved shepherds, even while we relegate *The Man of Feeling* and *The Vicar of Wakefield* to the ash heap of literary historical documents. Nonetheless, born the year of Chatterton's suicide, coming to manhood in a decade which enthusiastically read Helen Maria Williams, Anna Seward, Charlotte Smith, William Bowles, and Vicesmus Knox, the young Wordsworth shared with his age the taste for these and similar writers. It was a time when people read *Clarissa, La Nouvelle Héloïse, Die Räuber,* and *Werther,* not for the vitality of language and oddness of circumstance we might find in them, but for "sentiment," the exciting stimulation of fictional suffering. Later on, certainly, Wordsworth would denounce "frantic novels, sickly and stupid German Tragedies, and deluges of idle and extravagant stories in verse" (*Prose,* I, 128). His juvenilia, however, reveal the extent to which the energy of denunciation came from the denial of a past self, the casting out of the daemon of sensibility.

To later readers, sentimentalism, with its "eternal talking of *love,* and *woe,* and *delicious tears,*"[1] its repetitive depictions of virtue in distress, its orgy of sensibility with little enough sense, has often seemed mere foolishness. It is not quite that. Eighteenth-century sentimentalism is not naive, simple, or simple-minded, nor even primarily emotional. Coleridge accurately characterizes much of the literature Wordsworth read in his youth when he speaks of "the loaded sensibility, the minute detail, the morbid consciousness of every thought and feeling in the whole flux and reflux of the mind, in short the self-involution and dreamlike continuity of Richardson" (*BL,* II, 183). Sympathetic response to pathetic situations provides the emotional turbulence which such a consciousness demands. The central interest, however, is psychological, and even experimental. Thus, Henry MacKenzie, explaining the genesis of *The Man of Feeling,* writes, "I was somehow led to think of introducing a Man of Sensibility into different Scenes where his Feelings might be seen in their Effects."[2] Walter Scott said, in his essay on MacKenzie, that the purpose of such a work is to represent "the effect of incidents, whether important or trifling, upon the human mind";[3] it is also, one might fairly say, "to follow the fluxes and refluxes of the mind when agitated by the great and simple affections of our nature" (*Prose,* I, 126).

Sentimentalism is but one element of the late eighteenth century's quest for untapped emotion and unusual literary experi-

---

[1]This phrase is from an anonymous review of Helen Maria Williams' *Poems,* in *European Magazine* 10 (1786), 178.

[2]Henry MacKenzie, *Letters to Elizabeth Rose of Kilravock on Literature, Events, and People, 1768–1815,* ed. Horst W. Drescher (Edinburgh: Oliver and Boyd, 1967), p. 16.

[3]Walter Scott, *Lives of the Novelists* (London: Everyman, 1910), p. 298.

ence.[4] The craving for extremes present in Rousseau, Sterne, Lewis, Blake, Sade, Radcliffe, and the *Sturm und Drang* movement epitomizes the spirit of the age. The demand for artistic originality impelled writers to find new and outlandish forms of excitement. Sensibility's characteristic literary modes, the gothic and the sublime as well as the sentimental, reflect this reaching after exotic and extravagant fruit. Instead of an alp or a ghoul-haunted castle, sentimentalism focuses on human suffering, but it differs less than might be expected from other versions of the era's quest for emotional energy.[5] A contemporary heroine feels her compassionate heart *soften, melt,* or *dissolve* with *tenderness, enthusiastic sentiments,* or *sensibility* indiscriminately at the sight of a ruin, a waterfall, or an appropriate representative of suffering humanity. The flexibility with which the characteristic terms could be applied is evident as the title character of Wollstonecraft's *Mary* (1788) writes about "Sensibility." Having aided a bereft widow, Mary scribbles a "rhapsody" in the notebook she carries for such an occasion:

> It is this quickness, this delicacy of feeling, which enables us to relish the sublime touches of the poet, and the painter; it is this,

[4]For a general sense of what used to be called "pre-Romanticism," I am indebted to numerous studies of the literature of sensibility, notably: Louis Bredvold, *The Natural History of Sensibility* (Detroit: Wayne State University Press, 1962); Martin Price, *To the Palace of Wisdom* (Carbondale: Southern Illinois University Press, 1964); Walter Jackson Bate, *The Burden of the Past and the English Poet* (Cambridge: Harvard University Press, 1970); Northrop Frye, "Toward Defining an Age of Sensibility," in *Eighteenth-Century English Literature: Modern Essays in Criticism,* ed. James L. Clifford (New York: Oxford University Press, 1959), pp. 311–318; and Leo Braudy, "The Form of the Sentimental Novel," *Novel* 7 (1973), 5–13.

[5]It is a striking fact that there has been no really satisfactory study of the sentimental movement. The natural sublime, and the sublime of self-consciousness, no less conventional and extravagant than this human sublime, have been the subject of numerous thoughtful studies. Sentimentalism, however, has received relatively little attention, other than the useful compendia of such scholars as Ernest Birnbaum, Walter Wright, and Arthur Sherbo. Although W. P. Albrecht's *Sublime Pleasures of Tragedy* (Lawrence: University Press of Kansas, 1975) does suggest the ways in which the emotional response to suffering merged with the concept of the sublime in the late eighteenth and early nineteenth centuries, he does not relate the literary, or sub-literary, sentimental movement to contemporary theoretical statements about tragedy and the sublime.

which expands the soul, gives an enthusiastic greatness, mixed with tenderness, when we view the magnificent objects of nature; or hear of a good action. The same effect we experience in the spring, when we hail the returning sun, and the consequent renovation of nature; when the flowers unfold themselves, and exhale their sweets, and the voice of music is heard in the land. Softened by tenderness; the soul is disposed to be virtuous.[6]

[handwritten margin note: at beg. of Prelude?]

Universal responsiveness is the ideal of such an omnivorous sensibility. The enemy is ennui or apathy, and the critical need is for something to respond to. The mind of man or woman in its response to external stimuli is always the center of interest. The tears that flow like a great river through late-eighteenth-century literature represent an attempt, albeit crude and not a little silly, to bring within the text the response to tragic circumstances. The characters who shed them, as they respond to the sufferings of others, are meant as models for the reader.

What one might call the bipolarity of sentimental fiction reflects this concern with response. The sentimental author and reader are, to be sure, interested in human misery. But sentimentalism, in its fascination with suffering, essentially differs little from other, more respectable, forms of tragic literature. What distinguishes the sentimentalist is his profound interest in the man looking at the sorrow, in a word, himself. "The thing contemplated" shares center stage with "the Mind and Man / Contemplating."[7] Schiller's definition of the "sentimental poet"

[6]Mary Wollstonecraft, *"Mary, A Fiction" and "The Wrongs of Woman,"* ed. Gary Kelly (London: Oxford University Press, 1976), pp. 53–54.
[7]The reader will recognize the phrases of Wordsworth's "Prospectus" to *The Recluse; PW,* V, 6. In context, of course, they apologize for *The Prelude's* egocentricity, Wordsworth's justified sense that "it seems a frightful deal to say about one's self" (*EL,* p. 470). The turn from objective to subjective, however, is characteristic of the late eighteenth century. See Samuel Monk, *The Sublime* (New York: Modern Language Association, 1935); M. H. Abrams, *The Mirror and the Lamp* (New York: Oxford University Press, 1953); and Walter Jackson Bate, *From Classic to Romantic* (Cambridge, Mass.: Harvard University Press, 1946), for discussions of this glacial shift in perspective. The sentimental, with its self-conscious interest in response, shares with other contemporary sources of literary excitement the focus on the drama within. The same kind of historical and intellectual currents which result in a *Prelude* are responsible for such outlandish (as they now seem) movements as sentimentalism and gothicism.

24

suggests the self-consciousness which the eighteenth century brought to tragic art: "He *reflects* upon the impression that objects make upon him, and only in that reflection is the emotion grounded which he himself experiences and which he excites in us."[8] Thus, the central drama of sentimental fiction and poetry lies in reflection, the mind turning from externals to the exciting things happening within.

The extreme case of such self-involution is no doubt Laurence Sterne, who makes continual reference to "the impression that objects make," both upon himself as narrator and ourselves as readers. The turn from pathos to the observing self is exemplified in the episode of "The Captive" from *A Sentimental Journey:*

He was sitting upon the ground upon a little straw, in the furthest corner of his dungeon, which was alternately his chair and bed: a little calender of small sticks were laid at the head, notch'd all over with the dismal days and nights he had pass'd there—he had one of these little sticks in his hand, and with a rusty nail he was etching another day of misery to add to the heap. As I darkened the little light he had, he lifted up a hopeless eye towards the door, then cast it down—shook his head, and went on with his work of affliction. I heard his chains upon his legs, as he turn'd his body to lay his little stick upon the bundle—He gave a deep sigh—I saw the iron enter into his soul—I burst into tears—I could not sustain the picture of confinement which my fancy had drawn—I started up from my chair.[9]

[8]Friedrich von Schiller, *"Naive and Sentimental Poetry" and "On the Sublime,"* trans. Julius A. Elias (New York: Frederick Ungar, 1966), p. 116. Schiller's concept of *sentimentalisch* is, of course, a good deal broader than the English literary historical sense of *sentimental* which I am using. For Schiller, *sentimentalisch* is roughly the equivalent of our *sophisticated;* it is opposed in his dialectic by the naive, natural, unself-conscious poetry of Homer and the primitive ballads. Obviously, however, the kind of "sentimental" literature discussed in this study partakes of the characteristics of the modern self-consciousness that Schiller was describing. In German, the passage reads: "Dieser reflektirt über den Eindruck, den die Gegenstände auf ihn machen und nur auf jene Reflexion ist die Rührung gegründet, in die er selbst versetzt wird, und uns versetzt"; *Schillers Werke*, XX (Weimar: Hermann Bohlaus, 1962), 441.
[9]Laurence Sterne, *A Sentimental Journey through France and Italy,* ed. Ian Jack (London: Oxford University Press, 1968), p. 73.

Yorick's response intrudes upon the simple, exquisitely particularized sketch of the prisoner. Curiously, this description is not meant to be real, even in terms of the novel. It is only a "picture" created by Yorick's "fancy," a fiction within a fiction. Yorick has not visited a prison to look at the inmates, although in a different work, such as Wordsworth's "The Convict," he might well have. He is merely allowing "full scope to his imagination"[10] after having seen a caged starling. The scene is overtly and emphatically fictional, yet is no less moving for being so presented. Thus, Sterne has it both ways—he arouses emotion and provokes self-consciousness. In the movement between the pathetic object and the mind which half-perceives, half-creates it, Sterne is typical of the age, and it is not insignificant that, in August 1791, Wordsworth lists *Tristram Shandy* among his few "incursions into the fields of modern literature."[11] The Wordsworth of the great decade undoubtedly seeks originality in ways less flamboyant than *Tristram Shandy* and *A Sentimental Journey*. Nonetheless, the self-consciousness, ironic pathos, use of narrators, interest in obsession, and odd humor displayed in *Lyrical Ballads* likely owe not a little to the creator of uncle Toby and Parson Yorick.

A passage from another of Wordsworth's favorite works reveals a similarly self-conscious use of pathos.[12] *The Minstrel,* James Beattie's version of a poet's education, digresses a bit to retell the story of "The Children in the Wood":

> But when to horrour his amazement rose,
> A gentler strain the beldame would rehearse,

---

[10] *A Sentimental Journey,* p. 72.

[11] *EL,* p. 56. Five years later, Dorothy read *Tristram* and Henry Brooke's *A Fool of Quality* at Racedown and found them "very entertaining" (*EL,* p. 166).

[12] *The Vale of Esthwaite* and *An Evening Walk,* particularly, reveal Wordsworth's admiration of *The Minstrel*. Christopher Wordsworth's Hawkshead notebook, published as *The Early Wordsworthian Milieu,* ed. Z. S. Fink (Oxford: Clarendon, 1958), also suggests the kind of meaning Beattie's poem would have had to a sensitive and ambitious youth. Dorothy, in 1793, thought that "the whole character of Edwin [the minstrel] resembles much what William was when I first knew him after my leaving Halifax" (*EL,* p. 101). For a full discussion of Wordsworth and Beattie, see E. H. King, "James Beattie's *The Minstrel* (1771, 1774): Its Influence on Wordsworth," *Studies in Scottish Literature* 8 (1970–71), 3–29.

A tale of rural life, a tale of woes,
The orphan-babes, and guardian uncle fierce.
O cruel! will no pang of pity pierce
That heart, by lust of lucre sear'd to stone?
For sure, if aught of virtue last, or verse,
To latest times shall tender souls bemoan
Those hopeless orphan babes by thy fell arts undone.

Behold, with berries smear'd, with brambles torn,
The babes now famish'd lay them down to die:
Amidst the howl of darksome woods forlorn,
Folded in one another's arms they lie;
Nor friend, nor stranger, hears their dying cry:
"For from the town the man returns no more."
But thou, who Heaven's just vengeance dar'st defy,
This deed with fruitless tears shalt soon deplore,
When Death lays waste thy house, and flames consume thy store.[13]

Beattie's poem encloses the traditional ballad in a sophisticated and self-consciously literary framework. It is indicative of what he is doing that the ostensible quotation, "'For from the town the man returns no more,'" is no more a part of Bishop Percy's text than the rest of Beattie's réchauffé. The lines referred to are those which Wordsworth quotes in the "Preface" to *Lyrical Ballads,* "But never more they saw the Man / Approaching from the Town" (*Prose,* I, 154). The important thing for Beattie is that the reader *think* he is looking at a piece of the original text. The pseudo-quotation aims at making us feel as if we are re-experiencing the original.

The purpose in alluding to "The Children in the Wood" is to awaken the embers of past emotion; the sentimental reader, in recollecting the details of the story, is supposed to feel the original response revive within him. Having accomplished this, Beattie describes the poem's naive hero responding innocently, that is, for the first time, to the beldame's rehearsal of the well-known poem:

> A stifled smile of stern vindictive joy
> Brighten'd one moment Edwin's starting tear,

[13]I: 45–46; Chalmers, XVIII, 576.

"But why should gold man's feeble mind decoy,
And innocence thus die by doom severe?"
O Edwin! while thy heart is yet sincere,
Th'assaults of discontent and doubt repel:
Dark even at noontide is our mortal sphere;
But let us hope; to doubt is to rebel;
Let us exult in hope, that all shall yet be well.

Nor be thy generous indignation check'd,
Nor check'd the tender tear to Misery given;
From Guilt's contagious power shall that protect,
This soften and refine the soul for Heaven.
But dreadful is their doom, whom doubt has driven
To censure Fate, and pious Hope forego:
Like yonder blasted boughs by lightning riven,
Perfection, beauty, life, they never know,
But frown on all that pass, a monument of woe.

[I: 47–48]

For Beattie, the response is more interesting than the original story. Of four stanzas given to the ballad, thirteen lines suffice to recollect its plot; the rest goes to the intermediate figure of Edwin and to the "tender souls" who insure the story's immortality, that is, ourselves. Beattie, as a member of the Scotch establishment, wishes to defuse the vexing "Why?" and deflect indignátion from Fate or Heaven toward the evil uncle. Nonetheless, the ways of God are justified, insofar as they are scrutable at all, by means of sentimental vocabulary. It is "the tender tear to Misery given," not faith or good works, which will "soften and refine the soul for Heaven."

In their narrative structures, "The Captive" and *The Minstrel* are characteristic of sentimentalism. Typically, there is a character in late-eighteenth-century literature whose primary function lies in his response to sentimental objects. Figures such as Yorick, Tristram, Belford, Harley, and even Rasselas mediate between human suffering and its ultimate audience. We watch this person watch the victims, and often we watch him watch someone else who responds to the suffering. The sentimental plot delights in a complex layering of narrative. In *The Man of*

Feeling, for instance, an "editor" fortuitously obtains the mutilated manuscript from the curate with whom he is hunting. In this text, the narrator, "a grave, oddish sort of man,"[14] tells the story of Harley, who meets various sentimentally interesting figures. Occasionally there is a further narrative layer, as the people whom Harley meets tell of encounters with still other sentimental figures. Each person between reader and victim serves to guide the reader's response, but the sum of responses is anything but simple or naively emotional. Harley, with his weeping and insatiable generosity, shows only the simplest response. The editor tells us, "had the name of a Marmontel, or a Richardson, been on the title-page—'tis odds that I should have wept: But one is ashamed to be pleased with the works of one knows not whom."[15] An odd preface for a novel published anonymously! The narrator also provides ironic distance from, and sympathetic response to Harley's misadventures in London. At the novel's center, at considerable remove from the reader, are the tableaux of suffering, the mad girl, the beggar and his dog, the discharged soldier Edwards. All this elaboration appears in a narrative which speaks of itself as "simple to excess."[16] At one point the editor turns to the reader and ingenuously apologizes: "to such as may have expected the intricacies of a novel, a few incidents in a life undistinguished, except by some features of the heart, cannot have afforded much entertainment."[17] One is reminded of Wordsworth's similar assertion that "'Tis my delight, alone in summer shade, / To pipe a simple song to thinking hearts" ("Hart-Leap Well," ll. 99–100). In MacKenzie, as in Wordsworth, complication of narrative structure and voice displaces the complication of plot typical of romance.

Thus, in sentimentalism Wordsworth inherited an elaborate, highly artificial, and conventional literary system camouflaging

[14]Henry Mackenzie, *The Man of Feeling,* ed. Brian Vickers (London: Oxford University Press, 1967), p. 4.
[15]Ibid., p. 5.
[16]Ibid., p. 126.
[17]Ibid., p. 125.

itself in the guise of nature and spontaneous feeling. Characterized by what Northrop Frye calls "a strong sense of literature as aesthetic product,"[18] the novels and poetry of the late eighteenth century are artful and self-aware. In structure, as Leo Braudy has said, they strive to "imitate feeling rather than intellect, and to embody direct experience rather than artistic premeditation."[19] Paradoxically, the conscious attempt to create an unself-conscious form results in the most self-conscious of literary artifacts. Literature, once it knows itself literature, cannot return to innocence. Any simplicity which it achieves is necessarily sophisticated and complex. The simplicity for which Wordsworth's poetry reaches is no less artificial than that of his sentimental precursors. Indeed his work is rather more self-conscious and artful, which perhaps is one of the grounds of his extraordinary originality and success.[20]

II

In spring 1786, Helen Maria Williams' *Poems, in Two Volumes* appeared. Poetesses were in vogue in the eighties, as readers demanded multiple editions from Anna Seward, Hannah More, Charlotte Smith, and Ann Yearsley (the Poetical Milkwoman). Among these figures, Williams shone as "by no means the least elegant and pleasing of the constellation of females who have lately illumined the British Parnassus."[21] *Poems, in Two Volumes* provides a broad index of contemporary taste, for Williams was a bit of a magpie, tricking out her work with whatever sparkled or glittered in the poetry of the time. Her collection includes an ode "To Sensibility"; two stories of star-crossed lovers; "Paraphrases from Scripture"; "Part of an Irregular Fragment, Found

[18]Frye, "Toward Defining an Age of Sensibility," p. 316.
[19]"The Form of the Sentimental Novel," p. 5.
[20]For discussions of Wordsworthian "simplicity," see John Danby, *The Simple Wordsworth* (London: Routledge & Kegan Paul, 1960); and John Jordan, *Why the "Lyrical Ballads"?* (Berkeley and Los Angeles: University of California Press, 1976), pp. 84–102.
[21]*European Magazine* 10 (1786), 89.

in a Dark Passage of the Tower," in which a young man of artistic bent encounters the ghosts of murdered royalty; *Peru,* a sentimental mini-epic in six cantos describing the downfall of the Incas; an elegy; an epistle; a complaint; and sonnets to Twilight, Expression, Mrs. Siddons, and a fellow poetess. The impetus for this rampage through the day's poetically fashionable subjects is suggested in the "Advertisement" to *Peru:*

> To describe that important event with accuracy, and to display with clearness and force the various causes which combined to produce it, would require all the energy of genius, and the most glowing colours of imagination. Conscious of her utter inability to execute such a design, she [the author] has only aimed at a simple detail of some few incidents that make a part of that romantic story; where the unparalleled sufferings of an innocent and amiable people, form the most affecting subjects of true pathos, while their climate, totally unlike our own, furnishes new and ample materials for poetic description.[22]

For Williams, the romantic is enough. Her quest is for poetic objects which are "unparalleled," "most affecting," "totally unlike our own," "new." Scenery and suffering are equally interesting to her: the exotic and pathetic are both satisfactory sources of the excitement she craves.

Like Sterne and MacKenzie, Williams is primarily interested in human misery for the response it evokes in observer and reader. Questions of sympathetic emotion continually intrude upon the pathos she is presenting. In "An Ode on the Peace," mention of Major André brings to mind Anna Seward's "Monody on Major André" (1781). A response is then described which is both to André's demise and to the other poem:

> While Seward sweeps her plaintive strings,
>> While pensive round his sable shrine,
> A radiant zone she graceful flings,
>> Where full emblaz'd his virtues shine;

[22]Helen Maria Williams, *Poems* (London: Cadell, 1786), II, 53–54.

> The mournful loves that tremble nigh
> Shall catch her warm melodious sigh;
> The mournful loves shall drink the tears that flow
> From Pity's hov'ring soul, dissolv'd in woe.

"The tear 'tis luxury to shed," for Williams as for the age, is the central symbol of benevolent and sympathetic response. Addressing "Sensibility," the poet asserts

> 'Tis she that lights the melting eye
> With looks to anguish dear;
> She knows the price of ev'ry sigh,
> The value of a tear.[23]

The silliness of such lachrymose economics ought not to distract us from the importance and peculiarity of a poetry which dwells on response rather than the primary subject.

The predominant response of reviewers to Helen Maria Williams' *Poems* was polite apathy. The "two leading reviews,"[24] the *Monthly* and the *Critical,* each reprinted a poem and spoke vaguely of "our approbation of Miss Williams' poetical talents" or of her having obtained "no inconsiderable share of reputation."[25] The *Gentleman's Magazine* noted the publication of *Poems* in its "Catalogue of New Publications" (June 1786) but never reviewed it. Of the major journals, the *European Magazine* gave the most extensive, balanced and thoughtful reading. Williams' was the only poetic production of 1786 which it greeted with a review appearing in more than one issue. In August and September, a separate essay was given to each volume. The critic explains: "We have much exceeded our usual bounds in these remarks on the Poems of Miss Williams. Our good opinion of her happy genius led us into it." Despite reservations about "the very *mania* for *tenderness*" and the "tawdry tinsel richness of strained expression,"

---

[23]Ibid., I, 41, 18, 22.

[24]Robert Mayo, *The English Novel in the Magazines 1740–1815* (London: Oxford University Press, 1962), p. 204.

[25]*Critical Review* 62 (1786), 62; *Monthly Review* 75 (1786), 44.

the review offers a sympathetic criticism of "Miss Williams's poetical powers." It compliments her poetry by taking it sufficiently seriously to point out "blemishes" even while praising her "graceful ease and simplicity," "knack at similes," "many poetic thoughts and good lines," and "great and genuine poetic merit."[26]

In the north of England, a schoolboy at Hawkshead read Helen Maria Williams with rather less tempered enthusiasm. In all likelihood, William Wordsworth saw the *European Magazine*'s extensive review of *Poems, in Two Volumes.*[27] As would have been natural for a youth whom success as "the poet of the school"[28] had encouraged "to compose verses from the impulse of [his] own mind" (*PW*, I, 366), he wrote a sonnet to her. The short poem of recognition to a fellow poet was a minor genre popular in the late eighteenth century. In the works of most of Wordsworth's contemporaries, one finds poems like Coleridge's "To Schiller" and, in a perverse vein, Blake's challenge to Klopstock. Certainly the genre flourished in the poetry section of the *European Magazine*. In 1786, six such poems appear, five of them addressed to poetesses. There are "Stanzas to Mrs. Barbauld," a "Sonnet, Addressed to Miss Seward," three sonnets to Mrs. Smith, and an "Ode to the Author of the Triumph of Benevolence." Probably the *European*'s evident interest in Helen Maria Williams and its publication of several other similar poems encouraged Wordsworth to send his sonnet to the magazine in late 1786 or early 1787. At any rate, the March 1787 issue contains his first publication, "Sonnet, on Seeing Miss Helen Maria Williams Weep at a Tale of Distress":

> She wept.—Life's purple stream began to flow
> In languid streams through every thrilling vein;

[26]*European Magazine* 10 (1786), 89–93, 177–180.
[27]The magazine's availability to Wordsworth is suggested by the fact that Christopher's notebook cites an article of January 1788; *The Early Wordsworthian Milieu*, p. 93.
[28]Christopher Wordsworth, *Memoirs of William Wordsworth* (London: Moxon, 1851), II, 304.

Dim were my swimming eyes—my pulse beat slow,
And my full heart was swell'd to dear delicious pain.

Life left my loaded heart, and closing eye;
A sigh recall'd the wanderer to my breast;
Dear was the pause of life, and dear the sigh
That call'd the wanderer home, and home to rest.

That tear proclaims—in thee each virtue dwells,
And bright will shine in misery's midnight hour;
As the soft star of dewy evening tells
What radiant fires were drown'd by day's malignant pow'r,
That only wait the darkness of the night
To chear the wand'ring wretch with hospitable light.

AXIOLOGUS[29]

Worse poems, less interesting ones certainly, have been composed by enthusiastic sixteen-year-olds.

The sonnet's language, as might be expected, is conventional and derivative. The overdependence on adjectives signals a beginning poet's unwillingness to let nouns and verbs perform the labors of description. Much of the vocabulary, in fact, echoes Helen Maria Williams. "Purple flood" is her favorite epithet for blood, and "delicious tears" are her characteristic way of describing the response to "aching pleasure." "The soft star of dewy evening" could be straight out of a poetess whose descriptions continually dissolve into talk of things "soft," "tender," "mild," "gentle," "sweet," and "melting."

Nonetheless, the "Sonnet, on Seeing Miss Helen Maria Williams Weep at a Tale of Distress" is a remarkable performance, revealing much about the nature of Wordsworth's early relationship to contemporary popular literature. The poem's complex, involuted structure reflects a sensitive mind working within a literature fascinated by emotional response. The

[29]*European Magazine* 11 (1787), 202; *PW*, I, 269. The certainty of the attribution of this poem has been reestablished by Mark Reed who quotes a note in which Wordsworth says that his first publication was "a sonnet printed in the European Magazine . . . signed Axiologus," Reed *EY*, p. 71.

natural temptation in writing this kind of poem is simply to praise, advise, or describe one's response to the other poet's work. Another "Sonnet to Helen Maria Williams," appearing in the *Gentleman's Magazine* (June 1786), is a fair sample of the genre:

> Daughter of Verse—soft Pity's sweetest child—
> Meek virgin-priestess of the tuneful Nine!
> Wilt thou admit of breathings rude and wild
> Th'attempt to praise such heavenly strains as thine?
> All uncontroul'd to thy enchanting song
> I gave my feeling, nor the gift could rue;
> For every note they found, while led along,
> To nature faithful, and to passion true.
> What though no longer now thy numbers roll
> Peru's sad story on my list'ning ear,
> Still, sunk their charming tenour in my soul,
> I think I hear them, and could ever hear;
> While, like the thanks some blest oration draws,
> I can but murmur thus my hoarse applause.
>
> E.[30]

This is, obviously, a less interesting and complex poem than Wordsworth's. "E." is content merely to assert an emotional response to *Peru*. Wordsworth's poem evidences a sensitive reading of Williams' *Poems*, and, however misplaced the fervor, his response takes the form of imitation of language and dramatic structure.

Rather than merely effuse, Wordsworth's "Sonnet on Seeing Miss Williams Weep" devises an elaborate and fictitious situation. It is not clear how many characters people the sonnet. There is certainly a narrative "I," for the poem's primary subject is his feeling while he watches an emotionally sensitive woman respond to some pathetic stimulus. As we have seen, the presence of a respondent in the text and the intrusion of narrative layers between reader and suffering are characteristic of senti-

[30] *Gentleman's Magazine,* 56 (1786), 513.

mental literature. Such figures are plentiful in Williams' poetry; for example, in "Edwin and Eltruda," the heroine meets a widow and her family:

> Wild throbs her aching bosom swell—
> They mark the bursting sigh,
> (Nature has form'd the soul to feel)
> They weep, unknowing why.
>
> Her hands the lib'ral boon impart,
> And much her tear avails
> To raise the mourner's drooping heart,
> Where feeble utterance fails.[31]

The idea here is the one that closes Wordsworth's "Sonnet," that tears of sympathetic sensibility are like a dewy star which "chears the wand'ring wretch with hospitable light." The focus in both poems is on the girl weeping to contemplate misery. There is a peculiar, and characteristic, circularity of emotion in "Edwin and Eltruda"; the family, as they "weep unknowing why," show the reader how to respond to the heroine's response to them. Thus, the family is both the pathetic object and, at two removes, the respondent to a pathetic object. In Wordsworth's sonnet, "Miss Williams" functions analogously to Harley in *The Man of Feeling*. She is a woman of sensibility introduced into a situation where her feelings are seen in their effects. Wordsworth, however, places the original pathos further from the reader than it had ever been in MacKenzie; "Miss Williams" does not contemplate real or present suffering, but is only reading or hearing a tale of distress. We know nothing of what moves her to tears. Her book remains closed to us, so that we do not even have the second-hand pleasure of responding to the person(s) for whom she weeps.

In the sestet, the poem becomes ambiguous, perhaps sloppily so. For the first time, a "thee" is mentioned. It is unclear whether "she" and "thee" are identical, or if "thee" addresses the reader,

---

[31]Williams, *Poems*, I, 71.

thus including him in the poem. Either is possible, and certainly the tendency of sentimental literature is to bring the reader self-consciously into literary structures. It seems more probable, however, that "thee" is still "Miss Williams," and the poem has shifted from the distancing third person to the more intimate second. In any case, the thought and morality of the concluding simile are curious. As malignant sunlight drowns the "radiant fires" of the stars, so the lack of a pathetic object frustrates the activity of the lady's benevolence. Only in "misery's midnight hour" can sensibility exercise itself, and the young Wordsworth seems quite oblivious to the parasitism implied by his imagery. In his sonnet, response is all that is given, "Miss Williams'" tears and the speaker's emotions as he contemplates her response. The "wanderer" within each reader is more important than "the wandering wretch."

The language of "Sonnet on Seeing Miss Williams Weep" is often obscure, but the experience described is oddly like the central Wordsworthian moment when the light of sense goes out or the motion of the blood is almost suspended. "The pause of life," suggestive though it is of Wordsworth's later poetry, is also clearly derivative from the sentimentalist's way of charting extreme emotional experience. In "Fragment Found in the Tower," a moment of terror causes the narrator to cry, "hark!—I hear / Sounds that the throbbing pulse of life suspend."[32] The stopping and starting of the emotions, the rapid transition between excitement and relaxation, pity and terror, are always the central object of sentimental interest, and they become the main region of Wordsworth's song. As the "Sonnet on Seeing Miss Williams Weep" makes evident, this psychological interest, particularly as it applies to the psychology of tragic response, is present from Wordsworth's poetic beginnings.

III

Given its rather lugubrious subject matter, Wordsworth's earliest poetry contains curiously few references to sentimental

[32]Williams, *Poems,* II, 30.

morality. "Sonnet on Seeing Miss Williams Weep" states that a
"tear proclaims—in thee each virtue dwells," but otherwise this
commonplace sentimental rationalization does not appear in
Wordsworth until the late nineties. Only with *The Ruined Cottage*
and *Peter Bell* does he begin to emphasize a connection between
sympathetic emotion and moral improvement. Earlier, though
doubtless conversant with the platitudes of sentimental morality,
he is largely indifferent to the moral implications of finding
personal pleasure in the contemplation of other people's suffering.[33]

Wordsworth's juvenilia are concerned not with justifying the
power of sentimental emotion but with appropriating it. His
first poems reveal a poet in search of an effective way to provoke
tragic emotions. Genre, voice, and focus shift kaleidoscopically
as he tries, with little repetition, first one type of poetry, then
another. Inevitably, the young poet experiments with the
models of the past, imitating poems from the classical and English traditions. He translates a Virgilian "tale of sorrow," the
Orpheus and Eurydice segment from the *Georgics,* and a Greek
pastoral elegy, part of Moschus' "Lament for Bion." A watery
version of Catullus' playful elegy on a dead sparrow opens "Pity
mourns in plaintive tone / The lovely Starling dead and gone"
(*PW*, I, 263). Other poems draw from eighteenth-century notions of medieval poetry. "A Ballad" in the manner of Percy and
David Mallet tells of a girl dying after disappointment in love.
"Dirge, Sung by a Minstrel" takes its inspiration, and quotes a
few lines, from Chatterton's *Aella: A Tragycal Enterlude.* More
modern attempts to deal with sentimental material are a "Sonnet
Written by Mr. _____ Immediately after the Death of His Wife"
and a fragmentary ode "To Melpomene." None of these poems
is terribly good or even shows much promise of future greatness;

[33]O. J. Campbell's "Sentimental Morality in Wordsworth's Narrative Poetry,"
University of Wisconsin Studies in Language and Literature no. 11 (1920), pp. 21–57,
still provides a useful and compendious discussion of Wordsworth's later claims
that "there is often found / In mournful thoughts, and always might be found, /
A power to virtue friendly." Chapter 4 suggests why and how the idea began to
emerge in 1798–1800.

nonetheless, taken in sum, they dramatize a poet's attempt to find a way to exploit tragic energies. Their variety, particularly the lack of repetition in form and approach, testifies to persistence and dissatisfaction, but also to Wordsworth's continuing interest in bringing human suffering into his poetry.

Wordsworth's problem was that of his era. It was a time which believed that "the Sublime and the Pathetic are the two chief nerves of all genuine poesy,"[34] yet which for all its effort produced no second Milton or Shakespeare. One solution to this dilemma, successfully practiced by William Collins and attempted by Wordsworth in "To Melpomene," is what one might call the ode of poetic wishfulness. The subject of poetry becomes the desire to write another, inaccessible poem. Thus Collins requests of "Pity" that he be "Allowed with Thee to dwell" and of "Fear" that she teach him "but once . . . to feel" like Shakespeare. Wordsworth's effort in the genre is unfinished, but his address to the tragic muse expresses similar ambitions:

> *To Melpomene*
> Come then in robe of darkest blue
> And face of pale and sickly hue—
> Who *Moon-like* guid'st the liquid swell
> Of sounds that float upon the shell
> At whose soft touch whate'er is mute
> Talks with a voice like Pity's Lute
> —Like what the Sailor's Widow hears
> At Night dull-tingling in her ears
> While touchèd by the *moon-raised* Surge
> The wild rocks round her sing a wondrous Dirge,
> That floats around thy poet's shell of bluest night[35]

The main concern of "To Melpomene" is with sound, used as a palpable metaphor for poetic achievement. The would-be poet calls upon the personification of his own desire, to come with a

[34]Joseph Warton, *An Essay on the Genius and Writings of Pope*, 4th ed. (London: Dodsley, 1782), I, x.
[35]The text of this fragment is newly available in William Wordsworth, *Poems*, ed. John O. Hayden (New York: Penguin, 1977), I, 44.

"liquid swell of sound" and touch the muteness he knows within. Melpomene is wanted to "talk with a voice like Pity's Lute," and call up waves (of tears?) that would "sing a wondrous dirge." Hearing all this, so the convention goes, the poet will finally be able to write the tragic poem of his desires. The sheer lugubriousness of Wordsworth's early work suggests a poet who very much wants the muse to descend from "the regions of Terrour and Pity."[36]

The effort of much of Wordsworth's verse of 1786–1788 is toward a crude form of dramatic monologue. Voices not his own and utterances of narrative selves projected into fictional situations speak in a poetry that values interesting and lurid fictions over dull, everyday truth. "Sonnet on Seeing Miss Williams Weep" describes a purely imaginary situation; Wordsworth met Williams for the first time in 1820. Both situation and speaker of the "Sonnet Written by Mr. ____ Immediately after the Death of His Wife" are apparently as fictitious as they are pathetically interesting:[37]

> The Sun is dead—ye heard the Curfew toll,
> Come, Nature, let us mourn our kindred doom;
> My Sun like thine is dead—and o'er my Soul
> Despair's dark midnight spreads her raven gloom,
> Yes, she is gone—he call'd her to illume
> The realms where Heav'n's immortal rivers roll
>
> [*PW*, I, 265]

Mr. ____ proceeds to find consolation in "Religion's moonlight ray" and the promise of "Heav'n's bright Morn." Neither the triteness of language and central image nor our own familiarity with such literary gameplaying should divert our attention from

---

[36]This phrase forms the subtitle of Robert Dodsley's "Melpomene," in Chalmers, XV, 348.

[37]De Selincourt notes that "a search in the Hawkshead Registers has not revealed the name of the widower for whom Wordsworth wrote this lament" (*PW*, I, 367). T. W. Thompson's *Wordsworth's Hawkshead*, ed. Robert Woof (London: Oxford University Press, 1970) likewise finds nothing in local history to provide the subject for this poem.

the peculiar modernity of this little monodrama. On a crude level, Wordsworth's Mr. ＿＿ is like the nameless editor who happens upon the fragmentary MS. of *The Man of Feeling* or Lovelace's friend Belford who diligently collects the prodigious quantity of letters Richardson had written for Clarissa, Lovelace, Miss Howe, and the rest. The nameless speaker is a convenient fiction enabling Wordsworth to create a tragic situation even while indulging a taste for literary elaboration. The poet imitates the voice of "real and substantial suffering," and the poem itself rather than what it describes becomes the pathetic object. Mr. ＿＿ says that he feels "Despair's dark midnight," a phrase which echoes the sonnet on Williams where the poetess wept to contemplate "misery's midnight hour." She, however, is outside the tragedy, pitying; Mr. ＿＿, like the Sailor's Widow in "To Melpomene," knows tragic loss. Both sonnets, however, are notably displaced from straightforward description of suffering. The commonplace model of reader and pathos mediated by mimetic objectivity does not hold in either poem. In "Mr. ＿＿" the person suffering speaks directly; in the other sonnet, he (or they) had been entirely hidden. In both, a narrative voice that is not the poet's creates an essentially dramatic structure.

Another voice the young Wordsworth assumed was that of the ballad-mongering minstrel. For a poet coming of age in the 1780s, this, too, was probably inevitable. As the *European Magazine* (February 1787) remarked querulously, in a review of Sophia Lee's *A Hermit's Tale, Recorded by His Own Hand, and Found in His Cell,* "The success of Dr. Goldsmith, Bishop Percy, and one or two others, has occasioned [such] an inundation of Tales and Legendary Ballads . . . that we conceive it would shew more genius in a writer of character to chuse some other subject for the exercise of her muse, than one so hackneyed."[38] The eighteenth century's reimagination of the middle ages, which brought forth Ossian and Rowley, haunted castles and ruined abbeys, and hordes of minstrels, bards, hermits, knights, and

---

[38]*European Magazine* 11 (1787), 90–91.

gentle maidens, touched Wordsworth also. In "A Ballad" of William and Mary, he competently imitates the "simplicity" of Percy:

> "And will you leave me thus alone
> And dare you break your vow?
> Be sure her Ghost will haunt thy bed
> When Mary shall lie low."
>
> So spoke in tears—but all in vain
> The fairest maid of Esthwaite's vale,
> To love's soft glance his eye was shut
> His ear to Pity's tale.
>
> And oft at Eve he sought the bridge
> That near her window lay;
> There gayly laughed with other maids
> Or sung the hour away.
>
> [*PW*, I, 265]

The characteristics of primitive folk song—simple language, snatches of conversation, an evocative lack of explicitness—are well managed here. The rapid shift from Mary's complaint to the sadism only suggested in the lover is patterned after poems like "Sir Patrick Spens" and "Fair Margaret and Sweet William." No doubt, it is a modern, sentimental touch that the lover's ear is shut to "Pity's tale," for the mention of "Pity" brings up matters of response. The implication is that the reader, unlike the lover, will not be deaf to the tale "she" (and the poet) tell.

"A Ballad" proceeds to its predictable conclusion, but not before Wordsworth brings into it words of external personal significance. As the maiden lies on her deathbed, she tells a pretty story:

> She saw—she cried—"'tis all in vain
> For broken is my heart,
> And well I know my hour is nigh,
> I know that we must part.

Heaven told me once—but I was blind—
My head would soon lie low;
A Rose within our Garden blew
Amid December's snow.

That Rose my William saw—and pluck'd,
He pluck'd and gave it me;
Heaven warn'd me then—ah blind was I—
That he my death would be.

Folded into the account of William and the rose are words that William Taylor, Wordsworth's mentor at Hawkshead, spoke from his deathbed:

A week, or little less, before his death
He had said to me, 'my head will soon lie low;'
And when I saw the turf that cover'd him,
After the lapse of full eight years, those words,
With sound of voice, and countenance of the Man,
Came back upon me; so that some few tears
Fell from me in my own despite.

[*Prel* X, 501–507]

The tears that Taylor's speech calls from Wordsworth, even eight years later, are an index of the emotion that he attaches to "my head will soon lie low." The adolescent Wordsworth imports these words into the text of "A Ballad" because he wants to exploit their deep, if personal, emotional significance. He wants to give the poem added power and calls in the language of real life, even this early, to endow a conventional and imitative fiction with tragic emotions.

Wordsworth's other "medieval" juvenile poem is the "Dirge, Sung by a Minstrel." Here, too, he invokes language with a traceable external context:

List! the bell-Sprite stuns my ears
Slowly calling for a maid;
List! each worm with trembling hears

> And stops for joy his dreadful trade.
> For nine times the death-bell's Sprite
> Sullen for the Virgin cried
> And they say at dead of night
> Before its time the taper died.
>> Mie love is dedde
>> Gone to her deathbedde,
>> Al under the wyllowe tree.
> When friends around her death-bed hung
> To feel life's ebbing flood awhile,
> The fell disease had chain'd her tongue
> Yet still she gave—she gave—a smile.

[*PW*, I, 267]

The indented, pseudoarchaic lines are from a "Mynstrelles Songe" in Chatterton's *Aella*.[39] Allusion serves to point up the tradition in which the poet is working and his relation to that tradition. By quoting Chatterton, Wordsworth attaches the kind of literary pathos to his poem that Beattie had to *The Minstrel* by pretending to quote "The Children in the Wood." Quotation helps the poet lay claim to the sentimental energies of another text even while pointing self-consciously to the literariness of his own.

That the original passage from Chatterton has an ironic, as well as sentimental, significance reflects the sort of complication in which the sentimental reader delighted. The Mynstrelle in *Aella* is a tangential figure, uninvolved with the main plot of battle and betrayal. He is only a voice, occasionally called upon to perform by the principals. The song that Wordsworth quotes appears in the "enterlude" as the heroine Birtha and her servant Egwina await the outcome of the great battle with the Danes. Birtha states, "I cannote joie ynne anie thynge botte weere [grief]," and Egwina suggests a song to cheer her up: "I wylle call the mynstrelles roundelaie; / Perchaunce the swotie sounde maie

---

[39]Moorman, I, 59; [Thomas Chatterton], *Poems Supposed to Have Been Written at Bristol, by Thomas Rowley* (London: T. Payne, 1777; rpt., London: Scolar Press, 1969), pp. 136–139.

chase your wiere awaie."[40] When the Mynstrelle sings "Mie love is dedde," however, he expresses Birtha's deepest fears. Of course, the reader of Chatterton knows from the work's full title and the shape of the plot that Birtha's premonitions are well founded. Therefore, he is in a position to savor the ironic pathos of the dirge. In quoting "Mie love is dedde," Wordsworth brings into his "Dirge" not only the natural pathos of the refrain and the archaic ambience created by Chatterton's spelling, but also a reminder of a literary situation in which the reader had been aware of himself as reader and of the work as literary artifact.

Thus, from the beginning, Wordsworth's poetry experiments with voice and point of view. Such ventriloquism and narrative legerdemain are the stock-in-trade of the sentimentally self-conscious writers of the late eighteenth century. The speaking voice that is not the poet's own provides a refuge for the literarily sophisticated mind that yet values simplicity and spontaneity. Thus we find Chatterton impersonating a monk named Rowley, and Sophia Lee recording a hermit's tale "by his own hand." In such a milieu, Helen Maria Williams could speak through the voice of a young artist exploring the Tower, and William Wordsworth could adopt personae of minstrels and bereft husbands. The impulse toward the "poetry of experience," whose genesis Robert Langbaum has located in Wordsworth and the Romantics, would seem, then, to stem from late-eighteenth-century efforts to discover a literature which could be both "sentimental" and "simple." Wordsworth's "hovering on the edge"[41] of the dramatic monologue form reflects the implicit tendencies of the literature which he had read and imitated in his youth.

IV

The Vale of Esthwaite, even in its incomplete state, offers a virtual anthology of the poetry of sensibility. A solitary *promeneur* wanders through a variable landscape in search of stimula-

---

[40]Chatterton, *Poems*, p. 135.
[41]Robert Langbaum, *The Poetry of Experience* (New York: Random House, 1957), p. 72.

tion, and he is not at all particular as to the means used to rouse interest. The images and language of contemporary poetry provide the energy by which *The Vale of Esthwaite* moves. The poem abounds with the quaint apparatus of gothicism: it is the world of *Otranto* and Williams' "Irregular Fragment," replete with skeletal "spectres," "moaning owls," "haunted castles," coffers marked with blood, "Murder," and "Suicide." There is even a *Lear*-like scene where "Edmund deaf to horror's cries / Trod out the cruel Brother's eyes."[42] In other, comparable modes, the young poet invokes the natural sublimity of lake country storms and imitates the melancholy nocturne of the *penseroso.* Far from exorcizing the beauty which has terror in it, as Geoffrey Hartman has suggested, Wordsworth's first long poem wallows in it. His yearning is not for "calmer pleasures," but for the gothic and the sublime.[43] Wordsworth, like his contemporaries, is greatly interested in the response to such extreme and outrageous forms of stimulus. *The Vale of Esthwaite* continually refers to such high-pitched emotional states as Fear, Horror, and Terror. Among such feelings, Pity is most piquant to the sentimentalist, and, inevitably, the poem invokes "tender tales" and "scenes of woe."

The version of Pity presented in *The Vale of Esthwaite*, however, is most often a feeling in search of an object. There are no human beings for the poet to vent his sympathy upon in the solipsistic valley of his imagination. His compassion can find no "appropriate human centre" there. Without another person upon whom to lavish attention, Pity either floats freely or exhausts itself in self-contemplation. The "floating" Pity is in evidence as the poet describes his feelings at sunset:

> Now holy Melancholy throws
> Soft o'er the soul a still repose,

[42]Lines 371–372 of the only text of *The Vale of Esthwaite* currently available, de Selincourt's rather confusing presentation in *PW*, I, 270–83.

[43]Geoffrey Hartman, *Wordsworth's Poetry, 1787–1814* (New Haven: Yale University Press, 1964), pp. 80–84. Although I take exception to Hartman's portrait of the young Wordsworth torn between "the apocalyptic tendency of his imagination" and "the social or socializing principle in human life" (p. 78), I am generally indebted to his sensitive discussion of this important early poem.

Save where we start as from a sleep
Recoiling from a gloom too deep.
Now too, while o'er the heart we feel
A tender twilight softly steal,
Sweet Pity gives her forms array'd
In tenderer tints and softer shade;
The heart, when pass'd the Vision by,
Dissolves, nor knows for whom nor why.

[ll. 121–130]

One recognizes again the vocabulary of sentimentalism.[44] Its map of emotion, charted by words such as "tender," "sweet," "soft," and "dissolves," describes the mind playing self-consciously around the "gloom too deep," some central vacancy beyond the reach of words. In this landscape, "sweet Pity" finds nothing specific to which to attach emotion: we never are told what the "forms" of Pity are, and it does not seem to matter for the purposes of such a free-floating Melancholy. Pity no longer gluts its sorrow upon a man mourning his wife, a disappointed lover, or even Helen Maria Williams weeping. In separating Pity from the pathetic, Wordsworth is following the general sentimental tendency. Sentimentalism's orientation toward response, taken to its extreme, fastens attention exclusively upon the emotions of the perceiver. As Frye suggests, "Where there is a sense of literature as process, pity and fear become states of mind without objects, moods which are common to the work of art and the reader, and which bind them together psychologically instead of separating them aesthetically."[45]

Ungrounded by any definite human object, Pity becomes a self-defining, if ill-defined, mode of autonomous feeling:

I trust the Bard can never part
With Pity, Autumn of the heart!

[44]Paul Sheats is probably correct in hearing an echo of Helen Maria Williams in the last line of this passage; *The Making of Wordsworth's Poetry, 1785–1798,* (Cambridge: Harvard University Press, 1973), p. 11. In the passage from "Edwin and Eltruda" quoted above, "They weep, unknowing why," describes the beggar family's sentimental response to Eltruda's highly wrought emotional state. In the solipsistic world of *The Vale of Esthwaite*, such an emotional interchange is impossible.
[45]Frye, "Toward Defining an Age of Sensibility," p. 316.

> She comes and o'er the soul we feel
> Soft tender tints of Sorrow steal;
> Each flaunting thought of glowing dye,
> The offspring of a brighter sky
> That late in Summer colours drest
> The laughing landscape of the breast,
> Is dead, or, ting'd with darkened shades
> In sickly sorrow droops and fades.
>
> [ll. 139–148]

This landscape "of the breast" describes a topography that has become entirely internal. The extended conceit linking "Pity" with the seasons, however, seems strained and overwrought. The inappropriateness of the metaphor tends to set the description free from its figurative meaning. Scenery replaces the response to human suffering.

As he moved from *The Vale of Esthwaite* to *An Evening Walk*, Wordsworth revised the description of the "landscape of the breast" several times.[46] In the final version, "Pity" disappears, and pathetic feelings attach entirely to the physical setting:

> —No purple prospects now the mind employ
> Glowing in golden sunset tints of joy,
> But o'er the sooth'd accordant heart we feel
> A sympathetic twilight slowly steal,
> And ever, as we fondly muse, we find
> The soft gloom deep'ning on the tranquil mind.
> Stay! pensive, sadly-pleasing visions, stay!
> Ah no! as fades the vale, they fade away.
> Yet still the tender, vacant gloom remains,
> Still the cold cheek its shuddering tear retains.
>
> [*An Evening Walk* (1793), ll. 379–388]

Sympathy no longer is the pity an observer feels in contemplation of human suffering; it becomes the feelings of the "accordant heart" beating in harmony with nature. The twilight, which had been metaphorical in *The Vale of Esthwaite,* becomes literal.

---

[46]Reed *EY*, pp. 21, 307–312; Sheats, pp. 10–11.

The emotion of the "soft" and "tender, vacant gloom" and of the "shuddering tear" is displaced from man to nature. The history of this passage reflects in small the movement of Wordsworth from sentimental to topographical verse, from "A Ballad" and "Sonnet on Seeing Miss Williams Weep" to *An Evening Walk.* The energies that originally focus on sentimental human objects shift to "the infinite variety of natural appearances" (*PW*, I, 319). Even the few sentimental figures of the topographical poems are firmly located in a natural setting.

The second refuge for objectless sympathy lies in self-pity. The involution of pity upon the self is evident in Wordsworth's first description of the "Waiting for Horses" episode:

> No spot but claims the tender tear
> By joy or grief to memory dear.
> One Evening when the wintry blast
> Through the sharp Hawthorn whistling pass'd
> And the poor flocks, all pinch'd with cold
> Sad-drooping sought the mountain fold
> Long, long, upon yon naked rock
> Alone, I bore the bitter shock;
> Long, long, my swimming eyes did roam
> For little Horse to bear me home,
> To bear me—what avails my tear?
> To sorrow o'er a Father's bier.
> Flow on, in vain thou hast not flow'd,
> But eased me of a heavy load;
> For much it gives my heart relief
> To pay the mighty debt of grief,
> With sighs repeated o'er and o'er,
> I mourn because I mourned no more.
> [*The Vale of Esthwaite,* ll. 416–433]

Even this early, Wordsworth needs to assert that things and places, all things and places if interpreted rightly, have emotional significance. Every "spot" potentially can make a claim upon the emotions. The content of the emotion is irrelevant; the poet is equally willing to shed "the tender tear" for joy or grief. The memory of the hawthorn and sheep is a potent way of asserting that "while I wandered round the vale / From every rock would hang a tale" (ll. 494–495). The pathos of personal experience, of the father's loss, is important primarily because it provides powerful substance from which to make poetry. The poet becomes his own sentimental object, and the response to self-description becomes the purpose of the exercise. The poet's eye is doubly on himself, on past emotion and present response, which he describes in cathartic terms; tears "eased him of a heavy load," and sighs "give the heart relief." He is relieved, not from sorrow, as one might expect, nor from guilt, as is the case in the *Prelude* XI version of events, but from emotional vacuity. "I mourn because I mourned no more" reflects the sentimentalist's eager interest in his own feelings and also his fear that even the most emotionally loaded topic can become void of power.

From his father's death, the poet turns to his own:

> A still Voice whispers to my breast
> I soon shall be with them that rest.
> Then may some kind and pious friend
> Assiduous o'er my body bend,
> Once might I see him turn aside
> The kind unwilling tear to hide.
>
> [ll. 444–449]

As in "Tintern Abbey," Wordsworth uses a "friend's" response to his being "where I no more can hear / Thy voice" as the ultimate pathetic device. Evoking his own death puts the most powerful complex of fears and longings at the poet's disposal. The source of this self-sentimentalizing move is, probably, the conclusion of Gray's *Elegy* where the poet imagines the memories others will have of him. At any rate, in conjuring up his own death, Wordsworth alludes to the earlier poem:

> Ah! may my weary body sleep
> In peace beneath a green grass heap,
> In Churchyard, such at death of day
> As heard the pensive sighs of Gray;
> . . . . .

And, what would even in death be dear,
Ah! pour upon the spot a tear.
Friend of my soul! for whom I feel
What words can never half reveal.

[ll. 456–459; 464–467]

By making himself the pathetic object, Wordsworth collapses the distance between the pitying observer and the suffering he contemplates. The source of emotion and the emotion itself are both located in the self. Wordsworth's, like all sentimentalism, is liable to turn into self-pity; the basically inward concerns, the focus upon one's own response, make the sentimentalist particularly vulnerable to a kind of solipsistic pathos.

V

What Schiller calls "reflection" is always characteristic of Wordsworthian pathos. Indeed my primary aim in this book is to explore the forms such sentimental self-consciousness takes in Wordsworth. Most of the time, I do not explicitly label such self-consciousness as "sentimental," but it can hardly be overemphasized that the assumptions underlying his delineation of "human passions, human characters, and human incidents" are those of his age. To stress Wordsworth's "sentimentalism," this chapter will conclude by presenting a few familiar, later passages where his sentimental education surfaces most noticeably.

The description of the Poet in the "Preface" to *Lyrical Ballads* (1802) is shot through with sentimental language and posturing. As elsewhere, Wordsworth turns from the poetic object to the man contemplating it. Though the Poet is "a man speaking to men," he is also an aristocrat of responsiveness: "a man . . . endued with more lively sensibility, more enthusiasm and tenderness, who has a greater knowledge of human nature, and a more comprehensive soul, than are supposed to be common among mankind; a man pleased with his own passions and volitions, and who rejoices more than other men in the spirit of life that is in him" (*Prose*, I, 138). The Poet is, in short, a Man of

Feeling. This part of Wordsworth's definition could apply to Yorick, Werther, Rousseau's self-projection in the *Confessions,* or virtually any sentimental hero or heroine. The Poet's "lively sensibility" defines itself in relation to "real and substantial action and suffering": "it will be the wish of the Poet to bring his feelings near to those of the persons whose feelings he describes, nay, for short spaces of time, perhaps, to let himself slip into an entire delusion, and even confound and identify his own feelings with theirs" (*Prose,* I, 138). The halting way in which the identification of self and other is pushed, "for short spaces of time, perhaps," emphasizes Wordsworth's consciousness that such submersion of the self is "an entire delusion." This illusion is not unlike the "pause of life" the narrator claims to feel in the "Sonnet on Seeing Miss Williams Weep." That such ultimate sympathy is not empirically valid does not make it less interesting or important to the Poet. Indeed, the mind's conscious passing of this sentimental fiction upon itself, coupled with the return from "delusion," helps define the boundaries of imagination. The voyage out and back again is that of the sonnet, where

> Life left my loaded heart, and closing eye;
> A sigh recall'd the wanderer to my breast;
> Dear was the pause of life, and dear the sigh
> That call'd the wanderer home, and home to rest.

The creation and contemplation of other people's misery make the Poet aware of the pleasures and limitations of sensibility. Wordsworth finds in human suffering the "freedom and power" which press the mind back upon itself. The pathetic, like the sublime, makes him more aware of his own passions and volitions. The sentimental poet looks out into the world of guilt and sorrow in order to discover himself.

During their stay in Germany (1799), Wordsworth and Coleridge engaged in a controversy regarding the merits of the popular balladeer Gottfried Bürger. A series of letters, now lost, passed between Goslar and Ratzeburg, discussing poetic incidents and the nature of character, as the two authors of *Lyrical*

Ballads (1798), in effect, debated the direction their work should take in the future. Surviving fragments of Wordsworth's opinions provide a glimpse of Wordsworth as reader of other people's poetry. Not surprisingly, his criticism of Bürger shows the characteristic sentimental move from pathos to the mind of man:

> As to Bürger, I am yet far from that admiration of him which he has excited in you; but I am by nature slow to admire; and I am not yet sufficiently master of the language to understand him perfectly. In one point I entirely coincide with you, in your feeling concerning his versification. In "Lenore" the concluding double rhymes of the stanza have both a delicious and *pathetic* effect—
> > "Ach! aber für Lenoren
> > War Gruss und Kuss verloren."
>
> I accede too to your opinion that Bürger is always the poet; he is never the mobbist, one of those dim drivellers with which our island has teemed for so many years. Bürger is one of those authors whose book I like to have in my hand, but when I have laid the book down I do not think about him. I remember a hurry of pleasure, but I have few distinct forms that people my mind, nor any recollection of delicate or minute feelings which he has either communicated to me, or taught me to recognise. [*EL*, p. 234]

Demonstrating the sentimentalist's concern with the beat of his own pulse, the letter to Coleridge is alert to the effects of poetry upon the reader. Wordsworth uses notably sentimental vocabulary to describe the way in which a technical poetic device strikes him. "Delicious and *pathetic*" describe that mixture of pleasure and pain which a Sterne or Williams continually refers to, in the very language they would have used. More significantly, the kind of inner space which sentimental self-consciousness opens up is in evidence as Wordsworth talks about Bürger. Wordsworth as reader goes from poetry into himself, exploring "delicate or minute feelings" and "distinct forms that people my mind." The literature he read in his youth made him sensitive to such movements of the mind and ambitious to describe them.

In the 1815 "Preface," Wordsworth lists "Sensibility" second among "the powers requisite for the production of poetry," commenting that "the more exquisite it is, the wider will be the range of a poet's perceptions; and the more will he be incited to observe objects, both as they exist in themselves and as re-acted upon by his own mind" (*Prose,* III, 26). "Re-action," the requickening of the mind in response to "objects," is the characteristic method of Wordsworth's poetry. Such objects can be either human or natural, and the mode of response is sublime or pathetic according to their status. When the objects are human in Wordsworth, most often the people before the poet's eye are such conventional recipients of sentimental attention as the beggar, the disappointed lover, the discharged soldier, the abandoned woman. The play between Wordsworth's mind and human suffering is no doubt more complex, and interesting, than what we find in most late-eighteenth-century sentimental texts. The difference, however, is in degree rather than in kind. The qualities that vivify Wordsworthian pathos—its psychological focus, its interest in tragic response, and its self-conscious art—are all to be found in those sentimental writers whom Wordsworth himself, rightly if not modestly, would have characterized as "the predecessors of an original Genius of a high order."

2 Suffering and Calm in the Early Poetry, 1788–1798

The tragedies of the Athenian poets are as mirrors in which the spectator beholds himself, under a thin disguise of circumstance, stript of all but that ideal perfection and energy which every one feels to be the internal type of all that he loves, admires, and would become. The imagination is enlarged by a sympathy with pains and passions so mighty, that they distend in their conception the capacity of that by which they are conceived; the good affections are strengthened by pity, indignation, terror, and sorrow; and an exalted calm is prolonged from the satiety of this high exercise of them into the tumult of familiar life.

—Shelley, "A Defence of Poetry"

I

Readers have often thought that the ending of *The Ruined Cottage* evades the poem's emotional and philosophical consequences. The tranquillity that pervades the closing lines has seemed incongruous after the relentless depiction of Margaret's disintegration. The general opinion has been that of F. R. Leavis, who sees this calm as an elegiac sleight-of-hand, in which the Pedlar's "consummate poetic skill" effects "a disciplined limiting of contemplation to the endurable, and, consequently, a withdrawal to a reassuring environment." Herbert Lindenberger has compared the poem's ending to Nahum Tate's desecration of *King Lear;* Florence Marsh has characterized it as the "evasion" of a "painful memory"; and E. E. Bostetter has said that "in affixing such a conclusion, Wordsworth has in effect repudiated the story as he has told it."[1] For such readers,

---

[1] F. R. Leavis, *Revaluation* (London: Chatto & Windus, 1936), pp. 181, 179; Herbert Lindenberger, *On Wordsworth's "Prelude"* (Princeton: Princeton Univer-

Wordsworth becomes a mere *zauberlehrling* who fears the emotions unleashed by his conjuration and desperately attempts to deny them. Their Wordsworth is an existentialist manqué, retreating from the abyss of universal evil and despair.

Whatever its attractions, such an interpretation ignores Wordsworth's obvious fascination with suffering. Through his poetry, after all, troops a veritable parade of victims; the insane, the miserable, the diseased, decrepit, dying, and dead populate his landscape to the virtual exclusion of the healthy and the normal. It seems likely that in such a poet the transition from suffering to calm has a more adequate explanation than repression or a sudden desire for decorum; indeed, as this chapter will suggest, calm or tranquillity represents the central response of Wordsworth's imagination to the fictional representation of human misery.

Paradoxically, the place to begin a discussion of the tranquil conclusion of *The Ruined Cottage*[2] is the poem's opening. Here the natural surroundings are completely unlike those in which the Pedlar and the young man "chearfully pursue" their "evening way."[3] The narrator wanders alone across a desolate plain; the summer sun beats down mercilessly, and the "uplands feebly glare" at him "through a pale steam" (ll. 2–3). He toils "with languid feet," baffled by "the slipp'ry ground" (l. 20). Finally, he collapses:

> when I stretched myself
> On the brown earth my limbs from very heat
> Could find no rest nor my weak arm disperse

---

sity Press, 1963), pp. 228–229; Florence Marsh, *Wordsworth's Imagery: A Study in Poetic Vision* (New Haven: Yale University Press, 1952), p. 61; E. E. Bostetter, *The Romantic Ventriloquists* (Seattle: University of Washington Press, 1963), p. 65.

[2] The texts of *The Ruined Cottage* used in this book are those presented in *RC & P*. Unless otherwise stated, passages are quoted from Butler's reading text for MS. D. The numbering of passages from *The Pedlar* (MS. D) is from Jonathan Wordsworth, *The Music of Humanity* (New York: Harper & Row, 1969), pp. 172–183.

[3] This is from the closing line of the "Addendum" to MS. B. *PW*, V, 404; *RC & P*, pp. 278–279. Numbering of passages from the "Addendum" throughout this book is from *PW*, V, 400–404.

The insect host which gathered round my face
And joined their murmurs to the tedious noise
Of seeds of bursting gorse that crackled round.

[ll. 21–26]

A digression about a dreaming man (ll. 10–18) appears in the midst of this description. His world is one of "soft cool moss," "dewy shade," and a wren's "soothing melody," yet Wordsworth makes clear that both traveler and dreamer experience the same countryside. The prostrating heat is, from the perspective of the dreaming man, "clear and pleasant sunshine . . . pleasant to him" (ll. 9–10). Among much else, this digression emphasizes the subjective nature of the narrator's experience.[4] It suggests that internal factors are responsible for his disharmony with the environment, that his weakness is more a mental than physical state. Like the Wordsworthian observer in the opening lines of *Salisbury Plain,* "A Night-Piece," and "The Climbing of Snowdon," he perceives nature as hostile and oppressive because of undefined psychological and spiritual burdens which he carries with him. Insignificant particulars, the insects and the bursting gorse seed, impinge upon a mind weak and easily distracted. Surrounded by petty annoyances, beset by a sense of profound futility, the narrator finds in nature a correlative and sympathetic image of the world within.

In the poem's narrative structure, this hostile landscape is antithetical to the closing scene. No empirical reason exists why evening should be less oppressive than noon. Out of the day's expiration, after all, suitably minded poets have often conjured gloom, despair, and melancholy intimations of mortality. One

[4]In "'Finer Distance': The Narrative Art of Wordsworth's 'The Wanderer,'" *ELH* 39 (1972), 87–111, Reeve Parker has traced the dreaming man motif in *Excursion* I. Parker's discussion of these opening lines emphasizes the dreamer's subjectivity; he, no less than the narrator, is the "prisoner of either an innocent or a willed illusion." The evidence for this is the "ambiguity of language" and "equivocal connotations" which describe the dreamer's view (p. 94). I would note that, for Wordsworth, the force of this dual subjectivity is positive rather than invidious—far from despairing that objectivity is impossible, he emphasizes the extent to which the mind creates the world in which it lives.

would think it appropriate for Wordsworth to have done as much after the Pedlar tells Margaret's story. Instead

> He ceased. By this the sun declining shot
> A slant and mellow radiance which began
> To fall upon us where beneath the trees
> We sate on that low bench, and now we felt,
> Admonished thus, the sweet hour coming on.
> A linnet warbled from those lofty elms,
> A thrush sang loud, and other melodies,
> At distance heard, peopled the milder air.
>
> [ll. 526-533]

The radical change in a sympathetic Nature reflects the traveler's psychological state. Something has worked a complete transformation, as almost paranoid irritability has given way to calm and a sense of universal harmony. Isolation and alienation dissolve in a world "peopled" by "melodies." But all that has happened has been the experience of listening to the tale of Margaret. If the change is not simply cosmetic, it derives from the contemplation of her suffering.

To emphasize this transformation, the conclusion of *The Ruined Cottage* presents three parallel conversions from uneasiness to calm. First, the Pedlar catechizes the young man:

> My Friend, enough to sorrow have you given,
> The purposes of wisdom ask no more;
> Be wise and chearful, and no longer read
> The forms of things with an unworthy eye.
> She sleeps in the calm earth, and peace is here.
>
> [ll. 508-512]

The Pedlar does not say the expected "She sleeps in the calm earth, and peace is *there*." The peace that the Pedlar finds, though connected to the earth where Margaret sleeps, is present in the immediate surroundings. Since previous descriptions of the cottage's environs have evoked only ruin and decay, clearly an internal response to Margaret's tale generates the peace found "here." Reading "the forms of things" is like reading about Margaret. When done properly, it evokes not "the impo-

tence of grief" (l. 500), but a cheerful and even exultant tranquillity.

In the Pedlar's subsequent reminiscence of the spear-grass
vision, he describes a similar, prior transfiguration of sorrow
into tranquillity:

> I well remember that those very plumes,
> Those weeds, and the high spear-grass on that wall,
> By mist and silent rain-drops silver'd o'er,
> As once I passed did to my heart convey
> So still an image of tranquillity,
> So calm and still, and looked so beautiful
> Amid the uneasy thoughts which filled my mind,
> That what we feel of sorrow and despair
> From ruin and from change, and all the grief
> The passing shews of being leave behind,
> Appeared an idle dream that could not live
> Where meditation was.
>
> [ll. 513–524]

Before seeing the spear-grass, his state had been roughly equivalent to the narrator's present emotionally excited, uneasy condition. The spear-grass, by impressing an "image of tranquillity"
upon his mind, provided an escape from temporal limitation.
"The passing shews of being" became, for the moment, "an idle
dream." Significantly, the Pedlar has earlier used the same
spear-grass as an image of desolation:

>   She is dead,
> The worm is on her cheek, and this poor hut,
> Stripp'd of its outward garb of houshold flowers,
> Of rose and sweet-briar, offers to the wind
> A cold bare wall whose earthy top is tricked
> With weeds and the rank spear-grass.
>
> [ll. 103–108]

This "visual peripety," as M. H. Abrams has termed it,[5] indicates
the reversal of the Pedlar's outlook. The brute stuff of nature

[5]M. H. Abrams, *Natural Supernaturalism* (New York: Norton, 1971), pp. 376–
377.

remains the same, but the mind of man changes, moving from despair to tranquillity. As has been seen, the young man accepts the vision, and the tranquillity of the past spear-grass vision is recapitulated in the evening calm. Thus, at the conclusion of *The Ruined Cottage,* a tripled experience of suffering and calm is meant to assert that a sense of tranquillity can result from the contemplation of human suffering.

Wordsworth's knowledge of *The Poetics* is uncertain, but in *The Ruined Cottage* he dramatizes a psychological process equivalent to Aristotelian *katharsis.*[6] Beginning in uneasiness and despair, the characters meditate upon the tale of sorrow, give themselves up to it, and are purged of their previous feelings. The calm of Nature is the metaphor by which the poet describes the cathartic effects of Margaret's tragedy. A striking parallel to the calm vision which closes *The Ruined Cottage* is the chorus's final speech in *Samson Agonistes:*

> His servants he with new acquist
> Of true experience from this great event
> With peace and consolation hath dismist,
> And calm of mind, all passion spent.
>
> [ll. 1755–1758]

Milton self-consciously incorporates an explicitly cathartic response within the text of his play. As watchers of Samson's demise, the Danites are analogues to readers; the "calm of mind" they feel is descriptive of tragic purgation. Though less conscious of the history of criticism than Milton is, Wordsworth too includes the response to tragedy within his fiction. His charac-

---

[6]Cleanth Brooks and Jonathan Wordsworth have suggested in passing that something like catharsis occurs in the spear-grass vision. Brooks, "Wordsworth and Human Suffering," in *From Sensibility to Romanticism: Essays Presented to Frederick A. Pottle,* ed. Frederick W. Hilles and Harold Bloom (New York: Oxford University Press, 1965), p. 387; *Music of Humanity,* p. 99. In "Wordsworth's 'Dependency Sublime'," *Essays in Criticism* 14 (1964), 352–362, Michael Irwin proposes a similar transformative role for suffering in Wordsworth's poetry. Using primarily Wordsworth's own terms, he suggests that the contemplation of suffering "obliterates the particular and adventitious," thereby bringing the mind into the realm of the "infinite."

ters, like Shelley's spectator peering into the Athenian tragic mirror, feel "an exalted calm" before returning to "the tumult of familiar life."[7]

Thus, the tranquillity criticized by Leavis and others is the statement of a complex, significant, and familiar response to suffering. Whether he had in mind Aristotle's terminology or not, Wordsworth could find, on the beat of his own pulse and in contemporary theories of the sublime and the pathetic, ample evidence of the cathartic value of pathos. Notably, *The Ruined Cottage* is only one of several early poems where natural tranquillity follows a tale of suffering. The dynamic juxtaposition of suffering and calm forms an important habit of the poet's imagination; time and again, human misery provides the psychic energy necessary to purge life of its petty irritations and to make accessible the cathartic calm. Far from being "mere literature,"[8] the outcast figures of the early poems are objects that provoke the young Wordsworth to intense sympathetic excitement and a consequent sense of tranquillity.

II

The earliest example of suffering and calm in Wordsworth's poetry is the episode of the vagrant family in *An Evening Walk* (ll.

[7]Wordsworth's early reading of *Samson Agonistes* is rather more certain than his familiarity with Aristotle; *An Evening Walk*, line 268, paraphrases line 89 of Milton's tragedy (*PW*, I, 26, 322). For comment on Wordsworth's awareness of the *Poetics*, see Ben Ross Schneider, *Wordsworth's Cambridge Education* (Cambridge: Cambridge University Press, 1957), pp. 95, 263. A passage in the "Preface" to *Lyrical Ballads* suggests only hearsay knowledge: "Aristotle, I have been told, has said, that Poetry is the most philosophic of all writing" (*Prose*, I, 139).

[8]Stephen Gill, "The Original *Salisbury Plain:* Introduction and Text," in *BWS*, p. 147. The rank sensationalism of the early attempts at pathos has often caused critics to regard them as juvenile excrescences, of little value for understanding the mature Wordsworth. Jonathan Wordsworth, for instance, emphasizes the distance between the pathos of *An Evening Walk* and that of *The Ruined Cottage*. The attempt to contrast early literary artificiality and later sincerity masks a discrimination based on admiration for the "compassionate restraint" of *The Ruined Cottage* and "Michael" and distaste for the gaudy sentimental style. *The Music of Humanity*, pp. 50–67; see also Mary Jacobus, *Tradition and Experiment in Wordsworth's "Lyrical Ballads" (1798)* (Oxford: Clarendon Press, 1976), pp. 133–183.

242–328).[9] In attempting to evoke pathos, the apprentice poet spares little. He hurls "torrent gales" and "bitter showers" upon the innocents, relishing such sentimental commonplaces as "frozen arms," "chattering lips," "dying" hearts, and "flooded" cheeks. Finally the children lie dead in their dead mother's arms:

> Soon shall the Light'ning hold before thy head
> His torch, and shew them slumbering in their bed,
> No tears can chill them, and no bosom warms,
> Thy breast their death-bed, coffin'd in thine arms.
>
> [ll. 297–300]

At this point, one might expect anger at a society which makes inevitable such occurrences, or sympathetic moralizing on human existence, or at the least, the justification that the sufferer will be rewarded in the afterlife.[10] The episode seems to demand response or comment; instead we immediately hear:

> Sweet are the sounds that mingle from afar,
> Heard by calm lakes, as peeps the folding star,
> Where the duck dabbles 'mid the rustling sedge,
> And feeding pike starts from the water's edge,
> Or the swan stirs the reeds, his neck and bill
> Wetting, that drip upon the water still;
> And heron, as resounds the trodden shore,
> Shoots upward, darting his long neck before.
> While, by the scene compos'd, the breast subsides,
> Nought wakens or disturbs it's tranquil tides.
>
> [ll. 301–310]

Without editorial upon the tale, or transition to the narrative present, the description of the frozen family ends, and the poet returns to an evening lakeside whose natural tranquillity is made

---

[9]Unless otherwise noted, all references to *An Evening Walk* are to the 1793 edition reprinted in *PW*, I, 4–38.

[10]Indeed, these are characteristic responses that poets of the "female vagrant" genre made to suffering they had evoked; see Cowper's "Crazy Kate," Southey's "The Widow," and many of the magazine poems cited by Robert Mayo in "The Contemporaneity of the *Lyrical Ballads*," *PMLA* 69 (1954), 494–506.

more pronounced, eerie, and moving by the frantic human struggle that has preceded it.[11]

The figure of a person suffering among the elements was common in eighteenth-century poetry. To satisfy an age that found literary pleasure in sentimental response, poets exploited material only too available in the wretches who wandered the countryside. John Langhorne, Robert Southey, George Crabbe, and William Cowper, among others, make such sketches of suffering rural humanity. None of them, however, places tranquillity after pathos in the manner of Wordsworth. Even the apparent literary source of *Evening Walk*'s freezing family, the anonymous "Winter Piece" in Vicesimus Knox's *Elegant Extracts*, expects no other response to suffering than emotion.[12]

Writers of topographical poems, particularly, exploited such sentimental interest by introducing pathetic episodes in the midst of their landscapes.[13] The popularizer, if not originator, of this device was James Thomson in *The Seasons*. The tale of Celadon and Amelia in *Summer* and the description of the man perishing in *Winter*'s snow provide variety and piquancy to the mass of description. Commentators on *The Seasons* were profuse in their praise of these episodes. Joseph Warton singled out among Thomson's "beauties" the man caught in the blizzard, and James Beattie, author of Wordsworth's much-loved *Minstrel*, wrote:

> Do not all readers of taste receive peculiar pleasure from those
> little tales or episodes, with which Thomson's descriptive poem on
> the Seasons is here and there enlivened? And are they not sensible,
> that the thunderstorm would not have been half so interesting
> without the tale of the two lovers; nor the harvest-scene, without

[11]Geoffrey Hartman has noted this apparently incongruous juxtaposition of suffering and calm, in *Wordsworth's Poetry, 1787–1814* (New Haven: Yale University Press, 1964) pp. 95–96. He, however, ascribes it to an anxious sense of nature's duality and asserts that "there is often no real harmony between what one again recognizes as sterner and milder nature."

[12]For "Winter Piece," see *The Music of Humanity*, pp. 52–53.

[13]See, for instance, James Grainger, *The Sugar Cane*, Book II; Joseph Cottle, *Malvern Hill*; Cowper, *The Task*, I: 534–56.

that of Palemon and Lavinia; nor the driving snows, without that exquisite picture of a man perishing among them? It is much to be regretted, that Young did not employ the same artifice.[14]

John Scott, whose rhetorically oriented *Critical Essays* Wordsworth read at Cambridge, also notes that "Our Author's description of scenes of horror, derives great force from this introduction of human beings actually suffering amidst them."[15]

The Seasons are, of course, much in the background of Wordsworth's topographical poetry; the "Essay, Supplementary to the Preface" reflects Wordsworth's particular interest in the episodes: "In any well-used copy of the Seasons the book generally opens of itself with the rhapsody on love, or with one of the stories" (*Prose*, III, 74). At any rate, the place in his reading where Wordsworth learned to express cathartic feelings by juxtaposing suffering and natural tranquillity was probably the tale of Celadon and Amelia in *Summer* (ll. 1169–1232).[16] Scott spends some eight pages discussing the linguistic devices which create the pathetic effect of this passage, and Wordsworth doubtless read both episode and commentary with attention.[17] In "Celadon and Amelia," the lovers wander through an "eternal Eden." Suddenly, a storm rises. To Amelia's expressions of fear, Celadon confidently responds that the innocent face no danger; only the "guilty heart" need shrink from the lightning. He embraces her, exclaiming " 'Tis safety ... thus / To clasp perfection." Divine providence, however, is not human justice; no sooner are these words spoken than "that moment to the ground, / A black-

---

[14]Joseph Warton, *Essay on the Genius and Writings of Pope*, 4th ed. (London: Dodsley, 1782), I, 50; James Beattie, *Essays on Poetry and Music* (Edinburgh: Dilly, 1778), pp. 36–37.

[15]John Scott, *Critical Essays* (London: Phillips, 1785), p. 384. For Wordsworth's use of Scott, see *PW*, I, 20, 321; Paul Sheats, *The Making of Wordsworth's Poetry* (Cambridge: Harvard University Press, 1973), pp. 53–61, 226–227.

[16]All references to *Summer* are from James Thomson, *Poetical Works*, ed. J. Logie Robertson (London: Oxford University Press, 1908), pp. 52–120.

[17]Scott, *Critical Essays*, pp. 338–346.

ened corse, was struck the beauteous maid." Turning from the embittered lover, Thomson describes the scene:

> As from the face of Heaven the shattered clouds
> Tumultuous rove, the interminable sky
> Sublimer swells, and o'er the world expands
> A purer azure. Nature from the storm
> Shines out afresh; and through the lightened air
> A higher lustre and a clearer calm
> Diffusive tremble.

It is as if the girl's death causes the heavens to seem sublimer, brighter, clearer, purer. The contemplation of suffering gives to experience an intensity and awesomeness it has previously lacked. The movement in Thomson to the "clearer calm" is identical to Wordsworth's shift from the pathetic to the tranquil.

The Windy Brow revision of *An Evening Walk*[18] retains the calm interval following the woman's death, but instead of one vagrant family, Wordsworth now presents two. The first, as in the 1793 version, is imagined by the narrator as he looks at a family of swans, "Haply some wretch has eyed them and called them blessed ... I see her now." At the climax, however, a second family enters the mind of the first woman:

> Oh, when the whirling drifts her paths assail,
> And like a torrent roars the mountain gale,
> Perhaps she knows that mother's pangs whose fate
> The shepherds of these hills shall long relate!
>
> [*PW*, I, 28]

This chain of surmise and legendizing is curious. Why bring in the shepherds and the second woman at all? Partially, of course, the insertion of these people puts the suffering at a more comfortable remove. No longer does the death seem solely the creation of the morbid authorial imagination; it becomes a matter of

[18]*PW*, I, 28–31; DC MS. 9.

communal knowledge and responsibility. For similar reasons, Wordsworth attempts to give fictive suffering the appearance of fact in a note inventing "the catastrophe of a poor woman who was found dead on Stanemoor."[19] These "extra" characters serve the additional purpose, however, of calling attention to the narrative process. In the revised version, two layers of response appear between the reader and the central core of suffering. As we have seen, such sentimental complication turns the focus from misery to the observer of misery.

At this point, the poet addresses someone who may be either vagrant woman, and is perhaps both:

> Poor Wanderer, when from forest, brook and dell
> Long sounding groans the storm's approach foretell,
> Thy memory in those groans shall live and cast
> Fresh horror o'er wide Stanemoor's wintry waste.
>
> [*PW*, I, 28]

The knowledge of suffering colors the landscape with ominous foreboding, as the groans of the approaching storm and a freezing woman coalesce. The association of ideas links the sounds of weather to those of human misery. Wordsworth's phrasing is ambiguous, perhaps intentionally so: "thy memory" may be the "mental faculty" of the first woman who recreates "that mother's pangs," thereby casting "fresh horror" over nature. Alternately, "thy memory" is the communal recollection of the second, dead woman, which lives in the minds of the shepherds and the first woman. Such ambiguity creates the impression of a continuing series. A present wanderer remembers past suffering and, in her turn, it is implied, becomes the stuff of future legend. The sense

---

[19]*PW*, I, 29. As Jonathan Wordsworth has pointed out, the creation of the frozen family episode c. 1788 antedated the actual deaths on Stanemoor (of three men!) by some six years, suggesting that Wordsworth was "trying to disguise its merely sentimental origin" (*The Music of Humanity*, p. 52). Moreover, the poet perhaps knew from his reading that Scott had praised Thomson for sometimes being "happy enough to bring real facts in example" in treating pathetic episodes (*Critical Essays*, p. 384).

of historical repetition is reinforced by a shift from the past tense
to the present:

> When blind she wildered o'er the lightless heath
> Led by Fear's icy hand and dogged by Death
> Who as she turned her neck the kiss to seek
> Broke off the dreadful kiss with angry shriek.
> —Snatched from her shoulder with despairing call
> She clasps them propped against that roofless wall
> Now ruthless tempest launch thy deadliest dart
>   but let us perish heart to heart
> Weak roof a cowering form two babes to shield
> And faint the fire a dying heart can yield
> Press the sad kiss fond mother! vainly fears
> Thy flooded cheek to chill them with its tears
> —Ah then to baffle the relentless storm
> She tries each fond device Despair can form
> Beneath her stiffened coats to shield them strives
> With love whose providence in death survives.
>
> [*PW*, I, 28–29; DC MS. 9]

It becomes impossible to tell precisely who is frozen when. The
tense used here is not the poem's narrative present, but a
visionary present—it can be read either as a rhetorical shift to
enliven a single death on Stanemoor or as a recapitulation of
that death in the present demise of yet another female vagrant.

At any rate, in the same vague present, the poet claims:

> When morning breaks I see the [   ] swain
> Sole moving object in all that boundless plain
> Start at her stedfast form by horror deck'd,
> Dead, and as if in act to move, erect.—
> The ear is lost in wonder thus to find
> Such quiet with such various sounds combined,
> And wondring ever knows not if 'tis more
> Hurry or stillness, silence or uproar.
>
> [*PW*, I, 29; DC MS. 9]

Sheats notes de Selincourt's error in reading "horror" for
"hurry" in DC MS. 9; he also criticizes *Poetical Works'* placement

of the last four lines so as to suggest that they "form the conclud-ing lines of the description of the vagrant."[20] In the manuscript, the lines in question are scribbled later in the right-hand margin; however, they are connected to the previous four lines, as in my text, with a dash, suggesting a link between the scene of horror and the subsequent tranquillity. The use of dashes in *An Evening Walk* is epidemic, and invariably a conjunction of thought is dis-cernible. Therefore, the shift here from suffering to calm is not simply "the most violent transition in the poem."[21] The passage belongs to both the morning calm where "I see" the swain and the woman, and to the evening landscape which is the poem's narrative present. The dynamic tension between hurry and still-ness, silence and uproar, finds a counterpoint in the woman's form, "stedfast" yet "as if in act to move."

Two instances of suffering and calm appear in *Descriptive Sketches*,[22] in the episodes of the Grison gypsy (ll. 184–282) and the chamois hunter (ll. 366–441). Wordsworth again follows Thomson's strategy of enlivening natural "scenes of horror" by the "introduction of human beings actually suffering amidst them." The gypsy and the hunter act as "appropriate human centres" in landscapes remarkable for sublimity and inhospi-tality; they are axes of suffering, the foci and yet the victims of their surroundings. In their deaths, the dynamic relationship of pathos and tranquillity provides the narrative's central paradox.

The description of the gypsy's death is recognizibly derivative from the self-imagined death of Hassan the camel-driver in Col-lins' second *Persian Eclogue:*

> —Bursts from the troubl'd Larch's giant boughs
> The pie, and chattering breaks the night's repose.
> Low barks the fox: by Havoc rouz'd the bear,
> Quits, growling, the white bones that strew his lair;
> The dry leaves stir as with the serpent's walk,

---

[20]Sheats, *The Making of Wordsworth's Poetry*, pp. 97–98, 269; DC MS. 9.
[21]Sheats, p. 57.
[22]All references to *Descriptive Sketches* are to the 1793 edition reprinted in *PW*, I, 42–90.

And, far beneath, Banditti voices talk;
Behind her hill the Moon, all crimson, rides,
And his red eyes the slinking water hides;
Then all is hushed; the bushes rustle near,
And with strange tinglings sings her fainting ear.
—Vexed by the darkness, from the piny gulf
Ascending, nearer howls the famish'd wolf,
While thro' the stillness scatters wild dismay,
Her babe's small cry, that leads him to his prey.
                [*Descriptive Sketches*, ll. 229–242]

O cease, my fears! all frantic as I go,
When thought creates unnumbered scenes of woe,
What if the lion in his rage I meet!
Oft in the dust I view his printed feet:
And fearful! oft, when Day's declining light
Yields her pale empire to this mourner Night,
By hunger roused, he scours the groaning plain,
Gaunt wolves and sullen tigers in his train:
Before them Death with shrieks directs their way,
Fills the wild yell, and leads them to their prey.
                [*Persian Eclogue* II, ll. 49–58]

Critics whom Wordsworth had read were lavish in their praise of the passage from Collins. John Scott thought it "one of finest instances of the horrid sublime our language can boast of." In "Observations" printed with most late-eighteenth-century editions of Collins, John Langhorne exclaims, "Nothing, certainly, could be more greatly conceived, or more adequately expressed, than the image in the last couplet."[23] Wordsworth eliminates Collins' prosopopoeia of Death and has a baby's cry "lead" the wolf "to his prey." The most significant variation on Collins, however, is the anxious quiet that accentuates the horror: "chattering breaks the night's repose"; "all is hushed; the bushes rustle near"; "thro' the stillness scatters wild dismay, / Her babe's small cry." Such silence represents not tragic catharsis but a form

---

[23]Scott, *Critical Essays*, p. 171; [John Langhorne], "Observations on the Oriental Eclogues," in *The Works of the English Poets with Prefaces, Biographical and Critical, by Samuel Johnson*, vol. 49 (London: Bathurst et al., 1779), 294.

of sublimity. Here, as in Burke's *Enquiry,* silence, with vacuity, darkness, solitude, and "all *general* privations,"[24] opens interestingly empty spaces in the mindscape. Though Wordsworth's gypsy obviously lacks the necessary physical distance from danger, the "sudden beginning, or sudden cessation of sound" evokes in the reader the "staggering, and hurry of the mind" central to sublime experience.[25]

After the wolf finds his prey, the tranquil plenitude of tragic response is invoked, though briefly:

> Now, passing Urseren's open vale serene,
> Her quiet streams, and hills of downy green
>
> [ll. 243–244]

For the moment, however, the poet withholds himself from cathartic serenity and plunges back into the sublime. The landscape that has destroyed the woman is recapitulated: after passing the quiet valley, we find "narrow walks of death," "floods," "Black drizzling craggs," and "Bare steeps, where Desolation stalks" (ll. 245–251). To such a vision of natural horror, one possible response is passive acceptance:

> By cells whose image, trembling as he prays,
> Awe struck, the kneeling peasant scarce surveys;
> Loose-hanging rocks the Day's bless'd eye that hide,
> And crosses rear'd to Death on every side,
> Which with cold kiss Devotion planted near,
> And, bending, water'd with the human tear,
> Soon fading "silent" from her upward eye,
> Unmov'd with each rude form of Danger nigh,
> Fix'd on the anchor left by him who saves
> Alike in whelming snows and roaring waves.
>
> [ll. 253–2€

---

[24]Edmund Burke, *A Philosophical Enquiry into the Origin of our Ideas of the Sublime and Beautiful,* ed. J. T. Boulton (New York: Columbia University Press, 1958), p. 71.
[25]Burke, *Enquiry,* pp. 82–83.

In the context of the gypsy's death, how are we to interpret such a description of primitive Catholicism? Clearly, Wordsworth rejects Christianity as blind and self-deluding. The image of Christian man is the kneeling peasant who scarcely knows where or what he is. Devotion, with its "cold kiss," stolidly ignores the sublime Alpine landscape which so excites the young apostle of fear's ministry. It may well be, too, that there are sardonic and ironic undertones in the 1793 text. The invocation of "him who saves / Alike in whelming snows and roaring waves," if not bland piety, is outright blasphemy. The footnote on the cells, similarly, seems to attack Superstition in Gibbon's manner: "The Catholic religion prevails here. These cells are, as is well known, very common in the Catholic countries, planted, like Roman tombs, along the road side" (*PW,* I, 56). At the least, an abyss of sensibility separates rational Englishman from superstitious Latin, the "sentimental traveller and the philosopher" (*PW,* I, 80) from the peasant groveling before his angry God.

A response to suffering, alternative to Christian self-delusion, appears in the subsequent lines:

> On as we move, a softer prospect opes,
> Calm huts, and lawns between, and sylvan slopes.
> While mists, suspended on th'expiring gale,
> Moveless o'er-hang the deep secluded vale,
> The beams of evening, slipping soft between,
> Light up of tranquil joy a sober scene;—
> Winding it's dark-green wood and emerald glade,
> The still vale lengthens underneath the shade;
> While in soft gloom the scattering bowers recede,
> Green dewy lights adorn the freshen'd mead,
> Where solitary forms illumin'd stray
> Turning with quiet touch the valley's hay,
> On the low brown wood-huts delighted sleep
> Along the brighten'd gloom reposing deep.
> While pastoral pipes and streams the landscape lull,
> And bells of passing mules that tinkle dull,
> In solemn shapes before th'admiring eye
> Dilated hang the misty pines on high,

> Huge convent domes with pinnacles and tow'rs,
> And antique castles seen thro' drizzling show'rs.
>
> [ll. 263–282]

This is the sole passage from *Descriptive Sketches* upon which the Fenwick notes comment: "I will only notice that the description of the valley filled with mist, beginning—'In solemn shapes,' was taken from that beautiful region of which the principal features are Lugarn and Sarnen. Nothing that I ever saw in nature left a more delightful impression on my mind than that which I have attempted, alas, how feebly! to convey to others in these lines" (*PW*, I, 324).

Arthur Beatty has remarked that the Lugarn and Sarnen Lakes "are included in that part of Switzerland spoken of in Wordsworth's note to lines 427–519," "the middle region of the Alps."[26] Though the poet's "sketching" has a somewhat random relation to his Swiss travels,[27] the poem's central section (ll. 184–567) follows the route of his tour. The description moves from the Grison gypsy's agony "where Viamala's chasms confine / Th' indignant waters of the infant Rhine" (ll. 184–185), past "Urseren's open vale serene" (l. 243), to "plunge with the Russ" (l. 245) into the Schöllenenthal (ll. 263–282). There follow "Uri's Lake" (ll. 283–316) and the "fane of Tell" (l. 349) on Lake Lucerne. After the chamois hunter's death, there are glances at the Unterwalden (l. 417), the Aar gorge (l. 415), and "Huge Pikes of Darkness named, of Fear and Storms" (l. 564), that is, the Schreck-Horn and Wetter-Horn. In this series of place names, the only notable disjunction from Wordsworth's itinerary is his placement of the valley-mist experience in the Schöllenenthal rather than in the Unterwalden. Apparently, as for the sunset over "Uri's Lake," the poet "consulted nature and [his]

[26]*Wordsworth: Representative Poems,* ed. Arthur Beatty (New York: Odyssey, 1937), p. 45; *PW*, I, 69.
[27]The poem leaps from Chartreuse (ll. 53–79) to Como (ll. 80–147), then back again to Simplon (ll. 178–183); Chamonix, in fact the second major sight on Wordsworth's tour, is reserved for the climactic denunciation of the *anciens régimes*. See *PW*, I, 325–326, for Wordsworth's itinerary.

feelings" (*PW,* I, 62). He appropriates the tranquillity of Sarnen to conclude the Grison gypsy episode in violation of geographical reality but in harmony with his emotions. The "calm huts," the "mists suspended," the "tranquil joy" of a sunset scene where "solitary forms" turn hay "with quiet touch" correspond to the internal response to the tale of female suffering.

In depicting the lost chamois hunter (ll. 366–441), Wordsworth consults not only nature and his feelings but also a travel book by Ramond de Carbonnières. As Émile Legouis pointed out, the picturesque details of *Descriptive Sketches* owed a good deal to Ramond's augmentation of *Lettres de M. William Coxe . . . sur l'État politique, civil, et naturel de la Suisse.* With much else, Wordsworth found in Ramond's book the hunter who slashes his feet in order to obtain traction:

> Des orages subits mouillent les roches et les rendent si glissantes, que la chaussure, quelque bien ferrée qu'elle soit, ne peut s'y cramponner; quelquefois la chaleur a tellement desséché leurs faces brulantes et les a couvertes d'une poussière si mobile, que le malheureux qui les gravit s'est vu forcé de les humecter avec son sang en se faisant à la plante des pieds et aux jambes de larges coupures.[28]

> Ye dewy mists the arid rocks o'er-spread
> Whose slippery face derides his deathful tread!
> —To wet the peak's impracticable sides
> He opens of his feet the sanguine tides,
> Weak and more weak the issuing current eyes
> Lapp'd by the panting tongue of thirsty skies.
>
> [ll. 392–397]

That the poet should select such a detail reflects an interest in the minutiae of suffering. Even this early, Wordsworth's imagi-

[28]Émile Legouis, *The Early Life of William Wordsworth,* trans. J. W. Matthews (London: Dent, 1897), p. 476. "Sudden storms moisten the rocks and make them so slippery that boots, however well fitted with iron they may be, cannot cling to them; sometimes the heat so dries the rock's burning surfaces and covers them with a dust so unstable that the unhappy man who climbs them is forced to wet them with his blood by making large cuts in the soles of his feet and in his legs" (my translation).

nation clings to the palpable. The episode of the chamois hunter proceeds toward its inevitable end by calling up all manner of Alpine horrors to torment the victim. Avalanches, cold, and starvation have a turn at the man, until finally scavengers, the eagle and an ironically unhelpful "raven of the skies," appear to await the end. Extending the pathos, Wordsworth describes the family's futile vigil and even a son's discovery, "in future days," of his father's bones.

On this occasion, a series of four questions appears between the description of suffering and the consequent tranquillity:

> Hence shall we turn where, heard with fear afar,
> Thunders thro' echoing pines the headlong Aar?
> Or rather stay to taste the mild delights
> Of pensive Underwalden's pastoral heights?
> —Is there who mid these awful wilds has seen
> The native Genii walk the mountain green?
> Or heard, while other worlds their charms reveal,
> Soft music from th' aereal summit steal?
>
> [ll. 414–421]

Grammatical and topical connections join these questions into two distinct pairs, which postulate alternative responses to pathos. The first questions refer to crude emotional responses: "Hence shall we turn . . . with fear" to listen to a torrent "or rather stay to taste the mild delights" of the melancholy Unterwalden?[29] This response approximates the ambivalent pleasure of emotional upheaval caused by the contemplation of suffering. The second pair of questions, however, like the spear-grass vision, implies a different order of experience; seeing "native Genii walk the mountain green" and hearing "soft music from th'aereal summit" suggest a realm where the "passing shews of being" become an "idle dream."

Wordsworth seems to choose the visionary tranquillity implied

---

[29]Wordsworth's note associates the Unterwalden with the "melancholy disposition." *PW,* I, 68.

by the second pair of questions; for the subsequent lines evoke
an extended natural calm:

> While o'er the desert, answering every close,
> Rich steam of sweetest perfume comes and goes.
> —And sure there is a secret Power that reigns
> Here, where no trace of man the spot profanes,
> Nought but the herds that pasturing upward creep,
> Hung dim-discover'd from the dangerous steep,
> Or summer hamlet, flat and bare, on high
> Suspended, mid the quiet of the sky.
> How still! no irreligious sound or sight
> Rouzes the soul from her severe delight.
> An idle voice the sabbath region fills
> Of Deep that calls to Deep across the hills,
> Broke only by the melancholy sound
> Of drowsy bells for ever tinkling round;
> Faint wail of eagle melting into blue
> Beneath the cliffs, and pine-woods steady sugh;
> The solitary heifer's deepen'd low;
> Or rumbling heard remote of falling snow.
>
> [ll. 422–439]

The landscape is that which has destroyed the chamois hunter.
The "dangerous steep," the eagle's "faint wail," and the "rum-
bling heard remote of falling snow" recall the pathetic scene just
narrated, yet it is "all changed, changed utterly." No longer is
there terror, but a pastoral tranquillity "mid the quiet of the
sky." The phrase "severe delight" is evidently borrowed from
Thomson's *Summer* where the poet "deep-roused" feels "A sacred terrour, a severe delight" (ll. 540–541). In Thomson, delight
has its source in a commonplace of eighteenth-century sublimity,
"the midnight depth / Of yonder grove, of wildest largest
growth" (ll. 516–517); Wordsworth, like Burke, finds a strenu-
ous delight in human suffering. As in the spear-grass vision, the
tranquillity which Wordsworth asserts is explicitly transcendental. No trace of humanity "the spot profanes"; the Alps
become a "sabbath region" ruled by a "secret Power."

III

Calm as the response to pity and terror becomes a dominant motif in *Salisbury Plain*.[30] In the poem's gross structure and at several critical points in the narrative, the contemplation of suffering provokes a feeling of tranquillity. As in *The Ruined Cottage*, Wordsworth presents "man and nature walking hand in hand through the poem, in overt congruity of mood."[31] A single traveler appears, wearily making his way across Sarum's Plain. Each step is "painful," and he looks backward "with a sigh." His sense of homelessness is acute—"in tears" he sees "the crows in blackening eddies homeward borne." Wherever he turns, he finds reflections of his situation. The sun sets in a "troubled west . . . red with stormy fire"; there are "no meads of pleasant green," "no shade," "no brook to wet his lips or soothe his ear," "no sound" except the lark's "wasted strain" and the melancholy wind. Traces of agriculture only reinforce his sense of isolation—he sees the corn, but the sower, the shepherd, the cottage are not to be found (ll. 37–60). An approaching storm is as much the image of turbulence within as it is a real storm.

On the following morning, the traveler draws utterly different perceptions from the same countryside:

> But now from a hill summit down they look
> Where through a narrow valley's pleasant scene

---

[30]This is MS. 1 of *Guilt and Sorrow*. The text used is from *SPP*, pp. 21–38. It has not been generally recognized that this original *Salisbury Plain* is organized much like *The Ruined Cottage*. At the beginning of each poem, a man travels on foot, acutely aware of oppressive natural surroundings. Then, in a deserted building he meets a fellow traveler who tells him a tale of great misery. As each poem concludes, the travelers move off together toward shelter in a transformed world of natural serenity. For a suggestive reading of *The Ruined Cottage* as an "excursus from *Salisbury Plain*," see Enid Welsford, *'Salisbury Plain'* (Oxford: Blackwell, 1966), pp. 66–70.

[31]John Jones, *The Egotistical Sublime* (London: Chatto & Windus, 1954), p. 76. Jones criticizes this use of pathetic fallacy as a "violent absurdity," but in the eighteenth century, such a depiction of nature was a respectable rhetorical device. In his discussion of tropes and figures, James Beattie notes that "the fancy, when roused by real emotions, or by the pathos of composition, is easily reconciled to those figures of speech that ascribe sympathy, perception, and the other attributes of animal life, to things inanimate" (*Essays on Poetry*, p. 276).

> A wreath of vapour tracked a winding brook
> Babbling through groves and lawns and meads of green.
> A smoking cottage peeped the trees between,
> The woods resound the linnet's amorous lays,
> And melancholy lowings intervene
> Of scattered herds that in the meadows graze,
> While through the furrowed grass the merry milkmaid strays.
>
> [ll. 406–414]

The very elements conspicuously absent in the opening scene have sprung up by a kind of Spenserian magic. The brook, the meads of green, the smoking cottage, the shady trees recall and repudiate the sense of vacuity that had overwhelmed the traveler on the previous evening. Obviously, on a literal level, it hardly needs a poet to tell us that the morning after a storm, with sunshine, sparkling water-drops, and singing birds, would be more pleasant than the evening described in *Salisbury Plain*'s first fifteen stanzas. This change in a psychological landscape, however, additionally suggests a radical transformation within the traveler's mind. As in *The Ruined Cottage*, all that has happened to the man is hearing a tale of sorrow—he has met the female vagrant in the dead-house and listened to her story. Nothing in her successive disasters directly encourages hope or cheerfulness, but the narration itself works the change. The best term available to describe such a freshening and revitalization brought on by a tale of suffering is catharsis.

In *Salisbury Plain,* Stonehenge appears as the symbol of "Superstition's reign" (l. 548), and, therefore, of all the reactionary forces responsible for the miserable condition of humanity. The association of Superstition and human suffering is apparent in the passage where the traveler tells the female vagrant "of the wonders of that boundless heath" (l. 172). He, like Wordsworth, is most impressed by the tradition that Stonehenge was the location of Druid sacrifices, "huge wickers paled with circling fire" (l. 424):

> And oft a night-fire mounting to the clouds
> Reveals the desert and with dismal red

Clothes the black bodies of encircling crowds.
It is the sacrificial altar fed
With living men. How deep it groans—the dead
Thrilled in their yawning tombs their helms uprear;
The sword that slept beneath the warriour's head
Thunders in fiery air: red arms appear
Uplifted thro' the gloom and shake the rattling spear.

[ll. 181–189]

Here the poet evidently remembers a vivid passage of Caesar: "Others [of the Druids] have images of immense size, whose members are woven of wicker work, which they fill with living men, which being set on fire, the men enveloped in the flames are burnt to death."[32] In *The Prelude*, Wordsworth claims this apocalyptic vision of human suffering as an actual experience of his rambles over Salisbury Plain:

I called upon the darkness; and it took,
A midnight darkness seem'd to come and take
All objects from my sight; and lo! again
The desart visible by dismal flames!
It is the sacrificial Altar, fed
With living men, how deep the groans, the voice
Of those in the gigantic wicker thrills
Throughout the region far and near, pervades
The monumental hillocks; and the pomp
Is for both worlds, the living and the dead.

[XII: 327–336]

The nightmare vision of man suffering, in both *The Prelude* and *Salisbury Plain,* is an intentional self-incitation. Whether in retelling traditional legends or in "calling upon darkness," there is a deliberate creation of sublime mental experience.

---

[32]*De Bello Gallico:* VI, 16, as translated in R. Huddlestone, *A New Edition of Toland's History of the Druids* (Montrose: James Watt, 1814), p. 321. For Wordsworth's contemporary interest in Druidism, see the notebook entry in DC MS. 12, transcribed by Gill in *SPP,* p. 35.

A radically different night-piece follows the vision of suffering
in *Salisbury Plain:*

> Not thus where clear moons spread their pleasing light.
> —Long bearded forms with wands uplifted shew
> To vast assemblies, while each breath of night
> Is hushed, the living fires that bright and slow
> Rounding th'aetherial field in order go.
> Then as they trace with awe their various files
> All figured on the mystic plain below,
> Still prelude of sweet sounds the moon beguiles
> And charmed for many a league the hoary desert smiles.
>
> > [ll. 190–198]

The sacrifice has cleared the fiery air, and we are brought into a
world of eternal wisdom and serenity. The calm "breath of
night" recalls the language of a rejected ending of *The Ruined
Cottage* where the narrator's cathartic response to Margaret's
suffering is "how sweetly breathes the air—it breathes most
sweet / And my heart feels it." (*RC & P*, pp. 258–259). There is a
similar movement to tranquillity in the *Prelude* version of the
experience on Salisbury Plain:

> I was gently charm'd,
> Albeit with an antiquarian's dream,
> And saw the bearded Teachers, with white wands
> Uplifted, pointing to the starry sky
> Alternately, and Plain below, while breath
> Of music seem'd to guide them, and the Waste
> Was chear'd with stillness and a pleasant sound.
>
> > [XII: 347–353]

The leap is again from suffering to calm, and the intermediaries
between heaven and earth, "the bearded Teachers," are the
bloody-handed Druids. The music of the spheres, a "pleasant
sound" which is paradoxically "stillness," is heard after the tab-
leau of suffering, just as, in the revised *Evening Walk,* the wo-

man's death leaves the poet "lost in wonder thus to find / Such quiet with such various sounds combined."

In the narrative present of *Salisbury Plain,* too, the contemplation of prehistoric misery evokes a kind of calm:

> While thus they talk the churlish storms relent;
> And round those broken walls the dying wind
> In feeble murmurs told his rage was spent.
>
> [ll. 199–201]

The vision of eternal suffering in this Spenserian poem causes storms to relent and winds to cease. Nature reflects the cathartic response to suffering. The Female Vagrant likewise feels some such calm as "With sober sympathy and tranquil mind" she begins her own tale (l. 202). Sympathy, with nature and with the suffering of others, moves the woman to present her history with unexpected serenity.

At its midpoint, the story reaches a dismal climax: "All perished, all in one remorseless year, / Husband and children" (ll. 320–321). The Female Vagrant's response to her losses is the refuge of semiconsciousness where she stays until "on board / A British ship" she wakes "as from a trance restored" (ll. 323–324). Having reached the furthest pitch of agony, her mind has turned round and been restored. At this juncture in *Salisbury Plain,* the boundary between past and present collapses. In the present, too, a kind of restoration takes place; no sooner does the woman tell of waking from her trance than the sun rises:

>   lo!
> Day fresh from ocean wave uprears his lovely brow.
> 'Oh come,' he said, 'come after weary night
> So ruinous far other scene to view.'
> So forth she came and eastward look'd. The sight
> O'er her moist eyes meek dawn of gladness threw
>   . . . . .
> They looked and saw a lengthening road and wain
> Descending a bare slope not far remote.

The downs all glistered dropt with freshening rain;
The carman whistled loud with chearful note.

[ll. 332-337; 343-346]

In the narrative present, restoration from the trance on ship-
board finds an analogue when the woman pauses, "of all present
thought forlorn" (l. 325), and then returns to find a tranquil
nature. In Gill's reading text, the change in nature expresses
catharsis, but in a variant, the psychological mechanism involved
is clearer:

He paused she of all present thought forlorn
While he in   was mute
Till Nature by excess of oerbourn
Did with discharge of tears hersel recruit
No other solace could such anguish suit
And saw the beams of breaking day upshoot
The yet [?]   his orient head
He feels his friendly beam a vital influence shed

[*SPP*, p. 111]

The same nature which gives man the solace of tears brings
sunrise. The function of dwelling on misery is to "discharge"
pent-up anguish through a sentimental catharsis. The "vital influence" of the sun parallels the "vivifying virtue" which "enables us to mount / When high, more high, and lifts us up when
fallen" in *Prelude* XI. In both cases, the quickening impulse
comes largely from the contemplation of suffering.[33]

The connection between past and present becomes explicit as
the Vagrant describes her sensations upon waking aboard ship:

Peaceful as this immeasurable plain
By these extended beams of dawn impressed,
In the calm sunshine slept the glittering main.
The very ocean has its hour of rest
Ungranted to the human mourner's breast.

[33]See the discussion of the "spots of time" in Chapter 7.

> Remote from man and storms of mortal care,
> With wings which did the world of waves invest,
> The Spirit of God diffused through balmy air
> Quiet that might have healed, if aught could heal, Despair.
>
> [ll. 352–360]

The mood of the passage contradicts the trite claim that the "hour of rest" is "ungranted to the human mourner." It is evident that, in the present and past, the woman is moved, by nature and the discharge of tears, to feel an unearthly calm. Two stanzas later, she speaks as if she has had an unmediated vision of eternity: "Some mighty gulf of separation passed / I seemed transported to another world" (ll. 370–371). Like the Pedlar at the close of *The Ruined Cottage,* she finds in natural tranquillity the means of surmounting the transient "shews of being." The intensity of suffering and feeling makes available the energy which carries her to "another world."

Thus, at the time he is finishing *The Ruined Cottage* in 1798, Wordsworth habitually describes his response to fictive suffering in terms of natural tranquillity. Repeatedly, in *Salisbury Plain* and the topographical poems, suffering moves the mind to deep serenity. I have identified this response to pathos with Aristotelian *katharsis* and suggested that the young Wordsworth receives a sense of purgation and revitalization from the contemplation of his gloomy fictions. There is good reason to doubt, however, that he would have imported the Greek term to describe such feelings. The poet himself would probably have seen the calm generated by suffering as an opposition of emotion and tranquillity. Indeed, the cathartic generation of repose is but one manifestation of a habitual movement from excitement to calm. The next chapter will digress a bit to explore other places in Wordsworth's writings where intense emotion leads to a serenity of transcendental value, where, as the third "Essay upon Epitaphs" phrases it, the excitement of language "upholds, and feeds, and leaves in quiet" (*Prose,* II, 85).

3 Excitement and Tranquillity

From nature doth emotion come, and moods
Of calmness equally are nature's gift,
This is her glory; these two attributes
Are sister horns that constitute her strength;
This twofold influence is the sun and shower
Of all her bounties, both in origin
And end alike benignant. Hence it is,
That Genius which exists by interchange
Of peace and excitation, finds in her
His best and purest Friend, from her receives
That energy by which he seeks the truth,
Is rouzed, aspires, grasps, struggles, wishes, craves,
From her that happy stillness of the mind
Which fits him to receive it, when unsought.

—*Prelude* (1805) XII: 1–14

I

The pattern of suffering and calm takes on yet greater significance when we recall how often Wordsworth refers to an apparently transcendental state which he calls variously serenity, tranquillity, or calm: "such a holy calm / Did overspread my soul"; "I stood and watch'd / Till all was tranquil as a dreamless sleep": "A tranquillizing spirit presses now / On my corporeal frame"; "The calm existence that is mine when I / Am worthy of myself!"[1] Perhaps the most famous such moment occurs in "Tin-

[1]*Prel* II: 367–368; I: 488–489; II: 27–28; I: 360–361. There has been considerable discussion of the function of calm in Wordsworth's poetry. In *The Egotistical Sublime* (London: Chatto & Windus, 1954), John Jones properly calls attention to the importance of the "Eye made quiet" to the Wordsworthian imagination (pp. 89–96). In *On Wordsworth's "Prelude"* (Princeton: Princeton University Press, 1963), Herbert Lindenberger sees the dichotomy between "violent emotions" and the "calm and gentle" as a version of Quintillian's distinction between *pathos* and *ethos*: "The quietude which makes possible the visionary state must come from *ethos*, but the intensity and range of his vision derive from *pathos*"

tern Abbey" as the poet recalls how memories of the landscape
have soothed him in periods of depression:

> But oft, in lonely rooms, and mid the din
> Of towns and cities, I have owed to them,
> In hours of weariness, sensations sweet,
> Felt in the blood, and felt along the heart,
> And passing even into my purer mind
> With tranquil restoration.

The mind passes through four distinct stages: initial weariness
or dejection, the creation of a picture in the mind's eye, emotional response to the picture, and transcendence into calm:

> that serene and blessed mood,
> In which the affections gently lead us on,
> Until, the breath of this corporeal frame,
> And even the motion of our human blood
> Almost suspended, we are laid asleep
> In body, and become a living soul:
> While with an eye made quiet by the power
> Of harmony, and the deep power of joy,
> We see into the life of things.

The movement of mind is remarkably like the response to suffering in *The Ruined Cottage* and elsewhere. The origins of the
excitement are different, but, in either case, the poet calls forth

---

(p. 34). In "The Wordsworthian Repose," *Tennessee Studies in Literature* 13 (1968),
39, David Rogers asserts that the calm is exclusively associated with pantheistic
feelings: "A psychic event frequently reflected in his poetry between 1797 and
1802 is one in which the exterior world seems part of himself, and whose chief
result is a seemingly divine repose." James Scoggins discusses two types of "calm"
paralleling the activities of Fancy and Imagination, in *Imagination and Fancy:
Complementary Modes in the Poetry of Wordsworth* (Lincoln: University of Nebraska
Press, 1966), pp. 79, 203. Christopher Salvesen meanwhile suggests, in *The Landscape of Memory* (London: Edward Arnold, 1965), that the activity of memory
creates tranquillity, pp. 92–93, 141–156. For the most part, however, critics have
explored the calm only as it touches their particular theses; the purpose of this
chapter is to suggest an overarching pattern.

images in anticipation of emotional stimulation and a consequent sense of calm.[2]

The most striking manifestation of a psychology of excitement and calm appears in trances experienced by various characters in Wordsworth's narrative poems. The previous chapter has discussed the trance and subsequent calm of the Female Vagrant (*Salisbury Plain*, ll. 316–378) as a response to the contemplation of suffering. Considered as a representation of psychological reality, however, the Female Vagrant's progression from "Agony" through "trance" to "calm" illustrates a more general principle. Her experience in "the western world" has been of wrenching personal dislocation:

> The pains and plagues that on our heads came down,
> Disease and Famine, Agony and Fear,
> In wood or wilderness, in camp or town,
> It would thy brain unsettle even to hear.
> All perished, all in one remorseless year,
> Husband and children one by one, by sword
> And scourge of fiery fever.
>
> [ll. 316–322]

The pressure of emotion was such that the woman could endure no more, and her mind retreated into unconsciousness: "every tear / Dried up, despairing, desolate, on board / A British ship I waked as from a trance restored" (ll. 322–324). This restoration is oddly like that which "Tintern Abbey" and "The Glad Preamble" chronicle. The overburdened mind suddenly, inexplicably, sloughs off its weariness and dejection and experiences a profound serenity. After being "restored," the Vagrant perceives

---

[2] In "The Structure of Imaginative Experience in Wordsworth's *Prelude*," *The Wordsworth Circle* 6 (1975), 290–298, John T. Ogden lays out a "paradigm" for the Wordsworthian spot of time: "The mind shifts from attention through confusion to illumination; or, as it may also appear, from expectation through frustration to fulfillment. This last stage of illumination or fulfillment may be divided into two stages: initial surprise and elation, and ensuing calm and satisfaction" (p. 292). Ogden emphasizes the role of "bafflement" and frustration in the process, where, as I shall demonstrate, such confusion is but one of several sources of emotion leading to calm.

"the calm sunshine" and the ocean in "its hour of rest." The calm of nature reflects a change in herself: "Some mighty gulf of separation passed / I seemed transported to another world" (ll. 370–371). This "gulf of separation" would seem equivalent to the alienation of the narrator from his "natural self" at the beginning of *The Prelude* (I: 23). Experience causes the woman's pastoral world-view to disintegrate and cuts her off from her original self and any faith in beneficent Providence. In its very intensity, however, the emotion apparently consumes itself, and her mind is left utterly tranquil, dimly sensing "The Spirit of God diffused through balmy air" (l. 359).

In *Adventures,*[3] the second version of *Salisbury Plain,* the traveler himself experiences a moment of calm. No longer simply the poet's alter ego, in this version he has evolved into a distinct character with his own story: he is a discharged sailor who, having robbed and murdered an innocent traveler, has wandered onto Salisbury Plain. Haunted by guilt, he walks through a landscape whose desolation reflects his own despair and weariness. Suddenly, he hears "a sound of chains" and looks up to see "on a bare gibbet nigh / A human body that in irons swang" (ll. 113–115). In *Prelude* XI, the same image of human misery energizes the "ordinary sight" of the girl with a water pitcher. For the sailor, however, the gibbet has additional force. In him, it calls up "a train / Of the mind's phantoms," the horror, guilt, and fear associated with the memory of his deed (ll. 121–122). The emotional pressure is such that "He fell and without sense or motion lay" (l. 125). This episode depicts, again, the Wordsworthian response to intense emotion, for when the "trance" is gone:

> As doth befall to them whom frenzy fires,
> His soul, which in such anguish had been toss'd,
> Sank into deepest calm; for now retires
> Fear; a terrific dream in darkness lost

[3]The text of MS. 2 of *Guilt and Sorrow* is from *SPP,* pp. 123–154.

The dire phantasma which his sense had cross'd.
His mind was still as a deep evening stream

[ll. 127-132]

Wordsworth's use of "As doth befall to them whom frenzy fires" to describe the traveler's condition is notable. The effort of a simile is to connect the thing being described to some known quantity. "My love is like a red red rose" works as a figure of speech because there is no doubt in poet's or reader's mind what a rose is. The assumption that animates the simile here is that those whom "frenzy fires" sink into "deepest calm"; the guilty sailor is one case among many. For Wordsworth, then, it is a given that intense emotion leaves the mind "still as a deep evening stream."

A similar sequence of excitement, trance, and tranquillity appears in *Peter Bell*, MS. 2.[4] At the conclusion of Part First, Peter falls into a trance:

His eyes will burst, his heart will break,
He gives a loud and frightful shriek,
And back he falls just like a stone.

[*PW*, II, 355]

The immediate cause of this faint is Peter's misapprehension of the drowned man as a "fiend with visage wan, / A live man-fiend."[5] Of course, the wandering potter has already had a troubled night. Like many a more respectable Wordsworthian fig-

---

[4]The text of *Peter Bell* is among the most complicated in the Wordsworth canon. I have had the advantage of working with Floyd G. Stoddard's unpublished dissertation, "Wordsworth's *Peter Bell:* A Critical Edition," Cornell University, 1965. Here, however, I give the approximate location in *PW*, II.

[5]In this scene, Wordsworth is imitating one of the most common plot devices of gothic fiction. Most of the apparently "supernatural" events in the novels of Radcliffe and Lewis turn out to have naturalistic explanations, thereby enabling the author to exploit the emotion of terror without really asking us to believe in supernatural beings. As revealed most plainly in the "Prologue," *Peter Bell* is consciously antigothic; perhaps the behavior of the title character in this episode parodies those Emilias and Ellenas of contemporary fiction who endlessly, breathlessly, explore haunted castles, abbeys, and other dark passages.

ure, he has become lost by taking the wrong path. He has been frustrated by the ass's obstinate refusal to leave the spot and awed by the animal's uncanny braying in the oppressive silence. At the point he discovers the ass's drowned master, his imagination is at the breaking point. The pressure of superstitious horror is overpowering, he passes out, and when he comes to,

> In Peter's brain there is no riot,
> His eye upon the stream he fixes
> And with the sight no terror mixes
> His heart is calm and quiet.
>
> [*PW*, II, 356]

Tranquillity again follows trance in the second canto of *The White Doe of Rylstone*. There, after the loyal Francis has broken with his family, "A phantasm, in which roof and wall / Shook, tottered, swam before his sight" (ll. 422–423) overcomes him. Almost inevitably,

> when he waked, his languid eye
> Was on the calm and silent sky;
> With air about him breathing sweet,
> And earth's green grass beneath his feet.
>
> [ll. 427–430]

Francis explicitly undergoes some kind of catharsis, for he is "cleansed from the despair / And sorrow" (ll. 439–440). The common element among these calm-inducing trances is strong emotion. The source of the emotion, whether grief, guilt, fear, or family conflict, is apparently irrelevant to the psychological mechanism involved. As the first "Essay upon Epitaphs" suggests, it is, for Wordsworth anyway, a common "progress," in both "the natural and the moral world" that "qualities pass insensibly into their contraries" (*Prose*, II, 53).

These trances are, one would suspect, literary as well as psychological phenomena. Characters of sentimental and gothic fiction were constantly blacking out, and thus one may well be skeptical of the mimetic pretentions of such trances. In *The Borderers,* however, Wordsworth presents a character who goes from stressful passion to unearthly calm without the intervention of anything so melodramatic as a trance. In Act III, the hero Mortimer enters alone, meditating upon his recent actions. Earlier he has been described as one whose soul "Is, after conflict, silent as the ocean, / By a miraculous finger stilled at once" (*PW,* I, 134). In the previous scene, driven by a misguided sense of justice and revenge, he has left the old, blind Baron Herbert alone upon the heath. The villain's insinuations have caused Mortimer to believe that Herbert had pandered Matilda, his own daughter and Mortimer's lover. Mortimer, however, was unable to murder the old man in cold blood and had decided to let the matter be determined through an ordeal by nature. It had been a scene full of pathos and emotion; anger, guilt, pity, jealousy, and grief raged through Mortimer's tormented mind. Yet, with such an experience in the immediate past, he utters these unexpected, enigmatic words:

> Deep, deep and vast, vast beyond human thought,
> Yet calm.—I could believe that there was here
> The only quiet heart on earth. In terror,
> Remembered terror, there is peace and rest.
>
> [*PW,* I, 186]

This is extraordinary, as if Hamlet were to fall into calm after learning of his father's murder, or Lear after his daughter barred him from the castle. After all, when Mortimer was last on stage, the pressure of events and conflicting emotions had driven him nearly mad. Now Wordsworth expects the audience to accept the claim that the man finds "peace and rest" in the "remembered terror"! Only a person experienced in drawing calm from vivid remembrance would be likely to create such a response in a character who had recently undergone Mortimer's ordeal. And, indeed, in *The Prelude,* Wordsworth calls before his mind the "spots of time," images of "all / The terrors, all the early miseries / Regrets, vexations, lassitudes," and claims that these "have made up / The calm existence that is mine when I / Am worthy of myself!" (I: 355–361). One who habitually used the energy of recollected emotion to produce a state of mind "Deep, deep and vast, vast beyond human thought, / Yet calm" would think that he was presenting a credible imitation of reality in Mortimer's unearthly tranquillity.

Lines in the Alfoxden notebook show the poet drawing energy and subsequent calm from natural beauty:

> To gaze
> On that green hill and on those scattered trees
> And feel a pleasant consciousness of life
> In the impression of that loveliness
> Until the sweet sensation called the mind
> Into itself, by image from without
> Unvisited, and all her reflex powers
> Wrapped in a still dream [of] forgetfulness.
>
> [*PW*, V, 341]

The act of "gazing," intense absorption in external nature, turns the mind in upon itself. The focus on particularized objects releases the poet's feelings in a kind of aesthetic trance. The "consciousness of life" he feels refers not to some vague pantheism so much as to his own emotions. The beauty printed on his mind gives a profound sense of vitality. The life within meets external phenomena and knows itself alive because of its own sensation. Exquisitely conscious of "that loveliness," the mind takes off on a journey "into itself." Independent of "images from without," it enters a state in which the eye is "made quiet" and mental activity "almost suspended." As in "Tintern Abbey," the energy of emotional response provides the power which wraps the mind in its oblivious, and tranquil, dream.

Thus, in Wordsworth's poetry, guilt, fear, grief, remembered terror, or intense response to nature,—virtually any powerful emotion it would seem—is able to move the mind to profound tranquillity. When the emotion is pity, catharsis describes the psychological mechanism involved. For Wordsworth, however, the nature of the emotion is less important than the fact of it.

The subsequent calm is the result of a mind made self-conscious by the presence of emotion. The "reflex powers" of the mind contemplating itself paradoxically depend on emotional stimulus yet separate from it in "the still dream of forgetfulness." They are at once "unvisited" from "without," and dependent on the powerful emotions which make such seeming autonomy possible. Wordsworth makes "mystical" claims for a kind of transcendental serenity even while firmly locating the source of such elevation in the rag-and-bone shop of the heart.

II

For the young Wordsworth, the burden of the past is less an overpowering presence than a knapsack out of which he takes exciting poetic objects. As Legouis and Beatty showed years ago, the topographical poems are a constant, unanxious raid on poets from Milton to Beattie; in *The Borderers* the young poet appropriates *Lear* and *Othello* without being consumed.[6] This rummaging in the past is, in fact, a quest for power, for that in poetry which makes the mind "work like a sea." Not surprisingly, Wordsworth finds such power in the traditional sources of literary energy inherited from previous generations of poets, the complex of images and responses collectively known as the "sublime." In this section, I explore Wordsworth's use of four such sources of "sublimity": the cosmic space vision, the "mountain glory", the graveyard, and the "psychological sublime." As one might expect, such conventionally literary excitement, too, leads Wordsworth to a sense of tranquillity.

In "A Night-Piece" (1798), the excitement of cosmic sublimity ebbs into calm:

> The sky is overspread
> With a close veil of one continuous cloud

[6]Émile Legouis, *The Early Life of William Wordsworth,* trans. J. W. Matthews (London: Dent, 1897), pp. 120–160; *Wordsworth: Representative Poems,* ed. Arthur Beatty (New York: Odyssey, 1937), pp. 10–64. For Wordsworth's unanxiety of influence, see also James Rieger, "Wordsworth Unalarm'd," in Joseph A. Wittreich, ed., *Milton and the Line of Vision* (Madison: University of Wisconsin Press, 1975), pp. 185–208.

All whitened by the moon, that just appears,
A dim-seen orb, yet chequers not the ground
With any shadow—plant, or tower, or tree.
At last a pleasant instantaneous light
Startles the musing man whose eyes are bent
To earth. He looks around, the clouds are split
Asunder, and above his head he views
The clear moon & the glory of the heavens.
There in a black-blue vault she sails along
Followed by multitudes of stars, that small,
And bright, & sharp along the gloomy vault
Drive as she drives. How fast they wheel away!
Yet vanish not! The wind is in the trees;
But they are silent. Still they roll along
Immeasurably distant, and the vault
Built round by those white clouds, enormous clouds,
Still deepens its interminable depth.
At length the vision closes, & the mind
Not undisturbed by the deep joy it feels,
Which slowly settles into peaceful calm,
Is left to muse upon the solemn scene.[7]

The vertiginous effects which the eighteenth century typically gained by contemplative projection into outer space[8] Wordsworth achieves through an optical illusion experienced by an earthbound observer. The stars, of course, only seem to be moving relative to "the vault / Built round by those white clouds." The eye has lent apparent stasis to the cloud layer, which is closer and therefore bulks larger than the distant moon and stars. There is a momentary suspension of belief in Copernican cosmography as the traveler becomes profoundly conscious of celestial movement relative to a fixed earth. Although this sense of movement is overtly illusory, it does mimic actual movement in heavenly bodies. The observer thus feels himself drawn out of oppressive surroundings to participate in a uni-

[7]This is Beth Darlington's text of DC MS. 16, from "Two Early Texts: *A Night-Piece* and *The Discharged Soldier*," in *BWS*, p. 431.
[8]See, for instance, Edward Young's *Night* IX, Mark Akenside's *Pleasures of the Imagination*, I; and *Spectators* No. 420, 565.

verse of life. This poem of early 1798 anticipates "Tintern Abbey," where the "eye made quiet by the power / Of harmony, and the deep power of joy" sees into "the life of things." In "Tintern Abbey" the eye's quiescence follows the sense of harmony and joy; the "peaceful calm" of "A Night-Piece" is also apparently produced by a sense of celestial harmony and "deep joy."[9]

The excitement of "A Night-Piece," however, is as much the response to language as to any actual experience that occurred on the road to Alfoxden. The opening lines closely echo Dorothy's journal:

> The sky spread over with one continuous cloud, whitened by the light of the moon, which, though her dim shape was seen, did not throw forth so strong a light as to chequer the earth with shadows. At once the clouds seemed to cleave asunder, and left her in the centre of a black-blue vault. She sailed along, followed by multitudes of stars, small, and bright, and sharp. Their brightness seemed concentrated, (half-moon).
>
> [*DWJ*, p. 2]

This vivid description, as much as "real" experience, is the seed out of which the poem grows. It enables Wordsworth to realize imaginatively the poetic quality of the experience he probably shared with his sister.

Of the first thirteen lines of "A Night-Piece," only the "musing man whose eyes are bent / To earth" represents a significant addition to Dorothy's account.[10] The ending of the poem

---

[9]Jonathan Wordsworth has argued that "the deep joy felt by the poet at the scene—in spite of de Selincourt's note on the subject (*PW*, II, 503)—is not the joy of *Tintern Abbey,* but an ordinary pleasure that settles into calm instead of producing 'life and food for future years'" ("The Climbing of Snowdon," *BWS,* p. 455). Jonathan Wordsworth wants to emphasize the distance between the "ordinariness" of emotion in "A Night-Piece" and the perception of the One Life in "Tintern Abbey." Undoubtedly it is true that no grand claim is made in "A Night-Piece"; however, the structural similarities of the two passages and the "mental bombast" employed to describe what is, after all, only the moon coming from behind clouds, suggest a significance out of proportion to the natural sight being described.

[10]For a stimulating discussion of this *penseroso,* see Neil Hertz, "Wordsworth and the Tears of Adam," in *Wordsworth: A Collection of Critical Essays,* ed. M. H. Abrams (Englewood Cliffs, N.J.: Prentice-Hall, 1972), pp. 108–112.

(ll. 14–23), however, is entirely Wordsworth's, and, notably, it is characterized by a different kind of language. Gone are the fine observations and close descriptions: the poem's subject becomes the heavens and the mind of man. "The wind is in the trees" provides the only reference to the immediate surroundings, and one is inclined to think even this wind a "correspondent breeze." The presiding genius of the closing lines is Milton. First of all, the situation itself recalls a particular moment in *Paradise Lost:*

> Silence was pleas'd: now glow'd the Firmament
> With living Sapphires: Hesperus that led
> The starry Host, rode brightest, till the Moon
> Rising in clouded Majesty, at length
> Apparent Queen unveil'd her peerless light,
> And o'er the dark her Silver Mantle threw.
>
> [IV: 604–609]

This was a favorite passage of Wordsworth's. *The Guide to the Lakes* recalls that Milton "has given a *clouded* moon to Paradise itself" (*Prose,* II, 192); in defence of his sonnet, "With Ships the Sea Was Sprinkled," Wordsworth quotes the above lines in their entirety (*ML,* I, 148). The language of the second half of "A Night-Piece," too, recalls Milton and the eighteenth-century cosmic sublime. For example, in *Paradise Lost,* the verb "wheel" frequently describes the movement of the spheres: "Now Heav'n in all her Glory shone, and rowl'd / Her motions, as the great first-Mover's hand / First wheel'd thir course" (VII: 499–501); and again, "the Moon / Sits Arbitress, and nearer to the Earth / Wheels her pale course" (I: 784–786). Similarly, the sonorous negative infinites, "immeasurably distant" and "interminable depth," are from Milton and his poetic offspring. This is not to say that Wordsworth has specific passages in mind as he describes the illusion of the sailing moon, although he may well have. Such language was the common property of the cosmic sublime, and was used enthusiastically by Thomson, Young, and others.

Thus, in "A Night-Piece," Wordsworth exploits two verbal

sources of energy, Dorothy's mimetic language and the cosmic sublime, in order to evoke excitement from what is, after all, a rather ordinary event. The peaceful calm into which the musing man settles is primarily a response to literature and the process of writing, to Dorothy's and his own words on paper, rather than to the original visual experience. The energy of language disturbs the mind, purges it, and leaves it in a state of tranquillity.

In a peculiar and unexpected way, the cosmic sublime also enters the skating episode in *The Prelude:*

> then at once
> Have I, reclining back upon my heels,
> Stopp'd short, yet still the solitary Cliffs
> Wheeled by me, even as if the earth had roll'd
> With visible motion her diurnal round;
> Behind me did they stretch in solemn train
> Feebler and feebler, and I stood and watch'd
> Till all was tranquil as a dreamless sleep.
>
> [I: 482–489][11]

As in "A Night-Piece," the central action is an optical illusion which approximates scientific reality. The world, after all, does revolve, and, in his vertigo, the child perceives a kind of revolution. Here, too, the excitement of estrangement exalts the mind to deepest tranquillity.

Much of the excitement in Wordsworth's description of this incident is again verbal; it is less a question of "emotion recollected in tranquillity" than of the development and evocation of excitement during the act of writing. Words such as "wheel," "diurnal round," and "solemn train" are characteristic of the space catalogs of Milton and his heirs. Wordsworth uses this language because he finds it stimulating and resonant. In fact it has a life of its own, unrelated to what might or might not have

---

[11]In "The Sublime and the Beautiful in *The Prelude*," *The Wordsworth Circle* 4 (1973), 78–79, W. J. B. Owen notes that this kind of vertigo is mentioned by Burke as a possible source of the sublime. Burke's *Enquiry into the Sublime and Beautiful,* ed. J. T. Boulton (New York: Columbia University Press, 1958), p. 73, reads, "After whirling about; when we sit down, the objects about us still seem to whirl."

occurred on Esthwaite Water fifteen years earlier. "Train," originally descriptive of virtually any sequential occurrence or thing,
had become a specialized word in the poetry of space to describe
processions of heavenly bodies. In *Paradise Lost,* it is "these the
Gems of Heav'n, her starry train" (IV: 649); Thomson calls God
the "Informer of the planetary train" (*Summer*, l. 104) and duly
notes the "awful train" of the "rushing comet" (ll. 1708–1710);
Young requests his ninth Night to "Voluminously pour thy
pompous train" (Chalmers, XIII, 479). The "solemn train" of
wheeling cliffs is, then, apparently a recollection of the cosmic
sublime. As such, it represents an autonomous extension from
the mimetic into the realm of pure language. Poetry has a mo-
mentum of its own: once talk of wheeling and diurnal rounds
is introduced, it becomes appropriate to speak of cliffs stretching
in a solemn train. The phrase "feebler and feebler," while re-
ferent to the ebbing of illusion, might, more fittingly, describe
the diminishment of starlight with the coming of the full moon.
Thus, from a displaced space-journey "across the image of a
star," Wordsworth receives the excitement which enables him to
become "tranquil as a dreamless sleep." The feeling of calm
again has as much to do with the process of composition, and the
verbal constructs the mind spins out of its reading, as with the
original experience.

Perhaps more than any passage in Wordsworth, "The Crossing of the Alps" (*Prelude* VI) has been contorted by mis- and
over-reading. The figure of Imagination starting up before the
eye and progress of the song has exercised the ingenuity of a
generation of critics.[12] Ignored, or perhaps assumed, in such
discussions have been the eighteenth-century context and the
episode's function within the structure of Book VI.

---

[12]Geoffrey Hartman, *Wordsworth's Poetry, 1787–1814* (New Haven: Yale University Press, 1964), pp. 39–69, uses the passage as the exception which proves the
rule of *via naturaliter negativa,* as the time when the poet "under that pressure of
composition, came once, and only once, face to face with his imagination." See
also Harold Bloom, *The Visionary Company* (Garden City, N.Y.: Doubleday,
1961), pp. 147–150; and Albert O. Wlecke, *Wordsworth and the Sublime* (Berkeley:
University of California Press, 1973), pp. 101–105, for readings that emphasize
an anxious struggle between subject and object.

Most obviously, "The Crossing of the Alps" is an example of the natural sublime; Marjorie Nicolson has aptly pronounced it "the perfect expression of 'The Aesthetics of the Infinite.'"[13] The extent to which Wordsworth would have been aware of it as such, however, has only become apparent with the publication of "The Sublime and the Beautiful" in the Owen and Smyser *Prose Works* (II, 349–360). This fragment, an overflow from *Select Views in Cumberland, Westmoreland, and Lancashire,* offers a theoretical description of the mind's response to sublime natural objects. Wordsworth dissects the "whole complex impression" of sublimity into "three component parts: a sense of individual form or forms; a sense of duration; and a sense of power" (*Prose,* II, 351). Though drawing on earlier theorists, Wordsworth is, to a remarkable extent, his own man. As Smyser notes, "neither individual form nor duration figures in discussions of the sublime in natural scenery before Wordsworth" (*Prose,* II, 453).

In reference to individual form, Wordsworth says, "whatever suspends the comparing power of the mind & possesses it with a feeling or image of intense unity, without a conscious contemplation of parts, has produced that state of the mind which is the consummation of the sublime" (*Prose,* II, 353–354).[14] At the climax of "Crossing the Alps," the discrete elements of the landscape fuse into such a unity-in-multeity:

> The immeasureable height
> Of woods decaying, never to be decay'd,
> The stationary blasts of water-falls,

[13]Marjorie Hope Nicolson, *Mountain Gloom and Mountain Glory* (Ithaca, N.Y.: Cornell University Press, 1959), p. 393.

[14]It ought to be noted that the suspension of the comparing power is also important in Coleridge's conceptualization of the sublime; see Clarence D. Thorpe, "Coleridge on the Sublime," in *Wordsworth and Coleridge: Studies in Honor of George McLean Harper,* ed. Earl L. Griggs (Princeton: Princeton University Press, 1939), p. 197; Raimonda Modiano, "Coleridge and the Sublime: A Response to Thomas Weiskel's *The Romantic Sublime,*"*The Wordsworth Circle* 9 (1978), 115–118. For another linking of Coleridge, Wordsworth, and the sublime, roughly contemporary to Wordsworth's fragment on the sublime and beautiful, see Edna A. Shearer and J. T. Lindsay, "Wordsworth and Coleridge Marginalia in a Copy of Richard Payne Knight's 'Analytical Inquiry into the Principles of Taste,'" *Huntington Library Quarterly* 1 (1937), 63–99.

> And every where along the hollow rent
> Winds thwarting winds, bewilder'd and forlorn,
> The torrents shooting from the clear blue sky,
> The rocks that mutter'd close upon our ears,
> Black drizzling crags that spake by the way-side
> As if a voice were in them, the sick sight
> And giddy prospect of the raving stream,
> The unfetter'd clouds, and region of the Heavens,
> Tumult and peace, the darkness and the light
> Were all like workings of one mind, the features
> Of the same face, blossoms upon one tree,
> Characters of the great Apocalypse,
> The types and symbols of Eternity,
> Of first and last, and midst, and without end.
>
> [VI: 556–572]

Elsewhere in "The Sublime and the Beautiful," Wordsworth notes that the "absolute crown on the impression is infinity, which is a modification of unity" (*Prose*, II, 357). The "one mind," the "one tree," the one "Eternity" are, then, perceptions of a mind strongly affected by the sublime.

The second element of the natural sublime for Wordsworth is "the naked fact of being conscious of external Power at once awful & immeasurable."

> Power awakens the sublime either when it rouses us to a sympathetic energy & calls upon the mind to grasp at something towards which it can make approaches but which it is incapable of attaining—yet so that it participates force which is acting upon it; or, 2ndly, by producing a humiliation or prostration of the mind before some external agency which it presumes not to make an effort to participate, but is absorbed in the contemplation of the might in the external power. [*Prose*, II, 354]

In Wordsworth's version of the sublime, the soul is sent into itself, "to be admonished of her weakness, or to be made conscious of her power" (*Prose*, III, 83). At Simplon, external power operates to humiliate and prostrate the mind so as to make it feel "a deep and genuine sadness." The psychological sublime in which the internal power of Imagination "comes athwart the mind" is parallel to the natural sublime, where the power is external. The source, however, whether inside or outside, is less important to Wordsworth than the fact of power. If *The Prelude* is a quest for the sources of poetic energy, the most crucial need is that power be found. Simplon Pass is replete with natural energy: the blasts of waterfalls, winds thwarting winds, the raving stream, all become unified as "the workings of one mind."

The most obscure component of Wordsworthian sublimity is duration. In "The Sublime and the Beautiful," Wordsworth's example of duration is "the Rock in the middle of the fall of the Rhine at Chafhausen"; of "the rock & the Waterfall," he says, "these objects will be found to have exalted the mind to the highest state of sublimity when they are thought of in that state of opposition & yet reconcilement, analogous to parallel lines in mathematics, which, being infinitely prolonged, can never come nearer to each other" (*Prose*, II, 356–357). The crucial element of sublime duration is the clash and stasis of mighty forces. Of course, Simplon Pass is "a landscape riddled with opposites":[15] "Tumult and peace, the darkness and the light . . . first and last, and midst, and without end." Thus, "The Crossing of the Alps" exemplifies not only general eighteenth-century notions of the sublime, but also Wordsworth's specific ideas about it. In writing the passage, he consciously taps a traditional and vital source of energy which, in 1804, was available to himself and contemporary poets.

Most readers have viewed "The Crossing of the Alps" (VI: 488–572) as an autonomous episode closing with the vision of "Eternity" and "Apocalypse."[16] In fact, however, the continuity of the narrative does not break at "first and last, and midst, and

---

[15]Wlecke, *Wordsworth and the Sublime,* p. 102.

[16]W. J. B. Owen in "The Sublime and the Beautiful in *The Prelude,*" does note that "the famous passage in Book VI describing the Ravine of Gondo" is "placed in almost immediate contrast with the description of the pastoral regions of the Italian lakes" (p. 77). Owen, however, finds no connection between the experiences other than to list them as another example of the contrast between the sublime and the beautiful in *The Prelude.*

without end." The poet continues down the River Tusa to Locarno and Como after stopping overnight at an inn. Wordsworth, then, is interested in what happens after apocalypse. In a real sense, lines 549–616 form as discrete a unit as lines 488–572. The type of poem they approximate is the River-Poem,[17] a genre well known to Wordsworth and Coleridge. *The Brook*, of course, was the occasion for Coleridge's career as a "spy":

> I sought for a subject, that should give equal room and freedom for description, incident, and impassioned reflections on men, nature, and society, yet supply in itself a natural connection to the parts, and unity to the whole. Such a subject I conceived myself to have found in a stream, traced from its source in the hills among the yellow-red moss and conical glass-shaped tufts of bent . . . to the hamlet, the villages, the market-town, the manufactories, and the seaport. [*BL*, I, 129]

Further, *The River Duddon*, as Robert Aubin has claimed, is "the greatest river-poem of all."[18] By describing the journey from Simplon to Locarno, Wordsworth creates a segment which, taken by itself, could justly be called "Tusa's Stream."

This stream is a stream of consciousness. The river that flows along the poet's dreams is a recurrent motif in *The Prelude*. At the close of Book VI, a scant hundred lines after he has seen the Tusa into Lake Locarno, Wordsworth breaks off his re-vision of the journey to describe a correspondent stream:

> On the front
> Of this whole Song is written that my heart
> Must in such temple needs have offer'd up
> A different worship. Finally whate'er
> I saw, or heard, or felt, was but a stream
> That flow'd into a kindred stream, a gale
> That help'd me forwards, did administer

---

[17]See Robert Aubin, *Topographical Poetry in XVIII-Century England* (New York: Modern Language Association, 1936), pp. 225–241, 377–385, for an exhaustive catalog of the genre.
[18]Aubin, p. 241.

> To grandeur and to tenderness, to the one
> Directly, but to tender thoughts by means
> Less often instantaneous in effect
>
> [ll. 669–678]

The distinction between "grandeur" and "tenderness" is a variant of the commonplace polarity between sublimity and beauty. The need for indirection to perceive tenderness is striking. One would think that all that need be done is to look upon a tranquil, pastoral scene such as the countryside of Locarno or Como, but apparently terrors, miseries, and vexations are again necessary to make up a calm existence. The beautiful is defined only by contrast with the sublime. Interestingly, much the same thing occurs in Wordsworth's original narrative of his Swiss tour, the letter to Dorothy of September 1790: "At Brig we quitted the Valais and passed the Alps at the Semplon in order to visit part of Italy. The impressions of three hours of our walk among the Alps will never be effaced. . . . It was impossible not to contrast that repose that complacency of Spirit, produced by these lovely scenes [at Como], with the sensations I had experienced two or three days before, in passing the Alps" (*EL*, pp. 33–34).

Thus, the poem's movement down the Tusa parallels the mind's ebb from sublimity to tranquillity. The language by which Wordsworth traces the traveler's descent is resonant with significance and even allegory. The place of lodging after crossing the Alps is "an Alpine House, / An Inn, or Hospital, as they are named." There is historical justification for this—Wordsworth and Robert Jones did indeed stay the night at "Spital" (*PW*, I, 326), but why highlight one inn, among fifty-odd stopping places of an Alpine trek? This "Hospital" is, I would guess, one of those false refuges such as recur in *The Faerie Queene*, a place where the hero goes for succor and finds betrayal. The problem with the building is the problem of the sublime—it is too big, constructed on a scale that dwarfs the merely human:

> A dreary Mansion, large beyond all need,
> With high and spacious rooms, deafen'd and stunn'd

> By noise of waters, making innocent Sleep
> Lie melancholy among weary bones.

[ll. 577–580]

The stay at the spital continues the experience at Simplon Pass, but the prostration of the mind here is uncompensated by any perception of unity.

The language of the next morning, too, is resonant; it is the language of the man who, in D. H. Lawrence's phrase, has come through:

> Upris'n betimes, our journey we renew'd,
> Led by the Stream, ere noon-day magnified
> Into a lordly River, broad and deep.
> Dimpling along in silent majesty,
> With mountains for its neighbours, and in view
> Of distant mountains and their snowy tops,
> And thus proceeding to Locarno's Lake,
> Fit resting-place for such a Visitant.
> —Locarno, spreading out in width like Heaven,
> And Como, thou, a treasure by the earth
> Kept to itself, a darling bosom'd up
> In Abyssinian privacy

[ll. 581–592]

"Upris'n" and "renew'd" suggest a healing process which is confirmed by the landscape. Where before it was a "raving stream" the river's chief characteristic is now "silent majesty." The Alpine sublime is tempered by distance and genial neighborliness. The "Visitant" that rests in Locarno is at once the river and the poet, the geographical reality and the psychological.

The process allegorized in Book VI is explained theoretically in Wordsworth's essay on "The Sublime and the Beautiful":

The point beyond which apprehensions for our physical nature consistent with sublimity may be carried, has been ascertained; &, with respect to power acting upon our moral or spiritual nature, by awakening energy either that would resist or that [hopes?] to participate, the sublime is called forth. But if the Power contemplated

Elegy of Gray" (l. 500). The passage in question is from "The Epitaph":

> His merits, stranger, seek not to disclose
> Or draw his Frailties from their dread abode;
> There they alike in trembling Hope repose
> The bosom of his Father and his God.[20]

Reading a poet's epitaph, in a setting like that in which Gray had ostensibly written his poem, is an experience where the mind would be "not undisturbed by the deep joy it feels." Walking on, Wordsworth thinks "with pleasure of the Verses, graven / Upon his Tombstone" (ll. 509–510). Partially, this is the pleasure of ego, the proud sense of vocation, that Taylor "loved the Poets, and if now alive, / Would have loved me" (ll. 511–512); but "the pleasure of the Verses" is also that of the *penseroso,* who feels "that mood in which melancholy—instead of depressing the spirit—acts as a power that carries it upward to an elevation otherwise unattainable" (*Prose,* II, 297).

Taylor's death is also bound up with the recollection of Wordworth's schoolboy poetry. As we have seen, the words of the dying man had found their way into the last speech of a lovelorn maiden:

> A week, or little less, before his death
> He had said to me, 'my head will soon lie low'
> > [*Prel* X: 501–502]

> Heaven told me once—but I was blind—
> My head would soon lie low
> > ["A Ballad," ll. 41–42][21]

"My head will soon lie low" is a reminder of those "toilsome songs" which Taylor had him "spin" as well as a direct verbal

---

[20]*Prel,* pp. 600–601. In *The Vale of Esthwaite,* Wordsworth imitated Gray's *Elegy* in imagining his own death (ll. 456–465). *Prelude* X enacts a return to, and a making peace with, the poetry and poetics he admired in his youth.

[21]See Chapter 1, section iii.

connection to a time of deep emotion. The energy unleashed by personal and literary memories lifts Wordsworth into a state of tranquillity: "Without me and within, as I advanced, / All that I saw, or felt, or communed with / Was gentleness and peace" (ll. 516–518). As in "Tusa's Stream" or "A Night-Piece," this calm sense of communion is the aftermath of sublime experience. In this instance, however, the source of tranquillity, at least partially, is the lugubrious poetry Wordsworth had read, admired, and imitated in his youth and whose canons of taste he outgrew but never entirely discarded.

A fourth version of the sublime available to Wordsworth might be called the "psychological" sublime. Here interest and energy emanate from the internalization of the subject-object relation: the mental processes themselves are taken as sublime objects. Wordsworth refers to this kind of sublimity when he braves Milton in the "Prospectus" to *The Recluse:*

> Not Chaos, not
> The darkest pit of lowest Erebus,
> Nor aught of blinder vacancy, scooped out
> By help of dreams—can breed such fear and awe
> As fall upon us often when we look
> Into our Minds, into the Mind of Man—
> My haunt, and the main region of my song.
>
> [*PW*, V, 4]

The Prelude too exclaims, "How awful is the might of Souls, / And what they do within themselves" (III: 178–179). The mind looking into itself, contemplating the internal void, is at one with the mind grappling with external vacancy in space, death, or mountain chasms. Although we think of this "psychological" sublime as characteristically Wordsworthian and Romantic, there are eighteenth-century analogues for it, most notably in Edward Young's *Night Thoughts:*

> I tremble at myself,
> And in myself am lost! at home a stranger,

Thought wanders up and down, surpris'd, aghast,
And wondering at her *own:* How Reason reels!

[*Night* I]

Darkness has more divinity for me;
It strikes thought inward; it drives back the soul
To settle on herself, our point supreme!
There lies our theatre! there sits our judge.

[*Night* V][22]

For the self-conscious imagination, there is nothing more "dark, uncertain, confused, terrible,"[23] and therefore fascinating, than the mind's inscrutable workings. In a notebook of 1801, Coleridge comments on "Tintern Abbey":

—and the deep power of Joy
We see into the *Life* of Things—
i.e.—By deep feeling we make our *Ideas dim*—& this is what we mean by our Life—ourselves . . . let me think of *myself*—of the thinking Being—the Idea becomes dim whatever it be—so dim that I know not what it is—but the Feeling is deep & steady—and this I call *I*—identifying the Percipient & the Perceived—. [*STCNB*, I, 921]

The subject considered as object turns out to be a source, perhaps the ultimate source, of the sublime.[24]

At any rate, the abyss that the self-conscious mind enters within itself evokes a response equivalent to that which other

---

[22]Chalmers, XIII, 420, 439.

[23]Burke, *Enquiry,* p. 59.

[24]In *Wordsworth and the Sublime,* Wlecke argues that for Wordsworth, as for Coleridge, "the true source of the sublimity of anything, physical object or idea, is always the subject" (p. 79). "Sublime consciousness" becomes "a structure of awareness in which all conceptions tend to recede from shapeliness, and the mind is left groping in the darkness of its own subjectivity" (p. 81). For a superb discussion of the link between sublimity and self-consciousness, see Wlecke's chapter 4, "The Intuition of Existence," pp. 72-105.

types of sublimity provoke. Thus, Wordsworth describes the awakening self-consciousness of his college years:

> As if awaken'd, summon'd, rous'd, constrain'd,
> I look'd for universal things; perused
> The common countenance of earth and heaven;
> And, turning the mind in upon itself,
> Pored, watch'd, expected, listen'd; spread my thoughts
> And spread them with a wider creeping; felt
> Incumbences more awful, visitings
> Of the Upholder of the tranquil Soul,
> Which underneath all passion lives secure
> A steadfast life.
>
> [*Prel* III: 109–118]

The movement is again from arousal to tranquillity. The energized search for "universal things" reaches within. Self-dissection creates a sense of the interpenetration of subject and object, as the mind spreads in the vacuum of itself. From this diffusion of thought comes a sense of sublime visitation, and awful "incumbences" press down upon the poet. The distinction between the 1805 text, "Incumbences more awful," and the 1850, "Incumbencies more awful," may be only the substitution of one obsolete word for another meaning the same thing. In the *OED*, however, "incumbence" (overhanging or impending) seems more threatening than "incumbency" (a spiritual brooding or overshadowing); the sense of benevolent "brooding," nurturing, is missing in incumbence. Thus, the original text would seem to be closer to describing the ambivalent sublime experience of power. The "visitings of the Upholder," like the "visitings of awful promise" in "Crossing the Alps," descend in the self-conscious moment. It is worth noting that in all MSS. except E,[25] *Prelude* (1805) III: 115–116 reads: "visitings / Of the Upholder, of the tranquil Soul." The insertion of the comma omitted by de Selincourt puts "Soul" in apposition to "Upholder." The "Upholder," therefore, is not a transcendental being

---

[25]DC MSS. 52, 53, MS. verses 22–25.

but something from within which emerges in sublime and self-conscious moments. The force of such awful incumbence, of being lost at the edges of the mind, is to uphold that sense of inner tranquillity so vital for Wordsworth.

A second instance of the psychological sublime leading to calm appears in *Prelude* II:

> A tranquillizing spirit presses now·
> On my corporeal frame: so wide appears
> The vacancy between me and those days,
> Which yet have such self-presence in my mind
> That, sometimes, when I think of them, I seem
> Two consciousnesses, conscious of myself
> And of some other Being.
>
> [ll. 27–33]

The image of pressing down recalls the incumbences of the mind turning in upon itself, but, in fact, the "tranquillizing spirit" comes from a slightly different source. The space which is opened up is not that of the mind contemplating itself, but the abyss of "Tintern Abbey," of time and the two selves. The contemplation of the lost self provides not only nostalgic excitement but also a deep awareness of the obscurity of all identity. By postulating "two consciousnesses," Wordsworth casts into doubt the solidity of the present self, and out of this contemplation comes the energy that calls forth the tranquillizing spirit.

III

The revision of *Prelude* I indicates how critical the movement from excitement to calm is to Wordsworth's sense of poetic vocation. In the original conception (MS. JJ), the autobiographical tale starts with the usual "I am born." The Derwent travels over "the green plains / Near my sweet birthplace."[26] In contrast, the

---

[26]*Prel*, p. 633. I assert this with some reservations, for on the Z verso (p. 642), where Wordsworth may well have begun work in JJ, we find drafts toward the "Glad Preamble." These drafts, however, are fragmentary; whereas the remnant of JJ forms a narrative made even more coherent in MSS. U-V, the two-part *Prelude*.

"Glad Preamble" opens the 1805 *Prelude;* the revised poem thus begins, as M. H. Abrams points out, "not at the beginning, but at the end—during Wordsworth's walk to 'the Vale that I had chosen.'"[27] The original opening expresses uncertainty, even anxiety: "Was it for this . . . ?" The "finished" version confidently asserts the poetic and prophetic power to complete *The Recluse.* The "Glad Preamble" is meant to epitomize the kind of experience the *Recluse* poet will have while "musing in solitude." The structure of this exemplary experience is strikingly like the responses to the sublime and the pathetic which I have been describing. Beginning in "weariness," the mind feels a remarkable excitement and a consequent sense of calm.

The Prelude opens in the middle of the experience. The narrator has left the city, a metaphorical "house of bondage" where weariness, confusion, and spiritual desertion have overcome his soul. Retrospectively, it seems the place of deracination and alienation:

> it is shaken off,
> As by miraculous gift 'tis shaken off,
> That burthen of my own unnatural self,
> The heavy weight of many a weary day
> Not mine, and such as were not made for me.
>
> [*Prel* I: 21–25]

As de Selincourt notes, the language describing this past weariness is similar to that used in "Tintern Abbey": "the burthen of the mystery . . . the heavy and weary weight / Of all this unintelligible world" (*Prel,* p. 511). Like the exhaustion the travelers of *Salisbury Plain* and *The Ruined Cottage* feel, it is more psychological than physical.

Such a weariness has ruled the poet's mind immediately prior to the point in narrative time when *The Prelude* begins. Line one represents the moment at which the poet is roused from spiritual deadness—"Oh there is blessing in this gentle breeze."

---

[27]Abrams, *Natural Supernaturalism* (New York: Norton, 1971), p. 74.

In the fifty-three lines that follow, Wordsworth uses metaphors to define his inordinate excitement. Religious enthusiasm, revolutionary liberty, and the "corresponding mild creative breeze" serve as figures to ground an indefinite energy.[28] These images, which possess great power by virtue of their contexts, provide Wordsworth with the means of creating and expressing his own excitement.

Another kind of language used to define and create this excitement is taken from the eighteenth-century sublime: "I breathe again; / Trances of thought and mountings of the mind / Come fast upon me" (ll. 19–21). "Trances of thought" recall the trances of the literature of sensibility. Because the poet-narrator, not one of his characters, is said to achieve such subliminal consciousness, the experience claimed is mitigated to a trance of thought. Nonetheless, here as in *Salisbury Plain*, the trance implies a separation from the earlier, weary, "unnatural" self. "Mountings of the mind" employs a conventional description of sublime response. Wordsworth, following tradition, uses the language of ascension, "ex-alt-ation," "elev-ation," and "mounting," to describe and locate such feelings. The metaphor, comatose but not dead, imposes the topography of the natural sublime upon intense mental states which, in reality, are directionless.

This excitement is at once the source and proof of poetic genius. In the recapitulation of the "Glad Preamble" which opens *Prelude* VII, Wordsworth claims that:

> my favourite Grove,
> Now tossing its dark boughs in sun and wind
> Spreads through me a commotion like its own,
> Something that fits me for the Poet's task.
>
> [ll. 50–53]

[28]See M. H. Abrams, "The Correspondent Breeze: A Romantic Metaphor," in *English Romantic Poets*, ed. Abrams (New York: Oxford University Press, 1960), pp. 37–54; also *Natural Supernaturalism*, pp. 74–80, 363–372, for discussion of Wordsworth's use of the prophetic, revolutionary, and wind metaphors, and particularly for the traditional and contemporary contexts in which Wordsworth is working.

An internal "commotion" which mirrors the energies of nature is a defining and necessary characteristic of poetic election. The "Glad Preamble" is, then, centrally about the power that binds man and nature together in such a way as to produce poetic words. The metaphor that asserts this creative unity is provided by the weather:

> For I, methought, while the sweet breath of Heaven
> Was blowing on my body, felt within
> A corresponding mild creative breeze,
> A vital breeze which travell'd gently on
> O'er things which it had made, and is become
> A tempest, a redundant energy
> Vexing its own creation. 'Tis a power
> That does not come unrecogniz'd, a storm,
> Which, breaking up a long-continued frost
> Brings with it vernal promises, the hope
> Of active days
>
> [I: 41–51]

The act of composition becomes the subject of the "Glad Preamble." The poet's racing imagination is mirrored by the rapid expansion of the vehicle of the metaphor. The surge from a "mild creative breeze" to "A tempest, a redundant energy . . . a storm" reflects what is going on within the poet as he makes "a present joy the matter" of his song. The ambivalence of "redundant" and "vexing its own creation" recalls the talk about the process of composition in the Fenwick note to *The White Doe of Rylstone:*

> When, from the visit just mentioned, we returned to Town-end, Grasmere, I proceeded with the Poem; it may be worth while to note, as a caution to others who may cast their eye on these memoranda, that the skin having been rubbed off my heel by my wearing too tight a shoe, though I desisted from walking I found that the irritation of the wounded part was kept up by the act of composition, to a degree that made it necessary to give my constitution a holiday. A rapid cure was the consequence. Poetic excitement, when accompanied by protracted labour in composition,

has throughout my life brought on more or less bodily derange-
ment. [*PW*, III, 542]

However painful it might be, this excitement, with the accompanying loss of control, even frenzy, is, for Wordsworth, critical
to the process of compositon.

In the "Glad Preamble" the process that begins with the exploitation of natural and linguistic energy is completed by a calm
scene that parallels the ending of *The Ruined Cottage:*

> Whereat, being not unwilling now to give
> A respite to this passion, I paced on
> Gently, with careless steps; and came, erelong,
> To a green shady place where down I sate
> Beneath a tree, slackening my thoughts by choice,
> And settling into gentler happiness.
> 'Twas Autumn, and a calm and placid day,
> With warmth as much as needed from a sun
> Two hours declin'd towards the west, a day
> With silver clouds, and sunshine on the grass,
> And, in the shelter'd grove where I was couch'd
> A perfect stillness.
>
> [ll. 68–79]

The landscape, formerly characterized by a sprightly breeze,
becomes "calm and placid"; "a perfect stillness" falls. It may be, of
course, that on the day when Wordsworth left London or Goslar
(or as John Finch would have it, Coleridge at Ullswater),[29] the
morning winds died away. Such things happen in nature, and
because of the day's importance, the poet might well have remembered its meteorological events with remarkable clarity.
More likely, however, in the opening scene of this personal *Bil-
dungsroman*, Wordsworth arranges the weather much as a
novelist would. Nature has fallen into calm *because* tranquillity is,
for him, as much the proof of his vocation as the preceding
excitement. The absolute quality of the calm is striking. The

[29]John Finch, "Wordsworth's Two-Handed Engine," in *BWS*, pp. 1–13.

stillness is "perfect." Only "a sense of touch / From the warm ground" balances the poet, "else lost / Entirely, seeing nought, nought hearing" (ll. 89–91). In MS. A₂ he is indeed "lost mid the intense / And absolute silence" (*Prel*, p. 7). Such total negation of sense does not occur in nature but rather describes a state of mind. Thus, in the "Glad Preamble," as in "Tintern Abbey," there is a movement from emotional turbulence to a kind of absolute tranquillity. This process becomes not only the source, but the proof as well, of "That Genius which exists by interchange / Of peace and excitation."

The thrust of these two chapters has been to suggest the similarities between Wordsworth's responses to the pathetic and the sublime. In blending the experience of tragedy with that of sublimity, Wordsworth follows the current of his age. As W. P. Albrecht has shown, "the merger of the sublime and the tragic took place during the eighteenth and early nineteenth centuries, completing itself in the definitions of sublimity and tragedy offered by Hazlitt and Keats."[30] In Wordsworth, certainly, the merger is virtually complete, in terms of response if not theory. The pathetic, for him, is a source of psychic energy equivalent to other forms of the sublime. The "Essay, Supplementary to the Preface" gives the pathetic and the sublime as the two major sources which the poet can tap to "call forth and to communicate power" (*Prose*, III, 82). In their effects on the mind, there is little distinction between "the profound and the exquisite in feeling" and "the lofty and universal in thought and imagination." Both necessitate a correspondent imagination within the reader: "Because without the exertion of a co-operating *power* in the mind of the Reader, there can be no adequate sympathy with either of these emotions: without this auxiliary impulse, elevated or profound passion cannot exist" (III, 81). The sublime and the pathetic share a single aim, to move the reader by poetic power

---

[30]W. P. Albrecht, *The Sublime Pleasures of Tragedy* (Lawrence: University Press of Kansas, 1975), p. vii.

"to be excited, often to external, and always to internal, effort"
(III, 81-82).

There remains, however, a significant difference between the
pathetic and the sublime. Although almost any object, if rightly
considered, can provide sublime experience, the object of pathos
is another human being, usually one more unfortunate than the
poet and reader. To the unscrupulous or naive writer, this distinction is of little moment: the need for emotional power over-
rides all considerations. The young Wordsworth, as we have
seen, has few scruples about using people, such as the Female
Beggar and the Chamois Hunter, to give energy to his work. For
the poet of *Salisbury Plain,* poetry is indeed passion, and he is not
at all fastidious about how emotions are roused. In the late
nineties, however, Wordsworth's poetry becomes increasingly
self-conscious. It is no longer enough that the contemplation of
human misery provide a facile source of emotional excitement.
The poet is anxious about the moral implications of exploiting
suffering in literature. With the rise of such concerns, his relationship to the suffering upon which his imagination feeds becomes more complex. After *The Ruined Cottage,* the emotional
catharsis dramatized in the early poems tends not to appear. In
its place perhaps, Wordsworth self-consciously explores the
problematic moral and psychological questions raised by tragic
pleasure.

4 The Pleasures of Tragedy, 1798

> It is not easy to account for the pleasure we take in poetry and painting, which has often a strong resemblance to affliction, and of which the symptoms are sometimes the same as those of the most lively sorrow. The arts of poetry and painting are never more applauded than when they succeed in giving pain. A secret charm attaches us to representations of this nature, at the very time our heart, full of anguish, rises up against its proper pleasure.
>
> —Abbé du Bos, *Réflexions critiques sur la poésie,* quoted by Lord Kames, *"Our Attachment to Objects of Distress"*

I

Until 1798, Wordsworth's use of natural tranquillity to present cathartic feelings reflected a crude emotional response rather than any vigorous intellectual effort toward self-awareness. The calm felt right, and therefore it became a recurrent pattern in his poetry. In *The Ruined Cottage,* however, the poet settles on the spear-grass vision as the response to Margaret's story only after he explores several contemporary theories about the pleasures of tragedy. The calm here is the product of settled deliberation by a mind eager to know itself.

Recent studies have established that composition of *The Ruined Cottage* occurred in two steps, in April–July 1797 and January–March 1798. In summer 1797, Coleridge and Lamb heard a relatively integrated version of Margaret's story. This "ur-Margaret" probably consisted of the passages describing the family's disintegration (ll. 98–185); Margaret's final decline (ll. 431–492); and at least one of the Pedlar's recurrent visits. After a hiatus of six months, Wordsworth returned to the poem. At this time, he added the dramatic framework, composed of the opening lines (ll. 1–54), two interruptions in the narrative (ll. 185–237, 362–376), the conclusion, and *The Pedlar*.[1]

This revision essentially changes the poem's emphasis. Originally *The Ruined Cottage* had been the straightforward narrative of Robert's desertion and Margaret's subsequent tragedy of hope. As with Southey's "Hannah," Cowper's "Crazy Kate," and the less restrained contemporary novels, the anticipated response is what Wordsworth and his age called "delicious pain" (*PW*, I, 269). The reader commiserates with Margaret's sufferings and feels the pleasure of sympathy. In the revised *Ruined Cottage,* however, two layers of response intrude between reader and suffering: the Pedlar actively responds to the story he tells, and the narrator, as he listens, is also deeply moved. These intermediary figures complicate the sympathetic reaction; we become nearly as interested in their responses as in Margaret.[2]

In MS. B of *The Ruined Cottage,* material describing the responses of the Pedlar and narrator has, for the most part, been added to the original fair-copy text. Among such passages are lines describing the Pedlar as one "who could afford to suffer / With those whom he saw suffer"; the Pedlar's digression, "Sir, I feel / The story linger in my heart..." (MS. D, ll. 362–371); three tentative, rough-draft endings; and the so-called "Addendum." The first draft of a passage equivalent to MS. D, ll. 73–88, beginning "The Poets in their elegies and songs," also appears in MS. B.[3] It is not possible to date each of these passages precisely; but certainly, as Finch and Butler make clear, they post-

[1]*PW*, V, 377–378; John Finch, "*The Ruined Cottage* Restored," in *BWS*, pp. 29–49; Reed *EY*, pp. 321–328, 337–339; Jonathan Wordsworth, *The Music of Humanity* (New York: Harper & Row, 1969), pp. 9–22; James Butler, "Introduction" to *RC & P*, pp. 7–22.

[2]In *Wordsworth's Poetry, 1787–1814* (New Haven: Yale University Press, 1974), Geoffrey Hartman aptly characterizes the change in focus: "Instead of centering transparently on Margaret, the tale reflects also the narrator, and tends to become a story about the relation of teller to tale" (p. 139).

[3]See photographs and transcriptions in *RC & P*, pp. 130–279. Butler's introduction and notes present and discuss the available evidence regarding the dating of individual passages.

date March 5, 1798, and therefore represent a late stage in the poem's composition. Probably they were added in March 1798 as Wordsworth was working feverishly on *The Pedlar* and the "Addendum."[4] All in some way discuss the central problem of tragic response.

Why then did Wordsworth feel it appropriate or necessary to change the poem's focus? Nothing in the letters, notes, and journals of winter 1798 suggests artistic, philosophical, or rhetorical reasons for such a revision; thus, surmise must be drawn from the internal evidence of the poem and our general knowledge of Wordsworth's development in the late 1790s.[5]

Let us begin with the assumption that Wordsworth knew what he was about. If *The Ruined Cottage* dramatizes the relationship of teller to tale, it is because in early 1798 Wordsworth wants to explore the imaginative use of pathetic narrative. With his growing interest in the mind, and with the example of Coleridge's chronic self-monitoring before him, it would be only natural to begin asking questions about the response to fictional suffering. In the three previous years, after all, Wordsworth created *Adventures on Salisbury Plain, The Borderers,* and the first version of *The Ruined Cottage,* and he began the still more gruesome *Somersetshire Tragedy.* In January–March 1798, he wrote "The Discharged Soldier" and revised "Description of a Beggar" into "The Old Cumberland Beggar." The spring saw the "*poesie larmoiante*"[6] of *Lyrical Ballads,* featuring Goody Blake, the forsaken Indian woman, Martha Ray, Simon Lee, and the drowned man

[4]Reed *EY,* p. 339; Finch, *BWS,* pp. 45-49; *RC & P,* pp. 17-22, 130-131.

[5]Using such material, Jonathan Wordsworth has suggested that the dramatic structure serves "to distance Margaret's suffering, making bearable a story which in its original conclusion was too painful, too abrupt" (*Music of Humanity,* p. 150). He connects the expansion of the poem with the concept of the One Life: "unrelieved sadness is quite incompatible with the Philosophy of Joy now put forward in *The Pedlar*" (p. 19). The framework brings the reader "momentarily to believe in a philosophical resolution which outside the context of the poem is presumably unacceptable" (p. 92). Much of this seems plausible, and it is my purpose not so much to disagree with Jonathan Wordsworth as to point to another issue important to the poet at the time.

[6]So described by Dr. Charles Burney's review of *Lyrical Ballads* in *The Monthly Review* 29 (1799), 209.

of *Peter Bell.* For such a writer, looking self-consciously at his work necessitates coming to terms with the feelings generated by the literary use of human misery.

The question Wordsworth asked himself is that which he gives to the Pedlar:

> Why should a tear be in an old man's eye?
> Why should we thus with an untoward mind
> And in the weakness of humanity
> From natural wisdom turn our hearts away,
> To natural comfort shut our eyes and ears,
> And feeding on disquiet thus disturb
> The calm of Nature with our restless thoughts?
>
> [MS. D, ll. 192–198]

In context, this question is meant rhetorically: the Pedlar wants to reprimand his own weakness and to halt the narration. Nevertheless, the question is, of itself, important. The problem of evil is not what troubles Wordsworth here. Later, in *The Prelude* and *The Excursion,* he will indeed explore the perplexing *unde malum,* as any would-be philosophical poet and rival of Milton and Pope must. *The Excursion* presents Margaret's sufferings in the context of Despondency and Despondency Corrected, but, in 1798, the weakness of humanity is not the inability to confront and explain suffering. It lies in the "untoward mind" which consciously "shuts our eyes and ears" to nature and craves the morbid and pathetic. The weakness is that in man which causes him to write, read, and enjoy stories about the miseries of others, the part of Wordsworth's mind that writes such poems as "Michael" and "Ruth" to produce "an unusual and irregular state of the mind" (*Prose,* I, 146).

"The Old Cumberland Beggar," like MS. B of *The Ruined Cottage,* represents the revision in early 1798 of pathetic materials which had lain fallow for a half year or so. The textual history of this poem, too, reflects the turn of Wordsworth's interest from the pathetic object to questions of tragic response. Originally, "The Old Cumberland Beggar" had been a straightforward portrait of a decrepit old man. The earliest integrated version, "Description of a Beggar," on the Pierpont Morgan folio sheet, consists of "The Old Cumberland Beggar," lines 44–66, and "Old Man Travelling," lines 3–5, 8–12.[7] The focus of "Description" is on the beggar's agonizingly slow progress through the countryside. He is a borderer "dwelling betwixt life and death," tottering in a limbo between motion and not-motion. Significantly, "Description" dates from approximately the same time as MS. A of *The Ruined Cottage.* Both were part of a dismantled notebook of late 1796 and early 1797 reconstructed by Finch and Reed.[8]

In revision, "The Old Cumberland Beggar" becomes a poem about the imagination's relation to suffering. As in *The Ruined Cottage,* the question of evil does not particularly interest Wordsworth. Remarkably little religious or metaphysical justification is brought forward to vindicate the Beggar's Life-in-Death. There is indeed a nod toward "Nature's law":

> That none, the meanest of created things,
> Of forms created the most vile and brute,
> The dullest or most noxious, should exist
> Divorced from good, a spirit and pulse of good,
> A life and soul to every mode of being
> Inseparably link'd.
>
> [ll. 73–79]

The argument is a Coleridgean, pantheistic version of the syllogism that God is beneficent, God made the world, and, therefore, the world is entirely good. Wordsworth, however, seems barely concerned with the theological implications of his assertions. This passage is unrelated to subsequent descriptions of the Beggar's social function; and the poet apparently adopts the argument solely for the polemic attack upon the "proud / Heart-swoln" statesmen.

[7]Beth Darlington presents the Pierpont Morgan text of "Description of a Beggar" in "The Privileged Inmates of Deep Solitude: A Study of Wordsworth's Solitaries," Ph.D. dissertation, Cornell University, 1970, pp. 46–47.

[8]Reed *EY*, p. 346.

The central question in "The Old Cumberland Beggar" is about the response to suffering: what does looking at the Beggar do to the psychology of the viewer? The effect obtained in *The Ruined Cottage* by the interposition of the poet's speaking voice and the Pedlar-as-narrator is created in "The Old Cumberland Beggar" by the projection of multiple observers. The important verbs in the poem are those of visual perception: "I saw an aged Beggar" (line 1); "The sauntering horseman-traveller . . . / Towards the aged Beggar turns a look, / Sidelong and half-reverted" (ll. 26–32); a toll-collector "sees / The aged Beggar coming" (ll. 34–35); "the Villagers in him / Behold . . ." (ll. 80–81); "all behold in him / A silent monitor" (ll. 114–115); "the young behold / With envy, what the old man hardly feels" ("Old Man Travelling," ll. 13–14). Much is also made of the Beggar's own limited vision, "seeing still, / And never knowing that he sees" (ll. 53–54). Finally, the process of visual contemplation becomes pantheistic. Nature, as well as man, watches the Beggar: "As in the eye of Nature he has liv'd, / So in the eye of Nature let him die" (ll. 188–189). Vision is the metaphor of encounter, of interaction between subject and suffering object. Except for the description of the Beggar's vision, all this seeing and beholding first appears in the 1798 revisions of the poem. The effect of these additions, as in *The Ruined Cottage*, is to draw attention away from the sufferer to questions of tragic perception and response.

II

In early 1798 the question of what happens in the mind when it perceives such an object is critical. The problem of suffering for Wordsworth at this time is quite simply, "How does the mind respond to human misery, in fiction, memory, or reality? What kinds of feeling do we draw from it, and why do we take pleasure in watching others undergo experiences which we would not at all care to undergo ourselves?" These are the very questions raised by the ongoing eighteenth-century discussion of the pleasures of tragedy, and, not surprisingly, Wordsworth refers to the contemporary theories of tragic response as he revises *The*

Ruined Cottage and "Description of a Beggar." What is remarkable, however, is the variety of theory he draws upon; nearly every major formulation that his century had postulated to explain or justify the seemingly perverse interest in fictional suffering finds its way into these poems. The only prominent theory not mentioned is the Aristotelian mimetic theory that "in viewing the works of imitative art . . . we contemplate with pleasure, and with the *more* pleasure, the more exactly they are imitated, such objects as, if real, we could not see without pain."[9] The poet suggests and explores at various lengths: (1) the sensationalist theory that the emotional agitation of tragic response provides a stimulating alternative to ennui; (2) the sentimental commonplace that the tale of suffering engenders moral improvement; (3) the Lucretian "return" upon the self; (4) the stoic dictum that tragedy makes men conscious of their limitations; (5) Aristotelian *katharsis;* (6) a secularized mutation of the Christian explanation of suffering; and (7) what Earl Wasserman has called the "doctrine of sympathy."[10] Only after considering each of these theories does Wordsworth settle on the spear-grass calm which closes *The Ruined Cottage.*

"Why should we thus with an untoward mind," the Pedlar

[9]Thomas Twining, *Aristotle's Treatise on Poetry, Translated with Notes* (London: Payne et al., 1789), p. 70. Eighteenth-century variants of Aristotle's mimetic explanation include those of Samuel Johnson and David Hume. For Johnson, "the delight of tragedy proceeds from our consciousness of fiction; if we thought murders and treasons real, they would please no more. Imitations produce pain or pleasure, not because they are mistaken for realities, but because they bring realities to mind" ("Preface to Shakespeare," in Arthur Sherbo, ed., *Johnson on Shakespeare* [New Haven: Yale University Press, 1968], I, 78). Hume's "On Tragedy" locates tragic pleasure primarily in the medium of imitation, "eloquence," although he does nod toward Aristotle: "tragedy is an imitation, and imitation is always of itself agreeable" (*Of the Standard of Taste and Other Essays,* ed. John W. Lenz [Indianapolis: Bobbs-Merrill, 1965], p. 32). A theory emphasizing the artifice of tragedy clearly did not much tempt Wordsworth, who was interested in the imagination's response to the power of "real and substantial suffering."

[10]The references to the historical background in this chapter largely follow Earl R. Wasserman, "The Pleasures of Tragedy," *ELH* 14 (1947), 283–307; Baxter Hathaway, "The Lucretian 'Return upon Ourselves' in Eighteenth-Century Theories of Tragedy," *PMLA* 62 (1947), 672–689; and W. P. Albrecht, *The Sublime Pleasures of Tragedy* (Lawrence: University Press of Kansas, 1975).

asks, "feeding on disquiet, thus disturb / The calm of Nature with our restless thoughts?" The subsequent conversation suggests the first of the contemporary theories of tragic response. The narrator, "impelled / By a mild force of curious pensiveness" (MS. B, ll. 276–277), requests continuation of the "homely tale," and the Pedlar protests, rather too energetically, the innocence of the collective undertaking:

> It were a wantonness, and would demand
> Severe reproof, if we were men whose hearts
> Could hold vain dalliance with the misery
> Even of the dead, contented thence to draw
> A momentary pleasure, never marked
> By reason, barren of all future good.
>
> [MS. B, ll. 280–285]

Manuscript evidence suggests that lines 261–297 of MS. B represent the first passage written for *The Ruined Cottage* exploring the response to fictional suffering. On leaves 15^r and 16^v of the Alfoxden notebook, the interlude appears in Wordsworth's hand.[11] The poet, evidently uneasy about the nourishment obtained from feeding on Margaret's disquiet, is attempting to purify and moralize the act of writing and reading *The Ruined Cottage*.

The theory being rejected is that postulated by René Rapin and widely disseminated by du Bos: "of all Passions Fear and Pity are those that make the strongest Impressions on the Heart of Man. . . . when the Soul is Shaken by Motions so Natural and so Humane, all the Impressions it feels becomes [sic] Delightful; its Trouble pleases, and the Emotions it finds is a kind of Charm to it . . . in this *Agitation* consists all the Pleasure that one is capable to receive from Tragedy."[12] This idea had powerful effects in England and animated much of the theory of the tragic sublime. For Burke, the "rousing" of the emotions constitutes the momentary pleasure one finds in the sublime, whether of

[11]*RC & P*, pp. 110–117; Reed *EY*, p. 28.
[12]Rapin, *The Whole Critical Works* (1706), II, 206–207, quoted by Wasserman, "The Pleasures of Tragedy," p. 289.

tragedy, nature, or language: "Now, as a due exercize is essential to the coarse muscular parts of the constitution, and that without this rousing they would become languid, and diseased, the very same rule holds with regard to those finer parts we have mentioned; to have them in proper order, they must be shaken and worked to a proper degree."[13] Hazlitt, too, insists that the pleasure "derived from tragic poetry, is not anything peculiar to it as poetry. . . . It has its source and ground-work in the common love of strong excitement."[14] For the sensationalist, the experience of tragedy becomes merely a way of keeping the mind in shape, indistinguishable in effect from other kinds of stimulation.

Such a theory would present obvious temptations to one who believes poetry is passion, yet Wordsworth has his Pedlar denounce it. As so often when he attempts to control feelings or ideas toward which he is ambivalent, Wordsworth's vehemence is suspect. After all, the poet himself has caught "greedily" at stories of lonely widows and vagrant families (*Prel* VIII: 525–559). Nonetheless, a purely sensationalistic theory of tragic pleasure is impossible for him to accept. When the agitation of tragic response is seen as an end in itself, the relation of poet to suffering becomes rankly exploitative, even ghoulish. Human misery, which for the "Moralist" is "a sacred thing" (*PW*, I, 174), is evoked solely for trivial personal pleasure, as the most powerful source of emotion available. Whatever temptations this theory of tragic pleasure might present to him, Wordsworth is not one to revel in his own sinfulness, and, thus, the denial of momentary pleasure must be sharp and absolute. Where Burke, for one, accepts morbid curiosity as a portion of human nature, Wordsworth cannot rest with feelings he considers to be "coarse sympathies" (*PW*, I, 334). For him there must be a more adequate and exalted explanation. The additions to the tale of

[13]Edmund Burke, *Enquiry into the Sublime and Beautiful*, ed. J. T. Boulton (New York: Columbia University Press, 1958), p. 135.

[14]William Hazlitt, "On Poetry in General," in *The Collected Works*, ed. A. R. Waller and Arnold Glover (London: Dent, 1902–1904), V, 7.

Margaret's suffering and the "Description of a Beggar" reflect the struggle to find such a rationalization.

Wordsworth's first impulse is to assert a moral explanation. After rejecting "vain dalliance with the misery / Even of the dead," the Pedlar theorizes, "there is often found / In mournful thoughts, and always might be found, / A power to virtue friendly" (MS. B, ll. 286–288). In the first draft of these lines, the poet underlines *is* (*RC & P*, p. 116). Wordsworth rarely resorts to italicization, but here, untypically, he feels the need for a stress not present in the natural rhythms of language and syntax. At any rate, even while the Pedlar acknowledges the possibly dangerous power of suffering, he domesticates it with an expression of faith. The statement that the energy of tragedy "always might" be channeled into morality, however, temporizes even as it makes absolute claims.

In the interlude, the attempt to assert the morality of tragedy is purely rhetorical: "were't not so / I am a dreamer among men—indeed / An idle dreamer" (ll. 288–290). Apparently, however, Wordsworth has in mind the contemplation of suffering as a moral discipline, for the first two, discarded, endings to MS. B depict such a process:

> But to some eye within me, all appeared
> Colours & forms of a strange discipline
> The trouble which they sent into my thought
> Was sweet, I looked and looked again, & to myself
> I seemed a better and a wiser man.
>
> I turned to the old man, & said my friend
> Your words have consecrated many things
> And for the tale which you have told I think
> I am a better and a wiser man.
>
> [*RC & P*, pp. 256–259]

The narrator is less insistent than the Pedlar had been about the moral effects of contemplating suffering. "I seemed ... I think / I am a better and a wiser man" assert only a subjective experience. Nevertheless, the closing scene of *The Ruined Cottage,* as first conceived, dramatizes moral transfiguration. The young man is "moved," his heart "goes back into the tale" which has been told, and "returning from [his] mind," he, like Coleridge's Wedding Guest, has a sense of improvement.

Wordsworth is apt to credit such improvement to whatever excites him greatly. In "Tintern Abbey," after all, recollections of the Wye valley are responsible for "that best portion of a good man's life." But here he also draws on the sentimentalist's insistence that a tale of misery has a beneficial effect on the hearer's moral constitution. For eighteenth-century theorists on tragedy, the moral improvement wrought by the tale of suffering was a safe truism; as Earl Wasserman points out, however, the century "was inclined to accept the moral value of tragedy as a profound truth and to move on" to other matters.[15] Although there was abundant reference to the assumption that tragedy promotes virtue, little effort was made to explore precisely how. Thus, Hugh Blair states, "the intention of Tragedy may, I think, be more shortly and clearly defined, To improve our virtuous sensibility," and Lord Kames asserts that "a pathetic composition, whether epic or dramatic, tends to a habit of virtue, by exciting us to do what is right, and restraining us from what is wrong." The manner of Mrs. Barbauld's dissent from it suggests the very strength of the commonplace: "Having thus considered the manner in which fictitious distress must be managed to render it pleasing, let us reflect a little upon the moral tendency of such representations. Much has been said in favour of them, and they are generally thought to improve the tender and humane feelings; but this, I own, appears to me very dubious."[16]

Unlike many of his predecessors, Wordsworth attempts a serious exploration of the moral improvement induced by tragic

[15]Wasserman, "The Pleasures of Tragedy," p. 283.
[16]Hugh Blair, *Lectures on Rhetoric and Belles Lettres* (London: Strahan, 1785), III, 294; Henry Home, Lord Kames, *Elements of Criticism* (Edinburgh: Bell & Creech, 1785), II, 374; John Aikin and Anna Aikin [Barbauld], *Miscellaneous Pieces in Prose* (London: J. Johnson, 1773), pp. 210–211.

pleasure. The "Addendum" seeks to clarify how the contemplation of suffering leads us along "the path / Of order and of
good" (ll. 94–95); the discussion of "sympathy" later in this chapter will talk about this effort to explore the morality of tragic
response. For the present, I shall consider "The Old Cumberland Beggar," which, among much else, attempts to define how
the contemplation of other people's misery makes one "a better
and a wiser man."

In that poem, after briefly invoking the pantheistic "spirit and
pulse of good," Wordsworth settles down in lawyerly fashion to
enumerate the beneficial effects of the Beggar's remaining at
large. The first justification of the status quo is moral:

> While thus he creeps
> From door to door, the Villagers in him
> Behold a record which together binds
> Past deeds and offices of charity
> Else unremember'd, and so keeps alive
> The kindly mood in hearts which lapse of years,
> And that half-wisdom half-experience gives
> Make slow to feel, and by sure steps resign
> To selfishness and cold oblivious cares.
>
> [ll. 79–87]

The analogy between the old, nearly blind man and a parish
registry of charitable deeds tends to turn the Beggar into a piece
of writing, as if words only could bind our days and ways each to
each. Wordsworth's argument, however, is based on the combined principles of British empiricism and benevolism:

> Where'er the aged Beggar takes his rounds,
> The mild necessity of use compels
> To acts of love; and habit does the work
> Of reason, yet prepares that after joy
> Which reason cherishes. And thus the soul,
> By that sweet taste of pleasure unpursu'd
> Doth find itself insensibly dispos'd
> To virtue and true goodness.
>
> [ll. 90–97]

The optimistic necessitarianism of David Hartley and William Godwin permeates this statement. The jargon of "habit," "reason," "pleasure" make it apparent that Wordsworth has gone, if not to his books, at least to Coleridge, in order to find a terminology to describe the moral effects of suffering. Before he was through worrying the topic in "The Old Cumberland Beggar," he would go yet further, to the Lucretian and stoic theories of tragic response.

For the eighteenth century, the opening lines of *De rerum natura*, Book II, were an important *locus classicus* among explanations of tragic pleasure:

> Tis pleasant, safely to behold from shore
> The rowling Ship; and hear the Tempest roar:
> Not that anothers pain is our delight;
> But pains unfelt produce the pleasing sight.
> 'Tis pleasant also to behold from far
> The moving Legions mingled in the War[17]

The essential movement of thought in Lucretius is reflection, as the viewer compares his lot to that of the persons on the ship or in battle. The leading English source of this view is Addison's *Spectator* 418: "when we read of Torments, Wounds, Deaths, and the like dismal Accidents, our Pleasure does not flow so properly from the Grief which such melancholy Descriptions give us, as from the secret Comparison which we make between our selves and the Person who suffers." Time and again, commentators refer to this theory, either to reject or embrace it: Hartley speaks of "the secret Consciousness of our own Security," Burke of "the contemplation of our own freedom from the evils which we see represented," and George Campbell of the viewer "ready to congratulate with himself on his better luck."[18] "The Old Cumber-

---

[17]Lucretius, *De rerum natura*, Book II, lines 1–6, trans. John Dryden, in *Poems 1685–1692* (Volume III of the California *Complete Works*), ed. Earl Miner (Berkeley: University of California Press, 1969), p. 46.

[18]Joseph Addison, Richard Steele, et al., *The Spectator*, ed. Donald F. Bond (Oxford: Clarendon, 1965), III, 568; David Hartley, *Observations on Man* (London: Leake & Frederick, 1749), I, 428; Burke, *Enquiry*, p. 45; George Campbell, *The Philosophy of Rhetoric* (London: Strahan & Cadell, 1776), I, 332.

land Beggar" presents an argument clearly derivative from the
Lucretian return upon the self:

> The easy man
> Who sits at his own door, and like the pear
> Which overhangs his head from the green wall,
> Feeds in the sunshine; the robust and young,
> The prosperous and unthinking, they who live
> Shelter'd, and flourish in a little grove
> Of their own kindred, all behold in him
> A silent monitor, which on their minds
> Must needs impress a transitory thought
> Of self-congratulation, to the heart
> Of each recalling his peculiar boons,
> His charters and exemptions.
>
> [ll. 108–119]

"Self-congratulation" virtually echoes the phrasing of Campbell's "congratulating with himself," and the structure of the
safe observer and pathetic victim is the same as that in *De
rerum natura*.

A second, purely stoic return upon the self occurs in the *Meditations* of Marcus Aurelius: "Tragedies were at first introduced
to remind us of the calamities necessarily attendant on human
nature, and to teach us that such disastrous events as entertain
us on the stage, we should bear with patience on the more enlarged stage of human life. For we see that such incidents must
unavoidably befall us; and that even those illustrious persons
who are the subjects of these tragical representations, are forced
to submit to them."[19] The view that "we are induced to acquiesce
with greater patience in our own lot, by beholding pictures of
life tinged with deeper horrors, and loaded with more excruciat-
ing calamities" is also a neoclassical commonplace. André Dacier
quotes the passage from the *Meditations* in his commentary on
the *Poetics*, and Dryden speaks of purging "the soul from pride,

---

[19]Marcus Aurelius, *Meditation* XI: 6, trans. Richard Graves (London: Robinson, 1792), p. 335.

by the examples of human miseries, which befall the greatest."[20] Among the Scottish professors, Blair sees tragedy as a moral lesson: "If an Author interests us in behalf of virtue, forms us to compassion for the distressed, inspires us with proper sentiments, on beholding the vicissitudes of life, and, by means of the concern which he raises for the misfortunes of others, leads us to guard against errors in our own conduct, he accomplishes all the moral purposes of Tragedy." Kames is more purely stoic: "A pathetic composition['s] . . . frequent pictures of human woes produce, beside, two effects extremely salutary: they improve our sympathy, and fortify us to bear our own misfortunes."[21] Wordsworth is less sanguine about the tractability of human nature, gently rejecting such optimism and suggesting that a lesser moral effect might be achieved in contemplating the old Beggar:

> and perchance,
> Though he to no one give the fortitude
> And circumspection needful to preserve
> His present blessings, and to husband up
> The respite of the season, he, at least,
> And 'tis no vulgar service, makes them felt.
>
> [ll. 119–124]

The unspoken lesson of *The Ruined Cottage,* too, is one of eternal change, of a nature which ravens all human joys and accomplishments. The poem hardly tries to encourage fortitude and circumspection or to give any practical advice relative to the human condition, but it does instill a profound sense that

> we die, my Friend,
> Nor we alone, but that which each man loved

[20]John Aikin, "On Romances," in *Miscellaneous Pieces*, p. 44; *Aristotle's Art of Poetry. Translated . . . according to Mr. Theodore Goulston's Edition. Together with Mr. D'Acier's Notes Translated from the French* (London: Browne & Turner, 1705), pp. 78–79; John Dryden, "Dedication to the *Aeneis*," in *Of Dramatic Poesy and Other Critical Essays*, ed. George Watson (London: Everyman, 1972), II, 227.

[21]*Lectures on Rhetoric*, III, 294; *Elements of Criticism*, II, 374.

And prized in his peculiar nook of earth
Dies with him or is changed, and very soon
Even of the good is no memorial left.

[ll. 68–72]

For Wordsworth, the poet is a moral teacher, and part of his morality is always the omnipresent sense of change and human transience.

The eighteenth century explained Aristotle's *katharsis* in two ways.[22] The first was a version of sentimental morality, a synthesis of Aristotle and the unrelated Horatian notion that tragedy should instruct. This view appears in John More's critique of *The Seasons:* "Objects of distress are formed to operate on the mind mechanically. Yet we soften, at the touch of misery, with a pleasure not so much resembling what we feel in the discharge of animal functions, as that which accompanies the performance of our most important obligations."[23] The "strange discipline" which troubles the young man in the discarded ending to *The Ruined Cottage* is a version of this moral catharsis. As More's statement suggests, the century also had access to the more familiar (and correct) interpretation of catharsis which likens the effect of tragedy to physical purgation, the expulsion of "impurities from the human body."[24] This version was supplementary rather than contradictory to moral catharsis. In the prefaces to *Samson Agonistes* and Dryden's *Aeneis*, for instance, the two

[22]The two interpretations are described by W. D. Ross, in *Aristotle* (New York: Scribners, 1924): "The main opposition is between the views which take *katharsis* to be a metaphor drawn from ceremonial purification, and the object of tragedy to be a moral one, the purification of the emotions, and those which take *katharsis* to be a metaphor drawn from the purgation of evil bodily humours, and the object assigned to tragedy to be non-moral. The former view has the support of many famous names, and is chiefly associated with that of Lessing" (p. 282). See also Clarence Green, *The Neo-Classic Theory of Tragedy in England during the Eighteenth Century* (Cambridge, Mass.: Harvard University Press, 1934), p. 23; Leopold Damrosch, *Samuel Johnson and the Tragic Sense* (Princeton: Princeton University Press, 1972), pp. 22–25.

[23]J[ohn] More, *Strictures, Critical and Sentimental, on Thomson's "Seasons"* (London: Richardson & Urquhart, 1777), p. 190.

[24]Samuel Johnson's expression of purgative catharsis in James Boswell, *Life of Johnson*, ed. G. B. Hill, rev. L. F. Powell (Oxford: Clarendon, 1934), III, 39.

concepts coexist without disharmony. Tragedy not only made one a better man, it made him feel better.

In the "Addendum," disease and health, the prominent metaphors of purgative catharsis, are major terms of the Pedlar's speech. He attacks the rational intellect which beholds "solitary objects . . . / In disconnection dead and spiritless." Hyperrationality abstracts man into "fretful dreams / Of feverish nothingness." This disease of mind is the narrator's state at the opening of *The Ruined Cottage*. He has eyes for insect hosts and ears for bursting gorse, but he fails to perceive the "processes of things." Listening to the tale of misery purges him of "sickly wretchedness." "Thus disciplined," he once again can "drink in the soul of things." Tragic response enables the senses and intellect to "invigorate and sharpen and refine" themselves (ll. 52–85). Significantly, "refine" is an important term in the eighteenth century's understanding of the cathartic process. Thomas Twining claims that "the habit of *indulging* the emotions of pity, or terror, in the fictitious representations of Tragedy, tends . . . to *moderate* and refine those passions, when they occur in real life."[25] The first English translation of the *Poetics* renders the *katharsis* passage: "Tragedy . . . by means of Compassion and Terror perfectly refines in us, all sorts of Passions."[26] In the "Addendum," the senses and intellect are self-purifying; they "refine / Each other." This parallels the assertion of Aristotle that "pity and terror" effect "the *correction* and *refinement* of such passions."[27]

At one point, the exploration of tragic response even leads Wordsworth to invoke the traditional religious justification of

---

[25]Twining, *Aristotle's Treatise*, p. 240.
[26]*Aristotle's Art of Poetry* (1705), p. 70. In James Beattie's *The Minstrel*, the purification of catharsis is given a Christian twist; Edwin's response, "the tender tear to Misery given," is said to "soften and refine the soul for Heaven" (I: 48; Chalmers, XVIII, 576).
[27]The translation here is Twining's (p. 75), but Henry Pye, too, in *A Commentary Illustrating the Poetics of Aristotle* (London: Stockdale, 1792), insists on the self-reflexiveness of the purgation: "effecting through the means of pity and terror, the purgation of such passions" (p. 16).

suffering. In a passage drafted into the original MS. B, the Pedlar turns aside from the main thread of his narrative:

> It would have grieved
> Your very heart to see her. Sir, I feel
> The story linger in my heart. I fear
> 'Tis long and tedious, but my spirit clings
> To that poor woman
>
> [MS. D. ll. 361–365]

One remembers the Moralist of "A Poet's Epitaph," "to whose smooth-rubb'd soul can cling / Nor form nor feeling great nor small." Lingering over a story of distress gives the spirit forms and feelings to hold onto in a disjointed, mysterious, all too unintelligible world:

> so familiarly
> Do I perceive her manner, and her look
> And presence, and so deeply do I feel
> Her goodness, that not seldom in my walks
> A momentary trance comes over me;
> And to myself I seem to muse on one
> By sorrow laid asleep or borne away,
> A human being destined to awake
> To human life, or something very near
> To human life, when he shall come again
> For whom she suffered.
>
> [ll. 365–375]

It is an unusual moment in the early, "semi-Atheist" Wordsworth, for the Pedlar is calling up a version of Christian immortality. The phrase, "he shall come again," while it refers to Margaret's husband, has resonances of resurrection and apocalypse. Similarly, "for whom she suffered" recalls Christ's sacrifice for mankind. From musing on Margaret's suffering, then, the Pedlar would appear to claim a vision of immortality much like that contained in the Christian promise. Earthly suffering becomes transitory and unimportant except as the occasion for life everlasting. Of course, Wordsworth is not at all

Christian but very nearly blasphemous in his equation of mere humanity with God the Son. In Christian dogma, immortality solaces the sufferer;[28] here, suffering itself is "permanent, obscure and dark, / And has the nature of infinity" (*PW*, I, 188).

Except in regard to the moral theory, Wordsworth's stance in considering the various theories of tragic response is tentative. Writing poetry occasions alternative formulations of the effects of tragedy. Among such alternatives, however, the complex of ideas which Wasserman has called "the doctrine of sympathy"[29] most attracts the poet. Much of the theoretical superstructure that Wordsworth builds in 1798 over the poems of 1797 has to do with "sympathy." The concept, of course, is important in the late-eighteenth-century discussion of the sentimental interest people take in other, less fortunate people. Burke, Adam Smith, Kames, and Blair, among others, ascribe the pleasure of pathos to the "social passion" they interchangeably call sympathy, pity, or compassion. According to Burke, "the bond of sympathy" attracts mankind to tragic plays and natural disasters. Kames states that "by a good tragedy, all the social passions are excited,"—passions arising "from that eminent principle of sympathy, which is the cement of human society."[30] The Pedlar himself is a man of feeling: "by nature tuned ... To sympathy with man, he was alive / To all that was enjoyed where'er he went, / And all that was endured" (*RC & P*, p. 183). He is curiously indifferent to the lot of those whom he observes. The equality of "enjoyed" and "endured" suggests that the intensity of human passion, not its nature, is what stirs him and keeps him "alive." He can "afford to suffer" with those whom he

---

[28]In the final revision of *The Excursion* (1845), Margaret's suffering is indeed redeemed by the knowledge of Christ's resurrection: she becomes one who "learned, with soul / Fixed on the Cross, that consolation springs, / From sources deeper far than deepest pain, / For the meek Sufferer" (*Excursion* I: 936–939).

[29]Wasserman, "The Pleasures of Tragedy," p. 299.

[30]Burke, *Enquiry*, pp. 44–47; Lord Kames, *Essays on the Principles of Morality and Natural Religion*, 3d ed. (Edinburgh: Bell and Murray, 1779), pp. 12, 16. See Walter Jackson Bate, *From Classic to Romantic* (Cambridge: Harvard University Press, 1946), pp. 129–141, for a useful discussion of the eighteenth century's uses of "sympathy."

sees suffer, and out of his watching becomes "rich" in "our best experience." Clearly, the kind of experience which is "best" is not Margaret's, but his own.

In Wordsworth, pantheism complicates and enriches eighteenth-century sentimentalism. The word sympathy encompasses not only the Pedlar's feelings for mankind but also his relationship with natural objects.[31] He has "sympathies" with the life of things and finds "in all shapes . . . a secret & mysterious soul, / A fragrance & a spirit of strange meaning." He gives a "moral life" to "every natural form, rock, fruit, & flower / Even the loose stones that cover the highway" (*RC & P*, p. 181). This is the Wordsworthian "sympathy with [the] real or imagined Life" of objects that Coleridge denounces in an 1803 notebook.[32]

In early 1798 the two sympathies become fused. Wordsworth discovers "the great social principle of life, / Coercing all things into sympathy" (*Prel* II: 408–409). He comes to see "sympathy with man" as equivalent to sympathy with nature. This merger of concepts would eventually produce the doctrine of Love of Nature Leading to Love of Mankind, but in 1798 it is the product of Wordsworth's explorations of the response to suffering. The earliest manuscript evidence of this convergence lies in two Alfoxden notebook fragments, juxtaposed to and contemporaneous with work on "The Discharged Soldier," the revision of *The Ruined Cottage,* and *The Pedlar:*

> Why is it we feel
> So little for each other but for this
> That we with nature have no sympathy

[31]Wordsworth's dalliance with pantheistic sympathy has long been noted. For discussions of this subject, see H. W. Piper, *The Active Universe* (London: Athlone, 1962); E. D. Hirsch, *Wordsworth and Schelling: A Typological Study of Romanticism* (New Haven: Yale University Press, 1960), pp. 38–61; *Music of Humanity,* pp. 184–232.

[32]*STCNB*, I, 1616. Interestingly, in another notebook entry Coleridge connects this sympathy with an abiding sense of calm: "The rocks and Stones put on a vital semblance; and Life itself thereby seemed to forego its restlessness, to anticipate in its own nature an infinite repose, and to become, as it were, compatible with Immoveability" (*STCNB*, I, 1189).

Or with such things as have no power to hold
Articulate language

And never for each other shall we feel
As we may feel till we have sympathy
With nature in her forms inanimate
With objects such as have no power to hold
Articulate language. In all forms of things
There is a mind

[*RC & P*, pp. 120–123]

Although nature has priority, the relation between natural and human sympathy is symptomatic rather than causative. The poet does not assert that lack of natural sympathy causes lack of human sympathy; rather he suggests that pervasive dullness of soul blunts us equally to nature and man. Possession of either sympathy implies possession of the other, while to lack one is to lack both.

On versos of MS. B of *The Ruined Cottage,* Wordsworth again connects the two kinds of sympathy. There Wordsworth's earliest draft of *The Pedlar* (MS. D), lines 275–277, follows a passage toward lines 19–57, 81–86:

... nor this alone
Sufficed but many an hour in caves forlorn
And in the hollow depths of naked crags
He sat and even in their fix'd lineaments
He traced an ebbing and a flowing mind
Expression ever varying. In his heart
Love was not yet nor the pure joy of love
By sound diffused or by the breathing air
Or from the silent looks of happy things
Flowing, or from the universal face
Of earth & sky .. tuned by Nature
to sympathy with man

[*RC & P*, pp. 148–149]

Here, Wordsworth has linked "sympathy with man" to the pantheistic sympathy with the "ebbing and flowing mind." Significantly, this passage is the point from which he embarked on his lengthy description of the Pedlar's mind. The original fair copy of MS. B, Part First, did not include lines 70–264 of the Darbishire text (*PW*, V, 379–399) and, thus, described only the Pedlar's lowly background (ll. 48–69) and his "sympathies" with the life of things (ll. 264–300). No effort was made to show how his mind had developed. A draft of lines 70–113 appears on versos of the original fair copy (leaves 4 and 5). The MS. B *Pedlar* itself appears on the rectos of leaves 6 through 18 variously in draft and fair copy. The manuscript evidence suggests that after starting *The Pedlar* (ll. 70–113) on the MS. B versos, Wordsworth composed 113–161 elsewhere and had Dorothy copy 70–161 in a second notebook, where *The Pedlar* grew yet another hundred odd lines. Then, as Finch has suggested, the whole of lines 70–264 was stitched "as is" into MS. B.[33] For my argument, what is important is that the verso rough draft of 70–113 is the germ of the expanded *Pedlar*. The notion that "sympathy with man" is related to sympathy with nature lies at the very heart of Wordsworth's decision to turn his attention from tale to teller.

Another passage scribbled on MS. B versos discusses sympathy and the poetry of suffering. The lines expand the suggestion of fair-copy MS. B, ll. 135–136, "The Waters of that spring if they could feel / Might mourn. They are not as they were":

> The Poets in their elegies and songs
> Lamenting the departed call the groves
> They call upon the hills & streams to mourn
> And senseless rocks, nor idly; for, inspired
> By no fallacious oracle they speak
> Obedient to the strong creative power
> Of human passion. Sympathies there are
> More mild, yet haply of a kindred birth
> That steal upon the meditative mind
> And grow with thought. Beside yon spring I stood
> And eyed its waters till we seemed to feel

[33]See Finch, *BWS*, p. 46, and Butler, "Introduction" to *RC & P*, pp. 17–18, for discussions of this gathering. The reader is also referred to the photographs and transcriptions in *RC & P*, pp. 142–189.

> One sadness, they and I; for them a bond
> Of brotherhood is broken time has been
> When every day the touch of human hand
> Disturbed their stillness, and they minister'd
> To human comfort.
>
> [*RC & P*, pp. 194–199]

A tentative expression of natural sympathy has been replaced by a scheme that affirms a link of sentiment between man and nature and dares even suggest an equivalence in their "sympathies." The communication between man and his world is reciprocal. The poet calls, "nor idly," upon natural objects to mourn with him, and, in turn, "sympathies" from those objects "steal upon" his mind. "The touch of human hand" disturbs nature, and nature "ministers" to man. In claiming that these two kinds of sympathy, man outward to nature and nature inward upon man, are "haply of a kindred birth," Wordsworth stops just short of absolute affirmation of the One Mind. But again pantheistic sympathy is related to pathetic sympathy. The Pedlar, musing by Margaret's spring, has brought her story before his mind's eye, and felt the sympathy of compassion. Nature "seems to feel one sadness" with him, thereby sharing his response. It turns out, therefore, that the major role of a sympathetic nature is to share with man the sentimental sympathy with human suffering.

In the "Addendum" Wordsworth attempts to provide a theoretical connection between the pantheistic and pathetic sympathies. The fragment opens with a passage echoing the Alfoxden notebook's description of the language of sympathy: "Not useless do I deem / These quiet sympathies with things that hold / An inarticulate language . . . ." The subsequent argument of the "Addendum" is like that of "Tintern Abbey." The poet's morbid passions, his feelings of disquietude, vengeance, hatred, and contempt, are "softened down" by sympathy with natural objects. This relationship causes a "holy tenderness" to pervade his being, and he finds "all his thoughts now flowing clear / From a clear fountain" ("Addendum," ll. 14–17).

Sympathy with vestiges of human hands supplements the quiet sympathy:

> And further, by contemplating these forms
> In the relations which they bear to man
> We shall discover what a power is theirs
> To stimulate our minds
>
> [ll. 24-27]

In objects with human associations, we read "some sweet & tender lesson to our minds / Of human suffering or of human joy" (ll. 34-35). As in *The Pedlar,* the spectator *ab extra* cares little whether he contemplates suffering or joy, so long as he finds the stimulation "to quicken and to rouze" himself from "weariness." The desire is to experience a heightened sensibility whether in the "holy tenderness" of pantheism or the "tender lesson" of human sympathy. When the Pedlar exhorts himself and the narrator to "rise / From this oblivious sleep, these fretful dreams / Of feverish nothingness" (ll. 76-78), the fretful dream is not Margaret's story but the unstimulated, fragmented existence that the narrator had known at the beginning of *The Ruined Cottage.* In that state one "dimly pores on things minute, / On solitary objects, still beheld / In disconnection dead & spiritless" (ll. 60-62). Thus, Margaret's story, bringing significance and emotional associations to objects, has what Wordsworth elsewhere calls a "fructifying virtue."[34] The poet finds justification for the contemplation of suffering in the activity of mind it engenders, the imaginative growth which enlarges "our sphere of pleasure & of pain" (l. 82):[35]

> Whate'er we see,
> Whate'er we feel, by agency direct

[34]This phrase is from the "spots of time" passage in the two-part *Prelude.* In the original context, the spots of time were closely allied to the response to pathetic narrative. The promulgation of them came immediately following a discussion of "the tragic facts of rural history." For a full discussion, see Chapter 7.

[35]*PW,* V, 402, claims that "pain" is "clearly a copyist's error," and substitutes "power" from MS. D. However, in MS. D, "pain" is the original fair-copy reading; see *RC & P,* p. 374.

> Or indirect, shall tend to feed & nurse
> Our faculties & raise to loftier heights
> Our intellectual soul.
>
> [ll. 95–99]

At this point Wordsworth comes close to the Burkean sublime, where the "exercise" of the mind is good for its own sake: "as these emotions [pain and terror] clear the parts whether fine, or gross, of a dangerous and troublesome incumbrance, they are capable of producing delight; not pleasure, but a sort of delightful horror, a sort of tranquillity tinged with terror."[36] For Burke, any stimulation of the passions is explicitly cathartic, whether the source of powerful emotions is nature, literature, or real life. For Wordsworth, although the metaphor he chooses is of nourishment rather than of purgation, tragic response is also cathartic. It is moral as well, however; aroused by sympathy, "we shall move / From strict necessity along the path / Of order and of good." One suspects this "necessity" is imposed by the poet's desire.

In MS. B, the conclusion of *The Ruined Cottage* follows the Pedlar's discussion of "sympathies." In the original context, therefore, the spear-grass vision exemplifies how the contemplation of suffering consecrates natural objects. Reading "the forms of things" with a worthy eye, the Pedlar finds salvation in the particular, "those very plumes, / Those weeds, and the high spear-grass on that wall." These mere things convey "so still an image of tranquillity" that he can find a strange peace "Amid the uneasy thoughts which filled my mind." At the conclusion of *The Ruined Cottage,* "the eye made quiet" can "see into the life of things," or, as the Pedlar says in a similarly expansive metaphor, "we" can "drink in the soul of things" ("Addendum" line 92). It is another of those sublime moments in Wordsworth, but the source of sublimity is, notably, the pathetic. Thus, in *The Ruined Cottage,* Wordsworth arrives at the "calm of mind all passion

---

[36]Burke, *Enquiry,* p. 136.

spent" only after expending considerable thought on the question of fictional pathos and its imaginative importance. The spear-grass vision is the earned result of an investigation into the very sources of his poetic excitement.

One of the arguments in "The Old Cumberland Beggar" resembles that of the "Addendum":

> Some there are,
> By their good works exalted, lofty minds
> And meditative, authors of delight
> And happiness, which to the end of time
> Will live, and spread, and kindle; minds like these,
> In childhood, from this solitary being,
> This helpless wanderer, have perchance receiv'd,
> (A thing more precious far than all that books
> Or the solicitudes of love can do!)
> That first mild touch of sympathy and thought,
> In which they found their kindred with a world
> Where want and sorrow were.
>
> [ll. 97–108]

Clearly the poet is talking about himself: "minds like these, / In childhood" echoes the earlier statement that "Him from my childhood have I known" (line 22). By the "good works" which exalt "lofty minds," Wordsworth means books as well as charitable deeds. The words describing the "authors of delight"—"lofty," "meditative," "exalted"—are those by which he habitually describes the poetic mind. Thus, as in the "Addendum," a major function of human suffering is to stimulate the growth of poetic imagination. Here, however, the suffering person has priority over the natural object; the "first mild touch of sympathy" comes not from a pantheistic awareness but from the social passion of pity. The model is not Love of Nature Leading to Love of Mankind, but sympathy for man leading to a sense of kindred with the external world. The "mild" sympathies come from the child's contemplation of the Beggar rather than from a sense of feeling "one sadness" with Nature.

III

In early 1798, Wordsworth describes yet another encounter with a "wanderer of the earth," the Discharged Soldier. Here psychological complication and abstract justification are sheared away, and the relation between observer and sufferer is starkly simple. Wordsworth, in his most understated style, refuses to indulge his twin penchants for moralizing and theoretical hypothesis, yet the scene is, after all, the dramatization of a response to suffering. The motives are intended to be intuited, but they clearly revolve around the notion of sympathy.

In fact, the bimodal structure of the 1798 "Discharged Soldier"[37] recalls the "Addendum" to *The Ruined Cottage*, which appears on the immediately preceding leaves of DC MS. 16. The opening description of a calm evening walk expresses pantheistic sympathy, and the narrative of the meeting with the soldier explores a sympathetic interaction with a fellow human being. As "The Discharged Soldier" begins, the boy, like the narrators of *The Ruined Cottage* and "The Climbing of Snowdon," is in a state of weariness. He is "listless," "exhausted," "worn out by toil," "all unworthy of the deeper joy" of nature. Overcoming his internal resistance, the calm of nature moves his mind to a condition of tranquillity and extreme visionary sensitivity:

> On I passed
> Tranquil, receiving in my own despite
> Amusement, as I slowly passed along,
> From such near objects as from time to time
> Perforce disturbed the slumber of the sense
> Quiescent, & disposed to sympathy,
> With an exhausted mind worn out by toil
> And all unworthy of the deeper joy
> Which waits on distant prospect, cliff or sea,
> The dark blue vault, and universe of stars.
> Thus did I steal along that silent road,

---

[37]I use Beth Darlington's text from "Two Early Texts," *BWS,* pp. 433-48.

My body from the stillness drinking in
A restoration like the calm of sleep
But sweeter far.

[ll. 11–24]

The boy's mood is that described in the opening lines of the "Addendum"—"disposed to sympathy" recalls the Pedlar's assertion that "Not useless do I deem / These quiet sympathies with things that hold / An inarticulate language." The "near objects" which intrude upon the sense are like the "things" with which the Pedlar sympathizes. The effect of "quiet sympathy" in the "Addendum," too, is restorative: "feelings of aversion" are softened down, and "tenderness" pervades the soul. In both passages, the experience is suprasensual. The inarticulate language of things in the "Addendum" is the voice of the One Life speaking though the particular: such a sound is inaudible to the bodily ear. Similarly, the boy of "The Discharged Soldier" "looked not round, nor did the solitude / Speak to [the] eye, but it was heard & felt" (ll. 26–27). In the "Addendum" the quiet sympathy with things leads to love of man: "the man / Once taught to love such objects" becomes "compassionate and has no thought, / No feeling which can overcome his love" (ll. 3–4, 22–23). "The Discharged Soldier" exemplifies such a process, for, after feeling quiescent sympathy, the narrator encounters the Soldier and acts in a sympathetic and helpful manner.

As in "The Old Cumberland Beggar," words of perception emphasize the relation and separation of the poetic eye and its suffering object. Even in this most economical of poems, Wordsworth insistently reminds us that one person is watching another: "Presented to my view an uncouth shape" (l. 38); "I could mark him well, / Myself unseen" (ll. 40–41); "I looked at them / Forgetful of the body they sustained" (ll. 46–47); "I could mark / That he was clad . . ." (ll. 53–54); "Long time I scanned him . . ." (l. 68); "I wished to see him move" (l. 77); "I beheld / With ill-suppress'd astonishment" (ll. 123–124). The effect of all this beholding is to provide a filter between sufferer and reader analogous to the dramatic framework of *The Ruined Cottage*. Vision is also clearly related to sympathy. To see accurately is to feel deeply, for the Soldier's admonition is "My trust is in the God of heaven, / And in the eye of him that passes me" (ll. 164–165).

The actual psychology of response to the Soldier's suffering is intimated rather than explicit, but the grounds of the boy's actions are clear enough. In the "happy state" when "beauteous pictures now / Rose in harmonious imagery," he confronts "an uncouth shape" at a "sudden turning of the road" (ll. 28–38). Calling the man an uncouth shape evokes the strangeness of Otranto and Udolpho, and the youth's immediate perception seems indeed to be of a supernatural being. The Soldier is "a foot above man's common measure," his legs are "long and shapeless," "his mouth / Shewed ghastly" (ll. 42–51). He appears like the "tall thin Spectre" of *The Vale of Esthwaite:* "You might almost think / That his bones wounded him" (ll. 44–45) only tones down the anatomical horror of "His bones look'd sable through his skin" (*PW*, I, 277). Even when the Soldier's humanness is established, the young man is astonished by the "tall / And ghostly figure moving at my side" (ll. 124–125). It is an experience of the *Unheimliche*, the supernatural occurring to one who does not believe.

The uncanny, however, only charges more fully an experience laden with emotional significance, and it is as an encounter with human suffering that "The Discharged Soldier" primarily concerns us. The underlying assumption of the poem is that the reader shares a common bond of sympathy with the author and all civilized men, that he will be swept up by the painful simplicity of the description. But the relation of poet to sufferer, and no doubt, that of reader to sufferer, involves other factors than sympathy. Even when he knows that the soldier is only human, and a deeply suffering human at that, the poet-to-be remains in his covert: "Long time I scanned him with a mingled sense / Of fear and sorrow" (ll. 68–69). Fear one understands as the result of lingering superstitious awe, but the scansion with sorrow, the reading into the other person's pain, suggests that something other than "specious cowardice" prevents Wordsworth from accosting the fellow immediately. "Fear and sorrow" is a common eighteenth-century rendering of the Aristotelian tragic emotions. In a sense, therefore, the young Wordsworth experiences in a real situation the tragic pathos; or, at least, so the poet remembers and responds to it ten years later as he is writing the poem. He does not leave his cover for the same reason that one does not walk out of *Othello* or onto the stage where it is played. The pleasant pain, the interested expectation of the inevitable, leave him in suspension. The "mild force of curious pensiveness" which impels the *Ruined Cottage*'s narrator to ask the Pedlar to continue keeps this narrator in hiding.

There is a sense of "reproach" (l. 83) in all this, a knowledge of exploitation and "momentary pleasure," but even when he leaves his "shady nook," the narrator's primary interest is in the soldier's tragedy. The pattern of conversation is reminiscent of the first interlude of *The Ruined Cottage:* there, after the Pedlar breaks off the tale, "A while on trivial things we held discourse, / To me soon tasteless" (ll. 205–206). In "The Discharged Soldier," after the formality of salutation, "A short while / I held discourse on things indifferent / And casual matter" (ll. 90–92). Here, too, the narrator wants the "history" (l. 95). Though he knows the end is ruin and misery, he must learn what has happened; he cannot forbear "To question him of what he had endured / From war & battle & the pestilence" (ll. 138–139).

In the early manuscripts, Wordsworth ends the narrative abruptly, "And so we parted." In the 1805 *Prelude,* however, "Back I cast a look, / And linger'd near the door a little space; / Then sought with quiet heart my distant home" (IV: 502–504). E. E. Bostetter has noted the peculiarity of this ending:

> The word "quiet" comes as a disquieting shock.... For "quiet" is not an ambiguous word in the sense of suggesting a complex of meanings, but simply an inadequate and inhibiting word. It deliberately cuts off the flow of response, represses and denies the tremendous range of questions clearly evoked in the story.... A

"quiet heart" can be relevant only in the sense that the boy has seen the man safely taken care of for the night; that he knows that the man will somehow survive; that he has been assured of the fundamental dignity and worth of human nature as it has been revealed in the man. But, in any final sense, his heart could not be "quiet."[38]

In light of the pattern of suffering and calm discussed in Chapter 2, clearly the quiet heart does not indicate mere complacency or repression. Wordsworth's heart is quiet, as he contemplates the Soldier's suffering ten or fifteen years later, because it is a natural response for him to make to suffering. His lingering near the door recalls the narrator's clinging to the story of Margaret: "I turn'd away in weakness; and my heart / Went back into the tale which he had told" (*RC & P*, p. 257).

It would also seem probable that the calm of nature which, over the intervening years, Wordsworth remembers as peculiar to that night originated not from the actual weather but from conditions that the memory fabricated in order to bring fact into agreement with the feelings evoked by the Soldier. As Wordsworth in 1798 recollected the night's events, called to mind in vivid detail the man and his suffering, and typically responded with emotion first, then calm, he might easily have remembered that night as being extraordinarily calm, whether it was in point of fact or not. At any rate, reviewing the Soldier's story provides the emotional energy necessary for catharsis and the "quiet heart" which is a principal end of Wordsworth's poetry.

---

[38]*The Romantic Ventriloquists* (Seattle: University of Washington Press, 1963), pp. 57–58. In *The Quest for Permanence* (Cambridge, Mass.: Harvard University Press, 1959), David Perkins interprets the "quiet heart" in still another way: "The veteran finally proves, like the leech gatherer, Michael, and other characters who represent Wordsworth's hope for human nature, to have a 'demeanour calm,' to come close to being 'solemn and sublime.' In other words, he possesses all the qualities usually located in nature and none that Wordsworth usually associates with man. Hence at the end of the incident the poet finds himself able to continue on his way 'with quiet heart'" (p. 18).

5 Experiments in Pathos:
Lyrical Ballads (1798)

However painful may be the objects with which the Anatomist's knowledge is connected, he feels that his knowledge is pleasure; and where he has no pleasure he has no knowledge. What then does the Poet? He considers man and the objects that surround him as acting and re-acting upon each other, so as to produce an infinite complexity of pain and pleasure.

—Preface to *Lyrical Ballads* (1802)

I

The commonplace that the *Lyrical Ballads* are experimental poems derives from Wordsworth's own statements. The "Advertisement" to the first edition claims, "The majority of the following poems are to be considered as experiments" (*Prose*, I, 116). The "Preface," too, describes the poems as "an experiment . . . to ascertain, how far, by fitting to metrical arrangement a selection of the real language of men in a state of vivid sensation, that sort of pleasure and that quantity of pleasure may be imparted, which a Poet may rationally endeavour to impart" (*Prose*, I, 118). The experimentalism of *Lyrical Ballads* goes beyond language.[1] Reflecting the sentimental interest in the workings of the mind,

[1]In the assumption of Wordsworth's pervasive experimentalism, I share the opinion of Stephen M. Parrish, *The Art of the "Lyrical Ballads"* (Cambridge, Mass.: Harvard University Press, 1973): "His intention was not simply to experiment with the language of poetry or the psychology of passion. It was, beyond this, to work in experimental forms that were distinctive in several important respects: some were marked by heightened metrical patterns; some by a jocular, mock-heroic, almost comic manner; some were innovations in dramatic method; some were Wordsworth's versions of pastoral; some were designed to reduce the role of story or event in narrative, in favor of passion or feeling—to internalize the action" (p. x).

Wordsworth would have us understand that the poems are experiments in psychology: they contain "a natural delineation of human passions, human characters, and human incidents" (*Prose*, I, 116). The note to "The Thorn" asserts the intention "to exhibit some of the general laws by which superstition acts upon the mind"; further, "Poetry is passion: it is the history or science of feelings" (*PW*, II, 512-513). The "Preface" claims that the poems attempt "to illustrate the manner in which our feelings and ideas are associated in a state of excitement . . . to follow the fluxes and refluxes of the mind when agitated by the great and simple affections of our nature" (*Prose*, I, 126). Such poems as "The Idiot Boy," *Peter Bell*, "The Forsaken Indian Woman," "The Last of the Flock," "The Mad Mother," and "Goody Blake and Harry Gill" are, in the poet's view, primarily clinical studies of human behavior. The main interest is in what today we would call abnormal psychology.

Wordsworth's approaches to diction and psychology are symptomatic of a radically experimental cast of mind. His deliberate tentativeness probes human experience, casts up explanatory hypotheses, and proceeds to test these "general laws" in further poetry. Thus, in *The Pedlar*, the organ of pantheistic apperception is intentionally left indefinite:

> In the after day
> Of boyhood, many an hour in caves forlorn
> And in the hollow depths of naked crags
> He sate, and even in their fixed lineaments,
> Or from the power of a peculiar eye,
> Or by creative feeling overborne,
> Or by predominance of thought oppressed,
> Even in their fixed and steady lineaments,
> He traced an ebbing and a flowing mind,
> Expression ever-varying.
>
> [*RC & P*, pp. 152-155]

I have given the earliest version of this passage in the previous chapter. The most significant change is the addition of the three lines beginning "Or." Wordsworth, evidently dissatisfied with his initial formulation, has returned to the passage and is casting about for explanations of pantheistic experience. His uncertainty is the leisurely experimentalism of a man trying alternate theories to see which most accurately accounts for the phenomena at hand. He makes no attempt to locate, once and for all, pantheistic urgings in some particular mental faculty. There is, as well, little anxiety to achieve such a resolution. Lacking proof or definite knowledge, Wordsworth is willing to remain in a state of fruitful uncertainty. Thus, in a real sense, the passage from *The Pedlar* becomes an experiment in pantheism, a trying out of language and theory to discover a satisfactory general postulation.

The aim of this chapter is to take rather literally Wordsworth's claim that the *Lyrical Ballads* are poetic "experiments." I shall suggest that Wordsworth conducts an experiment with the stuff of poetry, radically, and perhaps intentionally, analogous to the contemporary experiments in natural philosophy. His experimental, even analytical, cast of mind leads to a wide-ranging, insistently tentative exploration of the relations between the poetic object and its audience. As we have seen, for Wordsworth such an exploration requires that he engage questions about human beings as poetic objects, about readers who enjoy tales of suffering, and about poetry that exploits pathos as a source of energy. It is an indication of his curiosity and honesty that, in 1798–1800, the poet continues to probe such difficult and uncomfortable questions. This chapter examines two such experiments in pathos, "Simon Lee" and "The Thorn"; first, however, I wish to discuss further the implications of Wordsworth's describing poems as "experiments."

II

Commonly, the question, "How are the *Lyrical Ballads* experimental?" is taken to be equivalent to "How are the poems original?" In fact, these are different questions. Originality has to do with priority and beginnings; whereas experiment describes a specialized process of mind, the method of intellectual abstraction from reality peculiar to modern science and empirical philosophy. In experimental procedure, there is a continual interplay between raw data and hypothetical general constructs. The experimenter observes natural phenomena, formulates vague theoretical notions to order them, sets up controlled situations to isolate effects, records new observations, and reconstructs theories in accordance with the new data. The important factor in experimentation is the mind's coming to terms with uncertainty. Dr. Johnson's definition places appropriate emphasis on the tentative nature of the process: "EXPERIMENT: Trial of anything; something done in order to discover an uncertain or unknown effect."[2] The *OED* uses similar terms: "a tentative procedure; a method ... adopted in uncertainty."

Given the inevitable association between experimentalism and science, it is significant that Wordsworth should evince a sudden interest in the physical sciences simultaneously with the writing of his "experimental" poems. Wordsworth's first mention of "science" in the modern sense of the word, occurs in blank-verse fragments of March 1798.[3] Both *The Pedlar* and the "Addendum" to *The Ruined Cottage* make room for science in the development of imagination. The young Pedlar lingers "in the elements / Of science, and among her simplest laws" (*RC&P*, p. 169); he studies the "triangles" of the stars and scans "the laws of light." The "Addendum," even as it warns of the dangers of excessive reductivism, reserves for scientific enquiry an important place in mental growth: science's "most noble end / Its most illustrious province" lies "In ministering to the excursive power / Of intellect and thought" (ll. 56–57).

Letters contemporary to the "Addendum" and *The Pedlar* reveal the reason for Wordsworth's sudden interest in science. On March 11, 1798, the poet writes enthusiastically to James Losh:

> We have a delightful scheme in agitation, which is rendered still
> more delightful by a probability which I cannot exclude from my

[2]Samuel Johnson, *A Dictionary of the English Language* (London: 1773).

[3]His previous uses of the word, in the schoolboy verses on Education (*PW*, I, 259–61) and in the 1794 revision of *An Evening Walk* (*PW*, I, 13), retain the etymological meaning of "science" as all knowledge. It is noteworthy that in the 1797 version of "Lines ... Left in a Yew-Tree Seat," the youth who is a figure of the poet is "by genius nurs'd." In the 1800 revision, "science" replaces "genius."

mind that you may be induced to join in the party. We have come
to a resolution, Coleridge, Mrs. Coleridge, my Sister and myself of
going into Germany, where we purpose to pass the two ensuing
years in order to acquire the German language, and to furnish
ourselves with a tolerable stock of information in natural science.
[*EL*, p. 213]

This scheme's underlying purpose is not difficult to discover. In
the subsequent paragraph, Losh is told that "I have been tol-
erably industrious within the last few weeks. I have written 1300
lines of a poem which I hope to make of considerable utility; its
title will be *The Recluse or views of Nature, Man, and Society*" (*EL*, p.
214). Wordsworth is undertaking Coleridge's project for a
philosophical epic; with the project, he has adopted the method
Coleridge had outlined in an April 1797 letter to Joseph Cottle:

I should not think of devoting less than 20 years to an Epic Poem.
Ten to collect materials and warm my mind with universal science.
I would be a tolerable Mathematician, I would thoroughly know
Mechanics, Hydrostatics, Optics, and Astronomy, Botany, Metal-
lurgy, Fossilism, Chemistry, Geology, Anatomy, Medicine—then
the *mind of man*—then the *minds of men*—in all Travels, Voyages
and Histories. So I would spend ten years—the next five to the
composition of the poem—and the five last to the correction of it.
[*STCL*, I, 320–321]

In early 1798 Wordsworth is preparing himself along Coleridgean lines. The "natural science" he intends to stockpile is equivalent to Coleridge's ambitious list of scientific pursuits. In going
to Germany to "settle if possible in a village near a university"
(*EL*, p. 213), he will be able to absorb, cheaply, the knowledge
required to write Coleridge's poem of "universal science."

A letter to James Tobin (6 March) mentions *The Recluse* for
the first time in Wordsworth's writings and asks a favor: "If you
could collect for me any books of travels you would render me
an essential service, as without much of such reading my present
labours cannot be brought to a conclusion" (*EL*, p. 212). Apparently Wordsworth, like Coleridge the previous year, intends to
read "all Travels, Voyages and Histories" to understand "the

minds of men." The travel book was a genre of randomly scientific intent; such works enabled generations of Englishmen to peep and botanize through all corners of the world from the comfort of their sofas. Although it is uncertain how many "books of travels" Wordsworth read in early 1798, one which he did obtain, from Tobin or someone else, was Samuel Hearne's *Journey from . . . Hudson's Bay to the Northern Ocean*. The Fenwick note to "Complaint of a Forsaken Indian Woman" states that the poem was "Written at Alfoxden in 1798, where I read Hearne's Journey with deep interest" (*PW*, II, 474). The incident upon which the poem is based occurs in the book's seventh chapter. Presumably Wordsworth took up Hearne as background reading for *The Recluse*, and the piquant tale of the woman abandoned by her people diverted his energies into "The Complaint."[4] In this poem the scientific attitudes and procedures in which Wordsworth was immersing himself are reflected in his treatment of the woman. The focus of interest is psychological, as the poet delineates the effects of isolation and alienation upon the confusion of a dying mind.

Thus, a book originally taken up to provide knowledge for *The Recluse* becomes the source of a *Lyrical Ballad*. Unable to create the comprehensive poem of Coleridge's pipe-dreams, Wordsworth focuses on a specific episode which has caught his attention and then develops it in a quasiscientific manner. This shift from generality to particular observation might serve as an emblem of Wordsworth's retreat from the onerous task demanded by Coleridge's, and his own, ambitions for the philosophic epic. As Wordsworth swerves away from writing the all-inclusive poem, his reading in science and his "philosophical" conversations with Coleridge lend a scientific tinge to the poems he wrote instead, his *Lyrical Ballads* of 1798.

Almost simultaneously with the reference to *The Recluse* in the letter to Tobin, Wordsworth writes Joseph Cottle "merely to

[4]For Wordsworth's continuing interest in travel books, see Charles Coe, *Wordsworth and the Literature of Travel* (New York: Bookman, 1953).

request (which I have very particular reasons for doing) that you would contrive to send me Dr Darwin's Zonoomia *by the first carrier*" (*EL*, p. 199). A week later, Dorothy informs Cottle that "we have received the books" and "they have already completely answered the purpose for which William wrote for them" (*EL*, pp. 214–215). The two volumes are returned with other books on 9 May (*EL*, p. 218). The Fenwick note to "Goody Blake and Harry Gill, A True Story" acknowledges that "the incident" of the poem is "from Dr. Darwin's *Zoonomia*" (*PW*, IV, 439). Readers, therefore, have understandably assumed that the "purpose" of Wordsworth's request was to look at *Zoonomia* "in connection with work on his *Lyrical Ballads*, possibly for a purpose like finding out in detail about or checking the story of *Goody Blake and Harry Gill*."[5] A glance at *Zoonomia*, however, suggests that Wordsworth had in mind a more ambitious purpose, one justifying the urgency of underlining "*by the first carrier*." The book itself is a ponderous medical treatise, which presents "a theory founded upon nature, that should bind together the scattered facts of medical knowledge, and converge into one point of view the laws of organic life."[6] Darwin's theory of animal life postulates "a spirit of animation" which responds to external stimuli in four "modes"—those of "irritation," "sensations of pleasure and pain," "volition," and "association." Theories of psychology, physiology, and pathology are then spun out from this central core. *Zoonomia* is, in short, the kind of book that Coleridge's systemolatrizing mind devoured, dissected, and eventually discarded. While selling subscriptions to *The Watchman*, Coleridge had met Erasmus Darwin at Derby; although they disagreed on religious matters, he wrote to a friend, "Dr. Darwin possesses, perhaps, a greater range of knowledge

[5]Reed *EY*, p. 224. See also Moorman, I, 389; Paul Sheats, *The Making of Wordsworth's Poetry* (Cambridge: Harvard University Press, 1973), p. 220; Mary Jacobus, *Tradition and Experiment in Wordsworth's "Lyrical Ballads" (1798)* (Oxford: Clarendon, 1976), pp. 274–275; John Jordan, *Why the "Lyrical Ballads"?* (Berkeley and Los Angeles: University of California Press, 1976), p. 36.

[6]Erasmus Darwin, *Zoonomia, or the Laws of Organic Life* (London: J. Johnson, 1796), I, 2. Hereafter *Z*.

than any other man in Europe, and is the most inventive of philosophical men" (*STCL*, I, 177). It seems entirely probable that Wordsworth, in order to begin his Coleridgean project, would want to glance at such a "philosophical" work as *Zoonomia*.

Zoonomia apparently proved of great interest, for traces of Darwin's language and thought are plentiful in Wordsworth's poetry of spring 1798. The immediate source of the associationist jargon present in the "Addendum" to *The Ruined Cottage* and in *The Pedlar* is likely to have been Darwin, not Hartley as has often been asserted.[7] The epigraph from *Aeneid* VI appearing on *Zoonomia*'s title page suggests the common pantheistic yearnings of the two men:

> Principio coelum, ac terras, camposque liquentes
> Lucentumque globum lunae, titaniaque astra
> Spiritus intus alit, totamque infusa per artus
> Mens agitat molem, et magno se corpore miscet.
> [ll. 724–728]

Darwin translates this:

> Earth, on whose lap a thousand nations tread,
> And Ocean, brooding his prolific bed,
> Night's changeful orb, blue pole, and silvery zones,
> Where other worlds encircle other suns,
> One Mind inhabits, one diffusive Soul
> Wields the large limbs, and mingles with the whole.

The highlighting of this familiar passage would have attracted a poet wanting to believe that the "sentiment of being" pervades all things. As Paul Sheats and others have pointed out, the language as well as the thought of "totamque infusa per artus" is echoed in "Tintern Abbey":[8]

[7]Arthur Beatty, the major disseminator of the Hartleian view, in *Wordsworth: His Doctrine and Art*, University of Wisconsin Studies in Language and Literature no. 24 (1927), mentions Darwin only in passing and *Zoonomia* not at all.

[8]Sheats, *The Making of Wordsworth's Poetry*, p. 220, was the first to note, in this connection, that the passage from Virgil provides the epigraph to *Zoonomia*; J. W. Beach, *The Concept of Nature in Nineteenth-Century English Poetry* (New York:

And I have felt
A presence that disturbs me with the joy
Of elevated thoughts; a sense sublime
Of something far more deeply interfused,
Whose dwelling is the light of setting suns,
And the round ocean, and the living air,
And the blue sky, and in the mind of man,
A motion and a spirit, that impels
All thinking things, all objects of all thought,
And rolls through all things.

Wordsworth's cadences, aggregative and undulant, imitate the rhythms of Virgil and his translator.

It is unlikely that Wordsworth read the entire *Zoonomia.* The profusion of his poetic output in early 1798 suggests that he found more important tasks than to wade through some 1300 pages of medicophilosophical prose, and one would suspect that he dipped into it as chance and inclination led him. The section where he found the anecdote of "Goody Blake and Harry Gill," however, undoubtedly interested him. The case of the "young farmer in Warwickshire" belongs to Darwin's discussion of "Diseases of Increased Volition" (Z, II, 359), "volition" being defined as "that superior faculty of the sensorium, which gives us the power of reason" (Z, II, 321). Diseases of volition, therefore, are what we now call mental illness. Darwin is particularly interested in obsession: "In every species of madness there is a peculiar idea either of desire or aversion, which is perpetually excited in the mind with all its connections" (Z, II, 350). In examining the various species of madness, he first offers a theoretical definition, then illustrates the general construct with specific case histories. The fate of Harry Gill, for instance, is one of seven examples of *mania mutabilis*, in which the patient substitutes "imaginations for realities," focusing obsessively on a "mistaken or imaginary idea" all the while carefully concealing "the object of his desire or aversion" (Z, II, 356). Other mutable maniacs include a

---

Macmillan, 1936), p. 576; Ben Ross Schneider, *Wordsworth's Cambridge Education* (Cambridge: Cambridge University Press, 1957), pp. 258–262.

country squire who orders his servants to strip at gunpoint and a woman who stops eating on orders from an angel.

Such cases are not without their fascination, but it is difficult to see how they might contribute to the first genuine philosophic poem. It is clear, however, that they influence the *Lyrical Ballads* (1798), which reflect the assimilation of Darwin's case history approach to external phenomena. "Goody Blake and Harry Gill," "The Thorn," "The Last of the Flock," "The Mad Mother," "The Idiot Boy," and "The Complaint of a Forsaken Indian Woman" each present the case of a person at psychological extremes. The scientific mentality which uses "local accidents" to illustrate "general laws" is shared by both Darwin and the Wordsworth of *Lyrical Ballads*.

Particular details in some of the poems, too, reflect Wordsworth's reading of Darwin's chapter on "Diseases of Increased Volition." For instance, the doctor suggests that, in cases of acute puerperal depression, "the child should be brought frequently to the mother, and applied to her breast, if she will suffer it, and this whether she at first attends to it or not; as by a few trials it frequently excites the storgè, or maternal affection, and removes the insanity" (Z, II, 360). In "The Mad Mother," the woman is relieved by nursing her child:

> Suck, little babe, oh suck again!
> It cools my blood; it cools my brain;
> Thy lips I feel them, baby! they
> Draw from my heart the pain away.
>
> [ll. 31–34]

The shepherd, who sells the last of his flock, has clearly invested manic energy in objects of property:

> Sir! 'twas a precious flock to me,
> As dear as my own children be;
> For daily with my growing store
> I loved my children more and more.
> Alas! it was an evil time;
> God cursed me in my sore distress,

> I prayed, yet every day I thought
> I loved my children less;
> And every week, and every day,
> My flock, it seemed to melt away.
>> ["The Last of the Flock," ll. 81–90]

According to Darwin, the man is in a bad way: "When a person becomes insane, who has a family of small children to solicit his attention, the prognostic is very unfavourable; as it shews the maniacal hallucination to be more powerful than those ideas which generally interest us the most" (*Z*, II, 360).

Ideas from *Zoonomia* are also present in *The Pedlar*, and, thus, in Wordsworth's earliest gropings toward the philosophic poem. Indeed, such traces are to be expected, if Wordsworth's "particular purpose" in borrowing the book from Cottle was to read for *The Recluse*. When the poet goes oddly out of his way to suggest the therapeutic value of science in resolving adolescent crisis, he is echoing Dr. Darwin:

> But now, before his twentieth year was pass'd
> Accumulated feelings press'd his heart
> With an encreasing weight; he was o'erpower'd
> By Nature—and his mind became disturb'd,
> And many a time he wish'd the winds might rage
> When they were silent: from his intellect,
> And from the stillness of abstracted thought,
> In vain he sought repose, in vain he turn'd
> To science for a cure. I have heard him say
> That at this time he scann'd the laws of light
> With a strange pleasure of disquietude
> Amid the din of torrents, where they send
> From hollow clefts, up to the clearer air
> A cloud of mist which in the shining sun
> Varies its rainbow hues. But vainly thus
> And vainly by all other means he strove
> To mitigate the fever of his heart.
>> [*RC & P*, pp. 168–173]

The hope is that science will provide a cure for psychological distress, the "accumulated feelings" which press with an "encreasing weight." Thus, the laws of light are given a function similar to that of mathematics in *Prelude* X, where "Sick, wearied out with contrarieties," the poet turns "towards mathematics, and their clear / And solid evidence" (ll. 900–905). In "Diseases of Increased Volition," Darwin suggests mathematics and science as cures of various forms of insanity. *Tedium vitae*, or depression, is aided by "the cultivation of science, as of chemistry, natural philosophy, natural history, which supplies an inexhaustible source of pleasurable novelty" (Z, II, 374). A "medical person, in London," suffering from *paupertatis timor*, the obsessive fear of poverty, "cured himself of this disease by studying mathematics with great attention; which exertions of the mind relieved the pain of maniacal hallucination" (Z, II, 377).

Thus, in spring 1798, we find Wordsworth first attempting to come to grips with the scientific and experimental temper of his age. Coleridge's concept of *The Recluse* demanded such an effort. The product of this reading and thought, however, was not the first genuine philosophic poem, but the *Lyrical Ballads*. In the "little cells, oratories, and sepulchral recesses" of *Lyrical Ballads*, Wordsworth embodied the scientific spirit to a degree he was never able to in his efforts to write *The Recluse*.

III

The dominant attitude of *Zoonomia* is its experimentalism. Darwin, like other contemporary natural philosophers, displays a fearless willingness to theorize and an eagerness to discover the proof confirming the hypothesis. Such boldness and imagination in *Zoonomia* leads to the formulation of the "first consistent, all-embracing hypothesis of evolution."[9] A continual play between theory and fact, general law and local accident, is characteristic of Darwin, whether he discusses the working of the eye or the sexual instincts of plants. A not entirely random example will illustrate: "You may assure yourself of the truth of this ob-

---

[9]"Erasmus Darwin," in *Dictionary of Scientific Biography*, ed. Charles Coulston Gillispie (New York: Scribner's, 1970–1976), III, 579.

servation [concerning the natural or universal language of grief], if you will attend to what passes, when you read a distressful tale alone; before the tears overflow your eyes, you will invariably feel a titillation at that extremity of the lacrymal duct, which terminates in the nostril, then the compression of the eyes succeeds, and the profusion of tears" (*Z*, I, 150). In Darwin, the desire to move from the "universal" to a particular example overwhelms the original sentimental interest in the tale of distress. The emotion unleashed by sympathy becomes less an end in itself than an object to be examined and used in other proofs. Something like this occurs also in many of Wordsworth's writings.

In the "Essay on Morals" of late 1798, Wordsworth digresses from an attack on the barren rationalism of Godwin and Paley:

> In a [strict?] sense all our actions are the result of our habits—but I mean here to exclude those accidental & indefinite actions, which do not regularly & in common flow from this or that particular habit. As, for example: a tale of distress is related in *a mixed company*, relief for the sufferers proposed. The vain man, the proud man, the avaricious man, &c., all contribute, but from very different feelings. Now in all the cases except in that of the affectionate & benevolent man, I would call the act of giving more or less accidental—I return to our habits—Now, I know no book or system of moral philosophy written with sufficient power to melt into our affections, to incorporate itself with the blood & vital juices of our minds, & thence to have any influence worth our notice in forming those habits of which I am speaking. [*Prose*, I, 103]

The appropriate response to pathos is uncomplicated and familiar. One hears a tale of distress, and, assuming he is a morally sound, "affectionate & benevolent man," contributes emotion and money in good faith. The operant principles are those of sensibility: the reader is tuned by narration to sympathy with man. More interesting, however, is the way that the topic is introduced: "As, for example: a tale of distress is related. . . . " The method of advancing a general principle by means of a specific example is, no doubt, a universal rhetorical device; it is, however, particularly characteristic of commonsense British empirical thought that abstract soarings should be grounded in the stuff of everyday life. Curiously, however, the example that pops into Wordsworth's mind to distinguish between accidental and habitual actions is the response to a tale of distress. Apparently the response to suffering is a kind of litmus test in matters of psychology. This attitude toward pathos transcends merely sensational interest and can best be characterized as experimental.

In the "Preface" to *Lyrical Ballads* (1800), a similar use of the pathetic occurs in the discussion of meter. Writing to justify his claim that poetry should imitate "the real language of men," Wordsworth finds it necessary to answer "an obvious question, namely, why, professing these opinions have I written in verse?" (*Prose*, I, 144). As a self-proclaimed literary revolutionary, he cannot fall comfortably back upon tradition and genre, as would a conservative facing such a question. Indeed, though Wordsworth gestures toward the "nakedness and simplicity" of the primitive ballad, his self-justification is largely couched in psychological terms. Against the "shock . . . given to the Reader's associations" by undecorated language, Wordsworth asserts the "power of metre" and hypothesizes about its effects on the reader's mind. The effects are twofold—to restrain and to excite. Meter enlivens dull poetry through the power of association, by means of "the feelings of pleasure which the Reader has been accustomed to connect with metre in general" (*Prose*, I, 148). Paradoxically, meter also provides an ordering principle to a mind overwhelmed by passion:

> The end of Poetry is to produce excitement in coexistence with an overbalance of pleasure. Now, by the supposition, excitement is an unusual and irregular state of the mind; ideas and feelings do not in that state succeed each other in accustomed order. But if the words by which this excitement is produced are in themselves powerful, or the images and feelings have an undue proportion of pain connected with them, there is some danger that the excitement may be carried beyond its proper bounds. [*Prose*, I, 146]

The flow of his argument leads Wordsworth to a commonplace of eighteenth-century theories of sublimity, the necessity for aesthetic distance between the observer and the object associated with pain. As we have seen, for Wordsworth and his age the tragic is a version of the sublime. Therefore, it is not surprising that the discussion immediately turns to the reader's experience of the pathetic:

> Now the co-presence of something regular, something to which the mind has been accustomed when in an unexcited or a less excited state, cannot but have great efficacy in tempering and re-straining the passion by an intertexture of ordinary feeling. This may be illustrated by appealing to the Reader's own experience of the reluctance with which he comes to the re-perusal of the distressful parts of Clarissa Harlowe, or the Gamester. While Shakespeare's writings, in the most pathetic scenes, never act upon us as pathetic beyond the bounds of pleasure—an effect which is in a great degree to be ascribed to small, but continual and regular impulses of pleasurable surprise from the metrical arrangement. [*Prose*, I, 146]

Whatever validity and appeal Wordsworth's theory may have, his method of argument is itself significant. Out of the blue sky, he chooses the responses to *Clarissa* and Shakespearean tragedy to justify the decision to write in meter. As an "illustration," the "Reader's own experience" of pathetic verse and prose is the local accident which helps formulate and maintain the general law.

Thus, the contemplation of suffering is important for Wordsworth not only for excitement, but also as a source of energy upon which he can draw to explore, clarify, and illustrate other questions about poetry and human psychology. I have labeled these two approaches to pathos as the sensational and experimental. The *Lyrical Ballads*, although they are undoubtedly *poesie larmoiante*, retain, as Wordsworth claimed in his "Preface," a scientific purpose. They attempt to "illustrate the manner in which our feelings and ideas are associated in a state of excitement" (*Prose*, I, 126). It is not only the fictional characters who are in a state of excitement; poet and reader are also aroused, and the poetry plays experimentally upon readerly expectations and the structure of the poetic experience itself.

The clearest and simplest illustration of these claims is "Simon Lee, the Old Huntsman," where an experimental play among subject, poet, and reader is readily apparent.[10] Simon Lee, having spent his youth following the hounds, must use his remaining strength to eke out a meager existence from the village common. Such a life could well become a moralistic reprise of the parable about the grasshopper and the ant. Wordsworth's attitude, however, is sympathetically ironic:

> And he is lean and he is sick,
> His little body's half awry
> His ancles they are swoln and thick;
> His legs are thin and dry.
> When he was young he little knew
> Of husbandry or tillage;
> And now he's forced to work, though weak,
> —The weakest in the village.
>
> [ll. 33–40]

It is, after all, not the huntsman's fault that "Of years he has upon his back, /No doubt, a burthen weighty" (ll. 5–6). He is primarily the victim of the human condition, and only his pride is gently satirized:

> He says he is three score and ten,
> But others say he's eighty.
>
> A long blue livery-coat has he,
> That's fair behind, and fair before;
> Yet, meet him where you will, you see
> At once that he is poor.
>
> [ll. 7–12]

[10]For a significant discussion of the reader's place in "Simon Lee," see Andrew L. Griffin, "Wordsworth and the Problem of Imaginative Story: The Case of 'Simon Lee,'" *PMLA* 92 (1977), 392–409.

The divergence between what the man claims as his age and what "others say" reveals a harmless vanity. The blue livery-coat which vainly attempts to hide the obvious fact of poverty functions similarly. The effect of the irony, as always, is to create a community of knowledge between narrator and reader from which the poetic object is excluded.

The narrator makes a particular effort to bring his audience into the structure of the irony by means of the colloquial "you"—"Meet him where you will, you see." Such irony becomes poignant in the fourth stanza: "His hunting feats have him bereft / Of his right eye, as you may see" (ll. 25–26). The juxtaposition of Simon Lee's blind eye and the reader's "seeing" calls attention to the separation between the man struggling in the fields and the one holding the book. In any rendering of the pathetic, this distance exists, but the purpose of the art here is to make the reader aware of it. Again:

> Old Ruth works out of doors with him,
> And does what Simon cannot do;
> For she, not over stout of limb,
> Is stouter of the two.
> And though you with your utmost skill
> From labour could not wean them,
> Alas! 'tis very little, all
> Which they can do between them.
>
> [ll. 49–56]

The activity expected of the reader is most peculiar. The urge to "wean" the two old people reflects the sympathetic response to their plight. Obviously an annuity of fifty pounds would handsomely accomplish such a purpose, but Wordsworth wants to emphasize that, despite all readerly wishfulness, these people, or those like them, must work in order to survive.

The early references to "you" in "Simon Lee" prepare for the self-conscious interruption of the narrative:

> Few months of life has he in store,
> As he to you will tell,

> For still, the more he works, the more
> His poor old ancles swell.
> My gentle reader, I perceive
> How patiently you've waited,
> And I'm afraid that you expect
> Some tale will be related.
>
> [ll. 65–72]

Here the connection between the colloquial "you" and "you" the reader becomes explicit. These stanzas proceed from Simon telling "you" that he has "few months of life ... in store" to the narrator's direct address of the reader. Having engaged sympathy with the description of Simon Lee's old age, Wordsworth overturns the expectations of narrative convention when the self-conscious voice enters abruptly. Wordsworth's awareness of the contract between author and reader appears in teasing mockery: "I'm afraid that you expect / Some tale will be related." The effect is to cause the reader to examine his expectations and, indeed, the entire enterprise of reading. He says to himself something like: "Why yes! Isn't that what I'm doing here, what I'm supposed to be doing?" From the process of questioning familiar assumptions evolves a more precise knowledge of what it means to be a reader.

The assault on the reader's complacency continues in the next stanza:

> O reader! had you in your mind
> Such stores as silent thought can bring,
> O gentle reader! you would find
> A tale in every thing.
> What more I have to say is short,
> I hope you'll kindly take it;
> It is no tale; but should you think,
> Perhaps a tale you'll make it.
>
> [ll. 73–80]

Expectation, the craving for the "moving accident," the desire for the stimulus of fictional suffering, becomes a symptom of deficiency. Because the reader does not have "such stores as silent thought can bring," he fails to find "A tale in every thing." The convention of eighteenth-century orthography by which *every thing* is two words allows an emphasis on "thing" which could not exist in the twentieth-century collective pronoun *everything*; "every thing," as it exists as a separate entity, deserves the attention of the sympathetic imagination. When Wordsworth tells the reader conditionally, "should you think, / Perhaps a tale you'll make it," he challenges him to invest serious thought in the casual act of reading. The experiment here is to explore the boundary area between reader and writer, and to invite the reader to partake in the poetic making. "Simon Lee" asks what the proper subjects for poetry are; it attempts to break down the barriers between the tale and the not-tale, the poem and the world outside it. In the "Preface" Wordsworth speaks of "Simon Lee" "placing my Reader in the way of receiving from ordinary moral sensations another and more salutary impression than we are accustomed to receive from them" (*Prose*, I, 126–128). "Ordinary moral sensations" refer to pity and sympathy for one's fellow man, the emotional outpouring for one of Somersetshire's hundred neediest cases. The "salutary impression" of the poem, however, has to do with bringing the "gentle reader" in touch with his complacent assumptions about poetry and human suffering. He becomes aware not only of Simon Lee but also of what it means to read "Simon Lee."

Only after the reader has confronted the underlying tenets of the act of reading, does Wordsworth narrate the "incident" promised in the poem's subtitle:

> One summer-day I chanced to see
> This old man doing all he could
> About the root of an old tree,
> A stump of rotten wood.
> The mattock totter'd in his hand;
> So vain was his endeavour
> That at the root of the old tree
> He might have worked for ever.

> "You're overtasked, good Simon Lee,
> Give me your tool" to him I said;
> And at the word right gladly he
> Received my proffer'd aid.
> I struck, and with a single blow
> The tangled root I sever'd,
> At which the poor old man so long
> And vainly had endeavour'd.
>
> [ll. 81–96]

By challenging his reader not to find a "tale" in this episode, Wordsworth obtains for it an importance not usually given to the slashing of a taproot, however thick. At the same time, he endows this simplest of actions with mythic force by the manner in which he presents the experience. The "rhetoric of interaction,"[11] mirroring the "old man" and the "old tree, / A stump of rotten wood," charges the incident. The assertion that "He might have worked for ever," though obvious hyperbole, makes Simon Lee an archetypal figure like the Leech Gatherer wandering "About the weary moors continually." The "single blow" against the root becomes a decisive gesture which cries out to be endued with significance. Yet it is only a simple favor by one man for another. Wordsworth wants a poetry where the master strokes are neither apocalyptic nor heroic, where all is muted with the ordinariness of everyday life yet given the excitement of fiction. Thus, in "Simon Lee," the "case" involved is not the psychological pathology of a given mad mother or aggrieved shepherd. It is the psychology of writing, reading, and response; every man becomes his own case.

IV

In *Zoonomia*'s exploration of "Diseases of Increased Volition," a section is given to a "species of madness" which Darwin calls

[11]Herbert Lindenberger uses this apt phrase to describe the recurrent imagery of mirroring and transference in *The Prelude* and elsewhere in Wordsworth's poetry. See *On Wordsworth's "Prelude"* (Princeton: Princeton University Press, 1963), pp. 41–98.

"*Erotomania.* Sentimental love." (Z, II, 363–365). Its extremes describe a condition that Wordsworth depicts in such poems as "The Mad Mother," "Ruth," and "The Thorn": "The third stage of this disease I suppose is irremediable; when a lover has previously been much encouraged and at length meets with neglect or disdain; the maniacal idea is so painful as not to be for a moment relievable by the exertions of reverie, but is instantly followed by furious or melancholy insanity." The disappointed lover described here is rather more a literary than a psychological type. In real life people usually compromise their desires, where in literature, the extremes of sentiment sweep away an Ophelia or an Othello. Indeed, Darwin's primary examples of this pathology are from literary texts. He cites Romeo and Juliet, Virgil's Dido, and Ovid's Medea as sufferers from the "disease." At some point, however, life imitates art—people "who have not read the works of poets and romance-writers are less liable to sentimental love" (Z, II, 363) than readers of fiction. The one actual case Darwin does cite is oddly connected to the Wordsworth household and to *Lyrical Ballads*: "suicide, or revenge, have frequently been the consequence. As was exemplified in Mr. Hackman, who shot Miss Ray in the lobby of the playhouse" (Z, II, 365).

The actress Martha Ray was the grandmother of little Basil Montagu, the Wordsworths' ward at Alfoxden. In reading *Zoonomia*, Wordsworth had apparently been reminded of this lurid event close to his own domestic circle; he then imported the name associated with the episode into "The Thorn," whose heroine is also named Martha Ray. One might say that the poet's taste in this instance was remarkably dubious. The crime in question was sufficiently notorious even one hundred years after the fact to merit inclusion in the *DNB*. In 1798, by the standards of British murderology, the blood was barely dry. It is as if, in the present day, one were to write a novel in which a character named Sharon Tate were enveloped in a monstrous and bloody chain of events. Just as it would not be of import if our fictional Miss Tate played a role in the novel like that her namesake played in life, for Wordsworth it does not matter that the real Miss Ray was the victim, his character possibly a murderess. The name, the real name associated with a sensationalistic event, has the desired effect upon the poem. The reader's consciousness of a play between fiction and reality is aroused, perhaps uncomfortably, as he comes to an uneasy knowledge of the tie between Martha Ray and "Martha Ray." He is brought face to face with the somewhat morbid interest people have in literary depictions of human suffering, and, further, he must confront the relationship of fictional suffering to the real thing.

The odd fact of the two Martha Rays is symptomatic of what Wordsworth is doing in "The Thorn." As a poem, its central purpose is to examine the relationship between the poet's desire to conjure passions up in himself and the actual fact of suffering which nourishes his imagination. In the figures of the old sea-captain and his listener, "The Thorn" confronts poet and reader with grotesque images of themselves, as it explores the uncertain ground between the misery we read about in books and that which we see too clearly in the world around us. It is Wordsworth's most extreme experiment in pathos.

It is not mere hobbyhorsical extravagance to suggest that "The Thorn" is meant as an experiment. In addition to the poem's source in *Zoonomia* and Wordsworth's remark that "The Thorn" is meant to "exhibit some of the general laws by which superstition acts upon the mind" (*PW*, II, 512), much in the poem suggests the scientific bent of Wordsworth's thinking. The narrator, whom Geoffrey Hartman has called "the ocular man in Wordsworth,"[12] appears as a kind of experimentalist. He carries a scientific instrument, the telescope. His passion for definite location recalls the exactness of scientific measurement, and may well parody it:

> Not five yards from the mountain-path,
> This thorn you on your left espy;

[12]Geoffrey Hartman, *Wordsworth's Poetry, 1787–1814* (New Haven: Yale University Press, 1964), p. 148.

> And to the left, three yards beyond,
> You see a little muddy pond
> Of water, never dry;
> I've measured it from side to side:
> 'Tis three feet long, and two feet wide.

[ll. 27–33]

He has a botanist's, as well as poet's, eye for detail:

> And mossy network too is there,
> As if by hand of lady fair
> The work had woven been,
> And cups, the darlings of the eye
> So deep is their vermilion dye.
>
> Ah me! what lovely tints are there!
> Of olive-green and scarlet bright,
> In spikes, in branches, and in stars,
> Green, red, and pearly white.

[ll. 40–48]

Of Martha Ray's turbulent pregnancy, he says, in the manner of a physician, "Sad case for such a brain to hold / Communion with a stirring child" (ll. 144–145). His obsession with "knowing" and its limitations, "I'll tell you all I know," "No more I know," "And this I know," has at least an etymological link to the "Science" of the "Addendum" which is "worthy of its name."

In recent years a controversy has arisen about the central subject of "The Thorn." Debate has centered upon whether to emphasize the loquacious narrator or the story of Martha Ray, what is told or the way in which it is told.[13] Attempts to give primacy to

---

[13]Stephen Parrish's claim, in "'The Thorn': Wordsworth's Dramatic Monologue," *ELH* 24 (1957), 153–163, that the poem is "not . . . about an abandoned mother and her murdered infant" but "first, about a tree, and second, about a man" began this controversy. The notion that the poem is "a psychological study, a poem about the way the mind works" (p. 154), has been repeatedly attacked by readers who, to greater or lesser degrees, wish to make Martha Ray more than a figment of a senile imagination. Among significant responses to Parrish have been John Danby, *The Simple Wordsworth* (London: Routledge & Kegan Paul, 1960), pp. 55–72; Albert Gérard, *English Romantic Poetry* (Berkeley

either narrator or narration seem to me ill-advised. The narrator is finally inseparable from the story that obsesses him. In *The Ruined Cottage*, biographical background and physical description inform us what sort of man the Pedlar is, but in "The Thorn" we hear only a voice. In the "Note" Wordsworth demurs that "this Poem ought to have been preceded by an introductory Poem, which I have been prevented from writing by never having felt myself in a mood when it was probable that I should write it well" (*PW*, II, 512). This "introductory" poem would presumably have been like the opening of *The Ruined Cottage* (MS. B), where the poet-narrator meets the Pedlar at Margaret's cottage and digresses some three hundred lines describing him. Wordsworth's ingenuous claim that he was never in the "mood" camouflages the fact that such an introduction is irrelevant to his interests in "The Thorn." The narrator has no character apart from that revealed in the re-creation of Martha Ray because only his obsessive interest in human guilt and sorrow concerns Wordsworth.

For similar reasons, the story of Martha Ray has no solid grounding in reality like that which the setting of *The Ruined Cottage* gives to Margaret's story. At several intervals the Pedlar invokes the material witnesses of Margaret's suffering, the over-

---

and Los Angeles: University of California Press, 1968), pp. 64–88; Thomas L. Ashton, "*The Thorn*: Wordsworth's Insensitive Plant," *Huntington Library Quarterly* 35 (1971–72), 171–187; and Donald Priestman, "Superstition and Imagination: Complementary Faculties of Wordsworth's Narrator in 'The Thorn'," *Journal of Narrative Technique* 5 (1975), 196–207.

Dissatisfaction with Parrish's reading arises from a feeling that "The Thorn" in some way reflects what Geoffrey Hartman has called "Wordsworth's own imagination-in-process" (*Wordsworth's Poetry*, p. 148). After all, the poem tells a story, and the subject of the story is familiar. Martha Ray is recognizably the sister of the Female Vagrant and Margaret, of Ruth and the dying woman of *An Evening Walk*. The narrator, too, for all his strange loquaciousness, seems less a "psychological study" than a hyperventilation of Wordsworth's usual self-projection. The obsessive hovering around the thorn recalls the "spot syndrome," which Hartman has shrewdly put at the heart of the poet's imagination. I am in closest agreement with Mary Jacobus among recent commentators. In *Tradition and Experiment*, she emphasizes the relation between teller and tale: "Its narrative method reflects Wordsworth's interest in the interplay between the two—in the imaginative processes by which the simple elements of Martha's tragedy take on their sombre impressiveness" (p. 248).

grown garden and the naked walls. The thorn, however, with its encroaching lichen and mysterious pond, exists only in the memory, or fantasy, of the storyteller. Wordsworth, of course, did not have to leave so much of the story in uncertainty. Had he chosen, he could easily have placed the telling of Martha Ray's tragedy at the scene of her passion: the most trivial dramatic machinery could have arranged a meeting between the sea-captain and his listener beside the thorn. A description of an encounter of the men with Martha, followed by the sea-captain's narrative, would have made clear and definite what is deliberately blurred in "The Thorn." Such obvious fictional devices would have removed the uncertainties that allow Parrish to argue that the story has no existence outside the narrator's imagination. However, Wordsworth had already presented such a precisely delimited tale in *The Ruined Cottage*, and in early 1798, he was not apt to attempt the same thing twice.

"The Thorn," in fact, is best seen as an experiment upon the formula of *The Ruined Cottage*. The similarities between the two poems are marked. The central figure in each is a deserted woman who lingers around a spot made significant by her suffering. Unlike "Simon Lee," "Ruth," or "Michael," these poems draw their titles from the place where the suffering occurs, suggesting the centrality of the physical objects that connect the present to the past history of the place. Surprisingly, only one major commentator has noted the similar uses of natural detail in *The Ruined Cottage* and "The Thorn"; Albert Gérard cites linguistic parallels as well as symbolic continuities to show that the little tree, like Margaret's garden, is "the emblem of a being overcome by the suffering inflicted by outside forces."[14] Gérard does not discuss the "Addendum" of *The Ruined Cottage*; clearly, however, the theoretical basis of "The Thorn" is underwritten there:

> And further, by contemplating these forms
> In the relations which they bear to man

[14]Gérard, *English Romantic Poetry*, p. 72.

> We shall discover what a power is theirs
> To stimulate our minds
>
> [*RC & P*, p. 263]

"The Thorn" depicts a mind stimulated, indeed overstimulated, by the contemplation of a "form" in its relationship to human suffering. The poem's narrative structure is also similar to that of *The Ruined Cottage*. A Pedlar of the seas, the retired "captain of a small trading vessel," tells the story of female suffering to an increasingly involved auditor. The central focus in both poems is on neither the narrator nor the sufferer taken separately, but on the imagination's involvement with human suffering.

The similarities are particularly suggestive because "The Thorn" is apparently Wordsworth's first major undertaking after *The Ruined Cottage*. Perhaps a week after work on the "Addendum," the poet decided to make a poem about a thorn. In MS. B$_2$ of *The Ruined Cottage* (Dorothy's letter of 5 March 1798 to Mary Hutchinson), there is no suggestion of lines after "Last human tenant of these ruined walls." Coleridge's letter to his brother George (circa 10 March) quotes the first eighteen lines of the "Addendum"; Reed, therefore, seems justified in suggesting that "probably shortly after 5 March, especially between 6 March and circa 10 March," Wordsworth had completed the entire "Addendum," including the calm spear-grass vision which became the ending of *The Ruined Cottage* (Reed *EY*, p. 28). In the week following, Dorothy's journal entry for 19 March reads: "William wrote some lines describing a stunted thorn" (*DWJ*, p. 10). The lines referred to are apparently the descriptive lines in the Alfoxden notebook (*PW*, II, 240), and "The Thorn" "is probably finished very shortly after, almost certainly by circa 16 May" (Reed *EY*, p. 227).

The contrast between the dignified pathos of *The Ruined Cottage* and the barbaric yawp of "The Thorn" has caused the relationship between the two poems to remain largely unnoticed. Nevertheless, "The Thorn" continues to explore the questions about tragic pleasure examined in *The Ruined Cottage*.

Wordsworth recapitulates the elements that constitute *The Ruined Cottage*, its subject, narrator, and audience, and pushes them to extremity. In the experimental method, too, the road of excess leads to the palace of wisdom; it is the extreme case, the critical point before the system collapses, which offers significance and helps one understand the whole structure. "The Thorn" takes the fine-tuned formula of *The Ruined Cottage* and distorts it into what would be parody if the fundamental undertaking were not serious. It goes behind the carefully controlled fiction of two men talking in the noon shade about the sad events of an earlier time. This fiction, which had been useful in *The Ruined Cottage* to explore eighteenth-century theories of tragic pleasure, is discarded when Wordsworth creates the extreme version of the pathetic structure of victim, narrator, and audience in "The Thorn."

Instead of the cool and philosophically optimistic Pedlar, in "The Thorn" we have as narrator a man obsessed, alternately fascinated and horrified by the dark truth to which he clings. The difference between the two, however, is primarily a matter of decorum. The Pedlar, although he returns to the spot where Margaret suffered and his "spirit clings / To that poor woman," has the decency to talk about her in a highly restrained blank verse, carefully pruned of excess and sensationalism. This restraint, although attractive, is palpably a fiction. The language of "The Thorn" gives the effect of being without control. Lurid, highly repetitive, charged with a morbid interest in human guilt and suffering, the words imitate in their rapid meter the chaotic and turbulent flow of the narrator's thoughts.

In *The Ruined Cottage*, the auditor of the tale is defined by the effect of Margaret's story upon him. He moves from irritation and weariness to wholeness and tranquillity as he responds to the tale of suffering. There are suggestions that his interest in Margaret is slightly morbid, particularly when he feels "impelled / By a mild force of curious pensiveness" to beg continuance of the story; for the most part, however, he remains a comfortable surrogate for the reader. He responds with decent sympathy and understanding, and the catharsis at the end hardly seems rankly exploitative.

The reader surrogate in "The Thorn," however, is nearly as hysterical as the narrator. This poem lacks the stabilizing dramatic framework of *The Ruined Cottage*. It begins with the story being told; at first, one assumes that it is a straightforward third-person narrative, without any external context of narrator and audience. There are references to a colloquial "you"—"In truth you'd find it hard to say, / How it could ever have been young" (ll. 2–3); "Now would you see this aged thorn" (l. 56). But it comes as a shock when a second voice breaks in at the eighth stanza:

> "Now wherefore thus, by day and night,
> "In rain, in tempest, and in snow,
> "Thus to the dreary mountain-top
> "Does this poor woman go?
> "And why sits she beside the thorn
> "When the blue day-light's in the sky,
> "Or when the whirlwind's on the hill,
> "Or frosty air is keen and still,
> "And wherefore does she cry?—
> "Oh wherefore? wherefore? tell me why
> "Does she repeat that doleful cry?"
>
> [ll. 78–88]

Here, as in "Simon Lee," the colloquial "you" becomes equivalent to the reader, and the image of oneself in the mirror of Wordsworth's art again proves disconcerting. This voice of the reader is virtually indistinguishable from the narrator's obsessive iterations. The redundancy that reflects "a craving in the mind" (*PW*, II, 513) is equally present in the reader:

> "But what's the thorn? and what's the pond?
> "And what's the hill of moss to her?
> "And what's the creeping breeze that comes
> "The little pond to stir?"
>
> [ll. 210–213]

The intensity and even the cadences of the narrator's tale infect the listener's voice—he becomes little more than an echo of the narrator's dominant interests. If *The Ruined Cottage* represents the communication of pantheistic awareness, "The Thorn" shows the transfer of obsession from "I" to "you." This transfer is a model of Wordsworth's attempt to signify for the reader otherwise insignificant particulars. In the course of the telling, the thorn, the pond, and the heap of moss become as important to the listener as they have been to the narrator. The same thing occurs in *The Ruined Cottage*, but there the restrained language makes the process seem less peculiar than in fact it is.

The third element that *The Ruined Cottage* and "The Thorn" share is the victim. The language of Margaret is the language of *The Ruined Cottage*. Even in her moments of most profound suffering, the means by which she evokes pathos is understatement:

> a chain of straw
> Which had been twisted round the tender stem
> Of a young apple-tree lay at its root;
> The bark was nibbled round by truant sheep.
> Margaret stood near, her infant in her arms,
> And seeing that my eye was on the tree
> She said, 'I fear it will be dead and gone
> Ere Robert come again.'
>
> [ll. 419–426]

The delicate, artistic play between nature and its victim provides much of the pleasure of reading *The Ruined Cottage*. Here, Margaret's simple utterance calls attention to the exquisite use of the apple tree as a correlative for her suffering. "The Thorn" lacks such piquancies. Martha Ray's only words are a naked cry of suffering:

> Now would you see this aged thorn,
> This pond and beauteous hill of moss,
> You must take care and chuse your time
> The mountain when to cross.
> For oft there sits, between the heap

That's like an infant's grave in size,
And that same pond of which I spoke,
A woman in a scarlet cloak,
And to herself she cries,
"Oh misery! oh misery!
"Oh woe is me! oh misery!"

[ll. 56–66]

Like Margaret, Martha Ray is the third speaker of the poem in which she appears. That she talks only "to herself" emphasizes the self-enclosed, isolated, even incommunicable nature of her suffering. This "doleful cry" acts as a refrain, recurring five times in the poem; it is the hard core of language to which the narrator's mind returns and from which he recoils as from an impenetrable mystery. "Oh misery! oh misery! / Oh woe is me! oh misery!" is language as it borders on the mere animal cry of pain. There is no decoration, no poetry, none of the delightful complication which links man and nature in an artistic whole. Words cannot be any plainer or more naked.

It remains for the narrator to provide the association of ideas by which the thorn itself becomes the object of imaginative obsession. In the course of the poem, the insignificant thornbush becomes one of the forms contemplated "In the relations which they bear to man." Again, "The Thorn" undresses the artistry of *The Ruined Cottage* by extending its artistic formula to the extreme. In *The Ruined Cottage* the correlative of Margaret's disintegration is the encroachment of natural entropy upon her garden; the state of the garden is the measure of order in Margaret's small world, and its destruction carries resonances of the loss of Eden. In the transfiguration which occurs at the conclusion, the garden represents the "calm oblivious tendencies of nature" and becomes the metaphor of cathartic feelings.

A thorn bush covered with lichen, a hill of moss, a "little muddy pond . . . three feet long, and two feet wide" possess no such intrinsic power. We should indeed ask how Wordsworth came to concenter this bizarre poem around such objects, if the Fenwick note were not greatly informative. The poem, says

Wordsworth in his old age, "arose out of my observing, on the ridge of Quantock Hill, on a stormy day, a thorn which I had often passed in calm and bright weather without noticing it. I said to myself, 'Cannot I by some invention do as much to make this Thorn prominently an impressive object as the storm has made it to my eyes at this moment?' I began the poem accordingly, and composed it with great rapidity" (*PW*, II, 511).[15] The intent to write about the thorn is, therefore, experimental; the primary purpose, or at least the earliest, is to discover if the poem can be written. "The Thorn," like "To the Small Celandine" or "To a Daisy," seeks to immortalize the transient moment in which Wordsworth noticed a natural object. That Wordsworth's initial impulse was simply descriptive is suggested by the lines in the Alfoxden notebook:

> A summit where the stormy gale
> Sweeps through the clouds from vale to vale,
> A thorn there is which like a stone
> With jagged lichens is o'ergrown,
> A thorn that wants its thorny points
> A toothless thorn with knotted joints;
> Not higher than a two years child
> It stands upon that spot so wild;
> Of leaves it has repaired its loss
> With heavy tufts of dark green moss,
> Which from the ground in plenteous crop
> Creep upward to its very top
> To bury it for evermore
>
> [*PW*, II, 240]

There is little suggestion that this passage will introduce a tale of distress. Most of the significant revisions of the description for "The Thorn," however, endow the plant with attributes describing human misery. It becomes, not merely "toothless," but "old and grey," "aged," "a wretched thing forlorn." The shroud of moss is originally affirmative, for the thorn is said to have "re-

---

[15] Jacobus has noted that de Selincourt misreads "prominently" as "permanently" (*Tradition and Experiment*, p. 241).

paired its loss" with a "plenteous crop" of "dark green moss." In *The Thorn* such positive connotations disappear, as the moss becomes a "melancholy crop" which weighs down the tree. The funereal implications of "bury" expand insidiously:

> Up from the earth these mosses creep,
> And this poor thorn they clasp it round
> So close, you'd say that they were bent
> With plain and manifest intent,
> To drag it to the ground;
> And all had joined in one endeavour
> To bury this poor thorn for ever.
>
> [ll. 16–22]

Clearly, as Gérard has observed, the thorn is "both a setting and a symbolic correlative for the tale and the human situation [it] illustrates."[16]

It is less clear why an innocent plant which a poet noticed at the side of a mountain path should become the dark center of a tale of guilt and sorrow. Citing Annette Vallon and various literary sources, Gérard asserts the probability of such a leap of imagination: "Nor is it surprising that the first element of 'invention' ·that occurred to him at the time should have been the association of the thorn with the theme of abandoned womanhood."[17] On the contrary, it is most strange that, wishing to make the thorn a "prominent" object, the poet should dream up

[16]Gérard, *English Romantic Poetry*, p. 77.

[17]Gérard, p. 76. Following *PW*, II, 513–514, Mary Jacobus, too, has claimed that the leap of imagination from thorn to tragic tale is conventional and literary in nature: "The commonest of all literary associations for a thorn tree were illegitimate birth and child-murder. In Langhorne's *Country Justice*, it is under a thorn that the pitying robber finds the body of an unmarried mother with her new-born child . . . and in Richard Merry's *Pains of Memory* (1796), a remorseful seducer recalls: 'There on the chilly grass the babe was born, / Beneath that bending solitary thorn.' The Scots ballad known as 'The Cruel Mother' shows how traditional the association would have been" (*Tradition and Experiment*, pp. 241–242). Jacobus also cites "the haunted graves and thorn of 'The Three Graves'" as an instance of this association in proto-*Lyrical Ballad* material. This literary context is indeed suggestive, for, as my argument has made apparent, Wordsworth is writing a poem which primarily attempts to come to terms with the imaginative and literary uses of suffering.

the story of Martha Ray, with its complicated machinery of narrator and listener. How does a tale of suffering grow out of a moment's pleasure in a natural object? We might look again at the question which Wordsworth claimed to be the source of the poem: "Cannot I by some invention do as much to make this Thorn prominently an impressive object as the storm has made it to my eyes at this moment?" The original experience is of the natural sublime. The turbulence of the storm provides the energy which fixes the image in the mind. In his search for something analogous to such an excitement, then, Wordsworth hits upon the story of Martha Ray. For him, as for Burke, Alison, and Hazlitt, sublime emotions are equivalent to tragic feelings. Attempting to convey the significance and impressiveness of this one thornbush among millions, it seemed natural for him to give up the labors of description and to invest the thorn with the kind of substitutive excitement available in human suffering.

Unusual among Wordsworth's poems concentering around a form contemplated in its relation to human suffering, "The Thorn" takes as its central object a thing without intrinsic connection to humanity. In *The Ruined Cottage*, "Hart-leap Well," "The Brothers," and "Michael," the object is artificial and, therefore, carries with it, quite naturally, human associations. Though the connection in the narrator's mind between the thorn and Martha Ray's misery is perhaps not entirely adventitious, the connection in the poet's mind between the bush growing on the Somersetshire hillside and the story of the forsaken woman certainly is. The desire for the stimulation of fiction is at the heart of Wordsworth's turn from natural object to tragic tale. It is the same craving he later describes in *The Prelude*:

> Through wild obliquities could I pursue
> Among all objects of the fields and groves
> These cravings; when the Foxglove, one by one,
> Upwards through every stage of its tall stem,
> Had shed its bells, and stood by the wayside
> Dismantled, with a single one, perhaps,
> Left at the ladder's top, with which the Plant

> Appeared to stoop, as slender blades of grass
> Tipp'd with a bead of rain or dew, behold!
> If such a sight were seen, would Fancy bring
> Some Vagrant thither with her Babes, and seat her
> Upon the turf beneath the stately Flower
> Drooping in sympathy
>
> [*Prel* VIII: 542–554]

In *The Prelude* Wordsworth is speaking of this tendency as a youthful foible. In "The Thorn" he accomplishes much the same distancing by presenting the extreme version of such cravings as a pathological case easily distinguishable from his own speaking voice. Nevertheless, Wordsworth's relation to the real thorn approximates the relation of the narrator to the one in the poem. The central subject of "The Thorn" is the process of mind by which pathetic poetry is imagined.

"The Thorn" is Wordsworth's most severe portrait of the sentimental artist and his audience. The premises implicit in the success of *The Ruined Cottage* are laid bare, and they are not so benign and normal as they seem in that poem. Such a version of the imagination's relation to human misery hardly lends itself to comfortable rationalization, yet Wordsworth's integrity makes it impossible to return to the largely pathetic mode of *The Borderers* and *The Ruined Cottage* (MS. A). On the other hand, his commitment to *poesie larmoiante* as a source of powerful emotion makes it difficult to abandon human subjects.

The questions before him are those posed by sentimental self-consciousness generally: How, in good conscience, can the writer continue to use the power of human suffering if he is fully aware of his exploitative relation to real suffering? Is it possible for poet and reader to have a relation to tragic materials which is not somewhat parasitic? If so, what kind of poetry would enable this sort of innocent relation to exist? The effort of the later *Lyrical Ballads* is to find a means by which the excitement of suffering could be tapped without the ghoulishness portrayed so vividly in the narrator and his listener in "The Thorn."

6 The Union of Tenderness and Imagination: *Lyrical Ballads* (1800)

> The merit of a novellist is in proportion (not simply to the effect, but) to the *pleasurable* effect which he produces. Situations of torment, and images of naked horror, are easily conceived; and a writer in whose works they abound, deserves our gratitude almost equally with him who should drag us by way of sport through a military hospital, or force us to sit at the dissecting-table of a natural philosopher. To trace the nice boundaries, beyond which terror and sympathy are deserted by the pleasurable emotions,—to reach those limits, yet never to pass them,—*hic labor, hic opus est.*
>
> —Coleridge, Review of *The Monk*

I

The facile exploitation of emotion increasingly becomes the object of Wordsworth's scorn in the years when the *Lyrical Ballads* are written. Time and again, he voices distaste for poetry that appeals to the reader in "low" or "vulgar" ways. Authors who cater to the "degrading thirst after outrageous stimulation" are "those dim drivellers with which our island has teemed for so many years" (*EL*, p. 234), "bad poets," "writers who seem to estimate their power of exciting sorrow for suffering humanity, by the quantity of hatred and revenge which they are able to pour into the hearts of their Readers" (*EL*, pp. 325–326). The Pedlar's rebuke of the narrator's "curious pensiveness" in *The Ruined Cottage* sets the tone of Wordsworth's attack on sensational literature:

> It were a wantonness and would demand
> Severe reproof, if we were men whose hearts

> Could hold vain dalliance with the misery
> Even of the dead, contented thence to draw
> A momentary pleasure never marked
> By reason, barren of all future good.
>
> [ll. 221–226]

Wordsworth's notes of his meeting with Klopstock (October 1798) also record contempt for a poetics of mere emotional response: "We talked of tragedy: he seemed to rate too highly the power of exciting tears. I said that nothing was more easy than to deluge an audience. That it was done every day by the meanest writers" (*Prose*, I, 95). With the same condescension, "Hart-leap Well" dismisses contemporary poetry: "The moving accident is not my trade, / To freeze the blood I have no ready arts," says Wordsworth, putting his rivals at the level of eager shopkeepers spreading goods for potential customers.

The "Preface" to *Lyrical Ballads* makes clear that it is not solely the desire to be different from the "meanest writers" that informs Wordsworth's suspicions of tragedy:[1]

> For a multitude of causes unknown to former times are now acting with a combined force to blunt the discriminating powers of the mind, and unfitting it for all voluntary exertion to reduce it to a state of almost savage torpor. The most effective of these causes are the great national events which are daily taking place, and the encreasing accumulation of men in cities, where the uniformity of their occupations produces a craving for extraordinary incident which the rapid communication of intelligence hourly gratifies. To this tendency of life and manners the literature and theatrical exhibitions of the country have conformed themselves. The invaluable works of our elder writers, I had almost said the works of Shakespear and Milton, are driven into neglect by frantic novels, sickly and stupid German Tragedies, and deluges of idle and extravagant stories in verse. [*Prose*, I, 128]

The adjectives chosen to describe the literature of extraordinary incident betray vehemence out of proportion to such works' es-

---

[1]One should not, by any means, underestimate Wordsworth's need to be "original"; for a wide-ranging discussion of the topic, see Brian Wilkie, "Wordsworth and the Tradition of the Avant-Garde," *JEGP* 72 (1973), 194–222.

sential frivolity. One suspects that the extravagant fictions of Radcliffe, Schiller, Bürger, and Lewis are not the only objects of Wordsworth's meditations on "gross and violent" literary stimulants, nor perhaps the primary ones. As we have seen, Wordsworth himself, or part of him, had felt the all-too-human craving for the extraordinary. Among his recent compositions, after all, are the "Gothic Tale," *Salisbury Plain*, and a "German" tragedy, *The Borderers*. "The Three Graves" and "The Somersetshire Tragedy," though unfinished, reveal hankerings to exploit the more spectacularly gruesome side of "low and rustic life." What attracted Wordsworth to such materials was what appealed to his times, the powerful emotional energies that the bizarre and terrible make available to poetry and fiction. What repelled him was the self-conscious awareness that the exploitation of such energies could be considered ghoulish and morally irresponsible.

This ambivalence is apparent in the "Preface." Even while he rejects contemporary poetry, Wordsworth accepts its basic tenets. The polemic against extravagant narrative attacks the means such works employ but not their intention of stimulating the reader. The claim that "the human mind is capable of excitement without the application of gross and violent stimulants" (*Prose*, I, 128) implicitly accepts the sensationalist's premise that the primary function of literature is excitement. Indeed, in the "Preface," poetry serves as a conduit of stimulation. "Such objects as strongly excite" (126) the poet are described in the "real language of men in a state of vivid sensation" (118) in order to achieve the end of poetry, "excitement in coexistence with an overbalance of pleasure" (146). One writes poetry, then, and reads it deliberately to stir up the embers of emotion. The desire for such excitement, "an unusual and irregular state of the mind" (146), is only too similar to the craving for the extraordinary and outrageous from which Wordsworth is at such pains to distance himself.

The primary sources of extraordinary incident exploited in the works criticized by Wordsworth are the supernatural and the pathetic. A writer of the "German" school, for instance Bürger, is equally likely to find excitement in a girl's midnight ride with a skeleton bridegroom (*Lenore*) and in a betrayed woman's murder of her infant (*Des Pfarrers Tochter von Taubenhain*). In his great years, Wordsworth was not much tempted by the supernatural. Alone among the English Romantics, he found "the common growth of mother-earth" sufficient. Indeed the "Prologue" to *Peter Bell* pokes gentle fun at "full-grown poets" who indulge fantasies involving ghosts, fairies, spirits, and such (*PW*, II, 334–337). In a late marginalia, too, there is no small condescension toward "poor dear Coleridge": "Not being able to dwell on or sanctify natural woes, he took to the supernatural, and hence his Ancient Mariner and Christabel, in which he shows great poetical power; but these things have not the hold on the heart which Nature gives, and will never be popular, like Goldsmith's, or Burns's."[2]

The other important means by which the age gratified its thirst after stimulation was not so easily dismissed. Even though the meanest writers could deluge an audience, the pathetic was too valuable a source of excitement for Wordsworth to stop writing poems about human characters and incidents. The claim of the "Preface" that "Poetry sheds no tears 'such as Angels weep,' but natural and human tears" (*Prose*, I, 134) assumes that causing such a sentimental response is a major function of poetry. "Michael," he writes proudly to Thomas Poole in early 1801, has "drawn tears from the eyes of more than one, persons well acquainted with the manners of the 'Statesmen, as they are called, of this country; and, moreover, persons who never wept, in reading verse, before" (*EL*, p. 322). There are, no doubt, radical differences of content and tone between Bürger's and Wordsworth's ballads; nonetheless, the end toward which both poets work is the same, to call from the reader the "natural and human tears" that are the measure of a work's power in an age of sensibility.

[2]Geoffrey Little, ed., *Barron Field's Memoirs of Wordsworth* (Sydney: Sydney University Press, 1975), pp. 100–101.

The problem Wordsworth faces in the *Lyrical Ballads* is to reconcile the sense that deluging an audience is vulgar with the belief that poetry should move one profoundly. Perhaps a true reconciliation of such opposites is impossible. Looked at with sufficient introspection and skepticism, any narration of human suffering might appear exploitative. This is not a problem that would bother Lewis or Bürger, but for Wordsworth it becomes critical to show that the human mind can be excited without "gross and violent stimulants." The effort of *Lyrical Ballads*, particularly the 1800 volume, is to create a poetry that accomplishes this paradoxical purpose.

In later years, when Wordsworth talked of these poems, he spoke of the poet's role in "spiritualizing" or "sanctifying" normally painful objects.[3] Probably he expressed similar ideas in the lost letter of winter 1801 which a bemused Charles Lamb paraphrased to Thomas Manning:

> . . . he was sorry his 2d.vol. had not given me more pleasure (Devil a hint did I give that it had *not pleased me*) and "was compelled to wish that my range of Sensibility was more extended, being obliged to believe that I should receive large influxes of happiness & happy Thoughts" (I suppose from the L. B.—) With a deal of stuff about a certain "Union of Tenderness & Imagination, which in the sense he used Imag. was not the characteristic of Shakesp. but which Milton possessed in a degree far exceeding other Poets: which Union, as the highest species of Poetry, and chiefly deserving that name, He was most proud to aspire to."[4]

Although Lamb's fragmentary and unsympathetic account obscures the meaning, one may reconstruct what the "Union of Tenderness and Imagination" meant to Wordsworth.

Tenderness is the less problematic of the two primary terms. Deriving from the vocabulary of sensibility, it refers to the raw

[3]Fenwick note to "Lucy Gray," *PW*, I, 360; *Barron Field's Memoirs*, p. 100.
[4]*The Letters of Charles and Mary Anne Lamb*, ed. Edwin W. Marrs (Ithaca, N.Y.: Cornell University Press, 1975–), I, 272. Wordsworth apparently went on to cite "Michael," ll. 339–343, and "The Brothers," ll. 98–99, as examples of the union of Imagination and Tenderness.

emotional material of literature, the presentation of human feelings in order to evoke sympathetic response. The narrator of *The Vale of Esthwaite*, for instance, finds it "sweet . . . To rove as through an Eden vale / The sad maze of some tender tale" (ll. 176–179). The sentimentalist would be particularly likely to shed "the tender tear" (l. 416) in contemplating the lost children, decrepit beggars, deserted women, and bereaved lovers and parents who populate the 1800 *Lyrical Ballads*.

For Wordsworth in early 1801, Imagination is not yet the power which endows, modifies, shapes, and creates. The definition he probably had in mind is given in the nearly contemporary note to "The Thorn." There, superstitious men such as the obsessive narrator are said to have "a reasonable share of imagination, by which word I mean the faculty which produces impressive effects out of simple elements" (*PW*, II, 512). This version of Imagination encompasses the ambitious, seemingly paradoxical effort of *Lyrical Ballads* to be both simple and impressive, that is, to have a powerful impact on the reader without employing extravagant means. Imagination would, therefore, make the power of human suffering available even while allowing the poet to escape the stigma he attaches to deluging the audience. Theoretically at least, it enables such unlikely material as a boy sleepwalking from a cliff ("The Brothers") or a girl drowned in a canal ("Lucy Gray") to open "large influxes of happiness."

However much Wordsworth's claim of a "Union of Tenderness and Imagination" may have been wishful thinking, it does reflect his interest in finding a compromise between the obviously ghoulish and the completely ordinary. In the end, perhaps, such a compromise in conjunction with self-knowledge is impossible. The effort, in itself interesting, has as its chief monument the second volume of *Lyrical Ballads* (1800). "Hart-leap Well," "The Brothers," the "Lucy" and "Matthew" poems, "Ruth," and "Michael" are only the most important of the poems related to this attempt to present the incidents of common life in ways that are interesting without being extravagant or degrading.

II

The continuities between the 1798 and 1800 volumes of *Lyrical Ballads* are sufficient for the "Preface" to encompass both without undue strain. There is, however, a difference in how their poems, particularly those delineating human incidents, approach the reader. The characteristic mode of 1798 is self-referential: in such poems as "The Thorn" and "Simon Lee," we are continually aware of ourselves as readers and of our relationship to human suffering taken as a poetic subject. In the 1800 volume, the effort to unite Tenderness and Imagination aims at reaching the reader's emotions. Narrative attention focuses almost exclusively on exciting sympathy and pity.

The versions of the Little Child Lost story presented in each volume reflect the differences between 1798 and 1800. "The Idiot Boy" (1798) and "Lucy Gray" (1800), though employing the same basic plot, are radically unlike in tone and intention. In each, a parent sends a child to town on a mission of responsibility, and the child's failure to return sets in motion a desperate search which leads, eventually and inevitably, to a neighboring stream. The variations on this common theme reveal Wordsworth's change to a poetry "more likely to please the generality of readers" (*EL*, p. 298) by appealing directly to their emotions.

The motif of children wandering in a wilderness, sought by worried parents, or perhaps uncared for, was "in the air" in the late eighteenth century. "The Little Boy Lost" and "Found" in Blake's *Songs of Innocence* quarry this material for a metaphor of man's relation to God the Father; in the more problematic "Little Girl Lost" and "Found" of *Experience*, the parents' discovery of the dead (or sleeping) child surrounded by lions becomes the image of the apocalyptic time when "the desart wild" will "become a garden mild." For Wordsworth, the primary source of the motif is "The Children in the Wood," praised by Addison and printed in Percy's *Reliques*.[5] The "Preface" to *Lyrical Ballads* quotes "one of the most justly admired stanzas of the '*Babes* in the Wood.'

> 'These pretty Babes with hand in hand
> Went wandering up and down;
> But never more they saw the Man
> Approaching from the town.' "
>
> [*Prose*, I, 154]

Lines very like these describe Lucy Gray:

> The storm came on before its time
> She wander'd up and down,
> And many a hill did Lucy climb
> But never reach'd the town.
>
> [ll. 29–32]

Thus, in "The Idiot Boy" and "Lucy Gray," Wordsworth is consciously working with a conventional, even archetypal, tragic plot. The poems represent two possible ways of handling such material so that the piquancy of fictional suffering would be available and yet still be legitimate by Wordsworth's increasingly rigorous standards. Characteristically, the 1798 ballad plays with literary conventions and situations, and that appearing in the 1800 volume attempts to affect the emotions without degrading either poet or reader.

Stephen Parrish and Mary Jacobus have made clear the extent to which "The Idiot Boy" mocks poetry that employs the supernatural as a source of extraordinary incident.[6] The particular

---

[5] *Spectator* No. 85; see Chapter 1 for discussion of James Beattie's reference to "The Children in the Wood" in *The Minstrel*, I: 45–48. A. Charles Babenroth, *English Childhood* (New York: Columbia University Press, 1922), pp. 234–238, provides a useful compendium of eighteenth-century references to this popular ballad. See also Irene H. Chayes, "Little Girls Lost: Problems of a Romantic Archetype," *Bulletin of the New York Public Library* 67 (1963), 579–592.

[6] Stephen Parrish, *The Art of the "Lyrical Ballads"* (Cambridge: Harvard University Press, 1973), pp. 88–89; Mary Jacobus, "The Idiot Boy" in *BWS*, pp. 241–248; also her *Tradition and Experiment in Wordsworth's "Lyrical Ballads" (1798)* (Oxford: Clarendon, 1976), pp. 209–261.

target of satire seems to have been Gottfried Bürger: the midnight ride of Johnny Foy parodies Lenore's gallop to the grave. Wordsworth's burlesque, however, is equally directed at the sentimental reader's expectations of a pathetic tale. "The Idiot Boy" takes a situation that, conventionally, carries the expectation of pathos and presents it mock-heroically. Throughout the poem there is a tension between incident and tone. The dangers to Johnny are imminent; a suitably minded reader can picture all manner of things happening, yet the humor is a continual promise that nothing of a distressing nature will occur. One can as soon imagine Tam O'Shanter, John Gilpin, or Ichabod Crane falling from their horses and breaking their necks.

Within the sheltering assurance of comic intent, Wordsworth brings conventional and personal images of human suffering. Thus, after failing to learn of Johnny's whereabouts from the doctor, Betty Foy exclaims:

> "O woe is me! O woe is me!
> "Here will I die; here will I die;
> "I thought to find my Johnny here,
> "But he is neither far nor near,
> "Oh! what a wretched mother I!"
>
> [ll. 272–276]

Her lament echoes the words that the narrator of "The Thorn" had ascribed to Martha Ray: "Oh woe is me! O misery!" Betty's description of herself as a wretched mother is particularly notable in light of the fact that immediately before "The Idiot Boy" in the 1798 *Lyrical Ballads* is "The Mad Mother," who is indeed wretched.

As Betty passes through the owl-haunted countryside, she comes to an oddly familiar body of water:

> Poor Betty now has lost all hope,
> Her thoughts are bent on deadly sin;
> A green-grown pond she just has pass'd,
> And from the brink she hurries fast,
> Lest she should drown herself therein.
>
> [ll. 302–306]

The "green-grown pond" reminds the reader fresh from "The Thorn" of the muddy pond where "some say" Martha Ray drowned her child. Already, in that poem, the attention given to the pond by the narrator had seemed excessive; here it is simply parodic. For the eighteenth century, suicide is one of few subjects as lurid as child murder. Works such as *The Gamester* and *Die Leiden des jungen Werthers* exploit the excitement it offers. "The Idiot Boy" deflates the idea of literary suicide, not only by the generally comic tone, but also by the immediate reversal of Betty's thought when she remembers that "the pony he is mild and good":

> Then up she springs as if on wings;
> She thinks no more of deadly sin;
> If Betty fifty ponds should see,
> The last of all her thoughts would be,
> To drown herself therein.
>
> [ll. 317–321]

The exuberance of "fifty ponds" and "the last of all her thoughts" channels the excitement associated with suicide into comedy.

The reader's expectations of the Little Child Lost genre are expressed within the text of the poem itself. Mockingly, they appear in the simple minds of Susan Gale and Betty Foy. When Johnny fails to appear,

> . . . Susan she begins to fear
> Of sad mischances not a few,
> That Johnny may perhaps be drown'd,
> Or lost perhaps, and never found;
> Which they must both for ever rue.
>
> She prefaced half a hint of this
> With, "God forbid it should be true!"
>
> [ll. 187–193]

Perhaps is the word that opens the floodgates of the imagination; it is the essence of fiction, transforming possibility into probabil-

ity. Once it is uttered, we are free to create, if only supposi-
tiously, all manner of horror, and indeed the reader of a poem of
this genre fully expects, even wants, the child to be drowned or
lost. The word recurs in Betty Foy's worries as she searches for
her son:

> So, through the moonlight lane she goes,
> And far into the moonlight dale;
> And how she ran, and how she walked,
> And all that to herself she talked,
> Would surely be a tedious tale.
>
> In high and low, above, below,
> In great and small, in round and square,
> In tree and tower was Johnny seen,
> In bush and brake, in black and green,
> 'Twas Johnny, Johnny, every where.
>
> She's past the bridge that's in the dale,
> And now the thought torments her sore,
> Johnny *perhaps* his horse forsook,
> To hunt the moon that's in the brook,
> And never will be heard of more.
>
> .   .   .   .   .
>
> 'Oh saints! what is become of him?
> '*Perhaps* he's climbed into an oak,
> 'Where he will stay till he is dead;
> 'Or sadly he has been misled,
> 'And joined the wandering gypsey-folk.
>
> 'Or him that wicked pony's carried
> 'To the dark cave, the goblins' hall,
> 'Or in the castle he's pursuing,
> 'Among the ghosts, his own undoing;
> 'Or playing with the waterfall."
>
> [ll. 212–226, 232–241; my italics]

Her imagination peoples the landscape and thereby parodies the
poet contemplating "forms / In the relations which they bear to
man" (*RC & P*, p. 263). The Pedlar sees Margaret in the place

where she had lived, "I see around me here / Things which you cannot see" (ll. 67–68); Betty Foy sees "Johnny, Johnny, every where." The mother's fear creates fictions similar to those of balladeering poets—the references to "goblins" and "ghosts" burlesque the supernatural, but the other suppositions governed by "perhaps" suggest the simpler tragedy of "The Children in the Wood." One is led by this "tedious tale" to see cravings after pathetic incidents as analogous to the foolishness of supernatural fairy tales.

The connection between the "perhaps" of Betty and Susan and the making of fictions is explicit when Wordsworth addresses the reader:

> Oh reader! now that I might tell
> What Johnny and his horse are doing!
> What they've been doing all this time,
> Oh could I put it into rhyme,
> A most delightful tale pursuing!
>
> *Perhaps*, and no unlikely thought!
> He with his pony now doth roam
> The cliffs and peaks so high that are,
> To lay his hands upon a star,
> And in his pocket bring it home.
>
> *Perhaps* he's turned himself about,
> His face unto his horse's tail,
> And still and mute, in wonder lost,
> And like a silent horseman-ghost,
> He travels on along the vale.
>
> And now, *perhaps*, he's hunting sheep,
> A fierce and dreadful hunter he!
> Yon valley, that's so trim and green,
> In five months' time, should he be seen
> A desert wilderness will be.
>
> *Perhaps*, with head and heels on fire,
> And like the very soul of evil,
> He's galloping away, away,

And so he'll gallop on for aye,
The bane of all that dread the devil.

[ll. 322–346; my italics]

Mary Jacobus has accurately characterized this passage as a teasing of the reader "for wanting to be thrilled or scared."[7] The silent horseman-ghost and the mysterious evil knight, possible subjects for Bürgerian fantasy, are merely absurd when equated to Johnny Foy riding backward on his horse. The thrust of "The Idiot Boy" is to put aside all romance, whether of the supernatural or the pathetic, as irrelevant to human concern. Having cleared the ground, Wordsworth attempts in *Lyrical Ballads* (1800) to replace such empty fictions with what he calls, in a letter of 1801, "the pathos of humanity" (*EL*, p. 325). He hopes thereby to neutralize the exploitative relationship of poet and reader to suffering and to achieve an innocent pleasure in pathos.

"The Idiot Boy" can maintain the illusion of such an innocence primarily because, after all, nothing tragic happens in the poem. No "moving accident" is perpetrated upon Johnny, and "all his travel's story" is finally "'The cocks did crow to-whoo, to-whoo, / 'And the sun did shine so cold.'" (ll. 460–461). In "Lucy Gray," however, the central fact is the girl "bewildered in a snowstorm," "the body . . . found in the canal." The material is pathetic, not mock-pathetic, and the interest in such events, inevitably, is sentimental. Wordsworth's problem is to exploit the pathos of the tale without employing means which he has come to regard as cheap and vulgar. In the Fenwick notes, such a concern with modulating the depiction of suffering is evident: "The way in which the incident was treated and the spiritualizing of the character might furnish hints for contrasting the imaginative influences which I have endeavoured to throw over common life with Crabbe's matter of fact style of treating subjects of the same kind" (*PW*, I, 360).

---

[7]*Tradition and Experiment*, p. 252.

The complexity and downright peculiarity of Wordsworth's arrangement of the story are apparent when contrasted to Coleridge's remembrance of it in the earliest version of "Dejection: An Ode." The verse-letter to Asra addresses the rising wind as it draws from an Aeolian harp "a Scream / Of agony by Torture lengthen'd out." By an extravagant, and typically Romantic,[8] correspondence, Coleridge equates the harp's sound to poetic expression: "Thou Actor, perfect in all tragic Sounds! / Thou mighty Poet, even to frenzy bold!" The poetry of the wind is the poetry of human suffering:

> What tell'st thou now about?
> 'Tis of the Rushing of an Host in Rout—
> And many Groans from men with smarting Wounds
> At once they groan with smart, and shudder with the Cold!
> 'Tis hush'd! There is a Trance of deepest Silence,
> Again! but all that Sound, as of a rushing Crowd,
> And Groans & tremulous Shudderings, all are over—
> And it has other sounds, and all less deep, less loud!
>   A tale of less Affright,
>   And temper'd with Delight,
> As William's Self had made the tender Lay—
>   'Tis of a little Child
>   Upon a heathy Wild,
> Not far from home—but it has lost it's way—
> And now moans low in utter grief & fear—
> And now screams loud, & hopes to make it's Mother hear!
>   [*STCL*, II, 795]

The imagined scenes represent two literary versions of human suffering. The "Rushing of an Host in Rout" is a metaphysical image of man's fate, much like Arnold's "confused alarms of struggle and flight, / Where ignorant armies clash by night." This is the uncontrolled, and unpleasant, contemplation of human suffering, of "images and feelings" which "have an

---

[8]See Abrams' discussion of the Aeolian lyre and the imagery of inspiration in "The Correspondent Breeze: A Romantic Metaphor," in M. H. Abrams, ed., *English Romantic Poets* (New York: Oxford University Press, 1960), pp. 37-54.

undue proportion of pain connected with them" (*Prose*, I, 146). The language Coleridge uses to describe "Lucy Gray," not surprisingly, accords with Wordsworth's own discussions of the pathetic. The reference to William's "tender Lay" recalls the "Union of Tenderness and Imagination" Wordsworth claimed for *Lyrical Ballads* (1800). The suggestion that "Lucy Gray" is "temper'd with Delight" reflects the statement of the "Preface" that poetry should "never act upon us as pathetic beyond the bounds of pleasure" (*Prose*, I, 146).

In one important feature, however, Coleridge misremembers "Lucy Gray." He dwells upon the feelings and cries of the lost child. There is no such business in Wordsworth. The last that we know of her, "many a hill did Lucy climb / But never reach'd the Town" (ll. 31–32). Coleridge's mistake is understandable and possibly strategic. The "plot" of "Dejection" needs the girl's moaning to echo the sound of the harp. Moreover, the focus on the child's anxieties is the conventional way to create pathos in such a story—"The Children in the Wood" and Blake's "Little Boy Lost" and "Little Girl Lost" employ this obvious device. Wordsworth, however, makes no attempt to represent the child's emotions; the only expressions of unhappiness are from her mother and father:

> The wretched Parents all that night
> Went shouting far and wide;
> But there was neither sound nor sight
> To serve them for a guide.
>
> [ll. 33–36]

The focus on the parents, who will survive and suffer when their child is dead, complicates and perhaps "sanctifies" the pathos of "Lucy Gray." The reader's relation to the lost child would be the usual contemplation of the helpless victim, but Wordsworth gives us little of Lucy's death. The relation of reader and the parents is more that of equals. The reader, after all, is also a survivor, one who is looking for Lucy Gray, if only out of curiosity to discover what has happened.

The union of the reader and parents, with poet as intermediary, is emphasized by verbs of seeing. In the opening
stanza, the poet claims, "I chanc'd to see at break of day / The
solitary child." When exactly the poet saw Lucy Gray is left unclear; the past tense refers ambiguously to time both before and
after her death, and therefore, as far as the reader can know, it
may equally be the living child or a wraith. The poet sees the girl
"at break of day," and later in the poem, the parents also look for
her at dawn:

> At day-break on a hill they stood
> That overlook'd the Moor;
> And thence they saw the Bridge of Wood
> A furlong from their door.
>
> [ll. 37–40]

The reader, too, is brought into the circle of those looking for
and perhaps seeing the lost girl:

> You yet may spy the Fawn at play,
> The Hare upon the Green;
> But the sweet face of Lucy Gray
> Will never more be seen.
>
> [ll. 9–12]

The elegiac statement that Lucy "will never more be seen" apparently contradicts the opening stanza, but it does establish that
this poem, like the other "Lucy" poems, is about a dead girl. The
verb *spy* reappears at a critical moment in the parents' search:

> And now they homeward turn'd, and cry'd
> "In Heaven we all shall meet!"
> When in the snow the Mother spied
> The print of Lucy's feet.
>
> [ll. 41–44]

The spying by the reader is mirrored by the parents' spying the
footprint. This "print," implicitly a pun on the print of words, is
a "sight" which will serve both parents and reader "for a guide."

As the poem leads inexorably to the discovery of the body, the reader's knowledge is strictly limited to the extent of the parents' vision. He sees only what they see:

> Then downward from the steep hill's edge
> They track'd the footmarks small;
> And through the broken hawthorn-hedge,
> And by the long stone-wall;
>
> And then an open field they cross'd,
> The marks were still the same;
> They track'd them on, nor ever lost,
> And to the Bridge they came.
>
> They follow'd from the snowy bank
> The footmarks, one by one,
> Into the middle of the plank,
> And further there were none.
>
> [ll. 45–56]

These lines' effectiveness derives from their exquisitely slow pace and careful enumeration of detail. The parents' anxious attentiveness is reflected by the "marking" of seemingly irrelevant natural objects. The "Bridge of Wood," already seen from the hill at daybreak, comes to symbolize the separation of two worlds, the living and the dead. At the middle of the bridge, the "marks," which had been "still the same," fail. The guides of the sense reach no further.

At this point, mirroring the break in the footmarks, there is an interruption in the narrative. The actual discovery of the girl's body is left unexploited, and instead Lucy is invoked as a sort of *genius loci*:[9]

> Yet some maintain that to this day
> She is a living Child,
> That you may see sweet Lucy Gray
> Upon the lonesome Wild.

[9]See Geoffrey Hartman, *Wordsworth's Poetry* (New Haven: Yale University Press, 1964), pp. 213–214.

> O'er rough and smooth she trips along,
> And never looks behind;
> And sings a solitary song
> That whistles in the wind.

[ll. 57–64]

There is no question of belief. Wordsworth does not believe in supernatural events, nor does he demand of his reader even the suspension of disbelief called for by *Lenore* or "The Rime of the Ancient Mariner." The concluding image which "you may see" of Lucy Gray is only a mirage; you may see her, but, then again, you may not. That "some maintain" she is still alive only calls attention to the fictitiousness of the poem's ending. The overtness of the fiction, however, does not destroy its effectiveness; quite the contrary, in proclaiming itself make-believe, it disarms the corrosive force of matter-of-fact criticism. A clear parallel is to "the wish for the Cumberland Beggar," remarked by Lamb, "that he may ha[ve] about him the melody of Birds, altho' he hear them not"; in both poems, "the mind knowingly passes a fiction upon herself . . . and, in the same breath detecting the fallacy, will not part with the wish."[10]

Thus, in "The Idiot Boy" and "Lucy Gray," Wordsworth employs radically different techniques to accomplish his paradoxical purpose. By the careful modulation of conventional pathetic material, he is able to exploit the excitement inherent in the situation without seeming to appeal to the vulgar.

III

Wordsworth's narrative poetry characteristically plays down, even suppresses, the plot's central episode. The inevitable event toward which the poem has been moving and from which it radiates is left blank. The subject matter arouses readerly expectations of violent stimulus, of horrible incident and morbid detail; yet finally such expectations are disappointed. In *The Ruined Cottage*, for instance, an arbitrary placement of the Pedlar

[10] *The Letters of Charles and Mary Anne Lamb*, I, 265.

at Margaret's deathbed would provide a pathetic scene like the carefully staged deaths of Clarissa and Little Eva. The death, after all, is what gives the poem its power, but Wordsworth artfully substitutes the disintegration of Margaret's garden for her actual physical dissolution. The German model for "The Thorn," Bürger's *Des Pfarrers Tochter von Taubenhain,* invites the reader to luxuriate in grisly sensation, even to noting a silver hairpin which the dishonored woman "prest against" her babe's "tender heart."[11] "The Thorn," however, shrouds the infanticide in mystery and speculation, at once exploiting and avoiding the central horror.

This evasion of the climax is the primary device shaping the plots of the 1800 *Lyrical Ballads.* Poem after poem appeals to the reader's sympathies, even while artfully withholding the interesting, if gruesome, particulars of the case. "Hart-leap Well" makes this denial explicit: "I will not stop to tell how far he fled, / Nor will I mention by what death he died" (ll. 30–31); although the death here is only the hart's, these lines are indicative of the poet's coy hesitations and refusals all the way through the volume. "Lucy Gray" brings us to the bridge and leaves us there. Similarly, the necessary event in "Ruth," the youth's abandonment of the girl, is described only by utmost succinctness: "the Youth / Deserted his poor Bride, and Ruth / Could never find him more" (ll. 166–168). Luke's betrayal of Michael might have provided the occasion for an extended Hogarthian denunciation of urban life with the concomitant prurient immersion in sin. For Wordsworth, however, Luke's action is a shadow only important as it darkens his father's life; the boy "slackens in his duty," gives himself "to evil courses," and, in a matter of six lines, seeks "a hiding place beyond the seas" (ll. 451–456).

The circumvention of such central episodes is clearly self-

---

[11]*Des Pfarrers Tochter* was available to Wordsworth in William Taylor's translation, "The Lass of Fair Wone," which had appeared in *The Monthly Magazine* in April 1796 (repr. in Jacobus, *Tradition and Experiment*, pp. 284–288). For the relationship of "The Thorn" to its German original, see Parrish, *Art of the "Lyrical Ballads,"* pp. 109–10, and *Tradition and Experiment*, pp. 242–247.

conscious. In fact, Wordsworth repeatedly mentions a narrative strategy of avoiding what he calls the moving accident. The phrase first appears in the Pedlar's defence of the story he is telling. Coming from a figure whom Wordsworth termed "chiefly an idea of what I fancied my own character might have become in his circumstances" (*PW*, V, 373), the Pedlar's words can be taken as the poet's statement of intent:

> 'Tis a common tale,
> By moving accidents uncharactered,
> A tale of silent suffering, hardly clothed
> In bodily form, and to the grosser sense
> But ill adapted, scarcely palpable
> To him who does not think.
>
> [ll. 231–236]

This speech suggests two distinct narrative possibilities: the "common tale" like that of Margaret, and the story made extraordinary by its use of moving accidents. The common tale is charactered by a void of physical sensation; its suffering is silent, and its narrative without "bodily form," "scarcely palpable," ill adapted "to the grosser sense." It is worth asking in what sense a story could ever be clothed in bodily form or palpable even to a thinking man. The gulf between words and physical objects is, after all, basic to the structure of language; and Wordsworth, as a practicing poet, is well aware of this separation.[12] In no literal way can tales, which are only words, be perceived by "the grosser sense." Blankness of perception is apparently a metaphor, using the commonplace religious dialectic of corrupt body and pure soul to cast out the improper kind of pathetic fiction. The sensational tale is associated with the grosser bodily sense, and the understated tale of silent suffering with the spiritual.

What Wordsworth meant by the "moving accident" is

---

[12]For discussion of Wordsworth's ambivalent attitude toward the separation of language from the things it describes, see Frances Ferguson, *Wordsworth: Language as Counter-Spirit* (New Haven: Yale University Press, 1977), particularly pp. 1–34; also Stephen K. Land, "The Silent Poet: An Aspect of Wordsworth's Semantic Theory," *University of Toronto Quarterly* 42 (1973), 157–169.

suggested by the phrase's original context in *Othello*.[13] There, under interrogation for bewitching Desdemona, the Moor offers the narration of a narration:

> Her father loved me, oft invited me;
> Still questioned me the story of my life
> From year to year, the battles, sieges, fortunes
> That I have passed.
> I ran it through, even from my boyish days
> To th' very moment that he bade me tell it.
> Wherein I spoke of most disastrous chances,
> Of moving accidents by flood and field,
> Of hairbreadth scapes i' th' imminent deadly breach;
> Of being taken by the insolent foe
> And sold to slavery; of my redemption thence
> And portance in my travels' history;
> Wherein of anters vast and deserts idle,
> Rough quarries, rocks, and hills whose heads touch heaven,
> It was my hint to speak. Such was the process.
> And of the Cannibals that each other eat,
> The Anthropophagi, and men who heads
> Do grow beneath their shoulders.
>
> [I: 3: 127–144]

Describing the splash that the outlandish story of his life made in Brabantio's household, Othello presents at once his story and the response to it. Moving accidents are here the exciting and emotionally stimulating adventures of an heroic soldier. The Duke's reaction to the tale, "I think this tale would win my daughter too," recognizes the attractions as well as dangers posed by the intrusion of the exotic upon the domestic.

The great love of Othello and Desdemona legitimizes the seduction by narrative in Shakespeare's play. Nonetheless, the idea that fiction might be a source of evil is implicit as Othello describes Desdemona's response:

> She'd come again, and with a greedy ear
> Devour up my discourse. Which I observing,

[13]*PW*, II, 515.

> Took once a pliant hour, and found good means
> To draw from her a prayer of earnest heart
> That I would all my pilgrimage dilate,
> Whereof by parcels she had something heard,
> But not intentively. I did consent,
> And often did beguile her of her tears
> When I did speak of some distressful stroke
> That my youth suffered. My story being done,
> She gave me for my pains a world of sighs.
>
> .   .   .   .   .
>
> She loved me for the dangers I had passed,
> And I loved her that she did pity them.
> This only is the witchcraft I have used.
>   [I: 3: 148–158; 166–168]

The "greedy ear" with which Desdemona listens, the "pliant hour" when the story is told, the "beguilement" though only of tears, suggest possibilities of betrayal.

In a sense, Wordsworth takes the side of the father by making a dearth of moving accidents the feature which distinguishes his poetry. Indeed, the Pedlar's description of the "tale of silent suffering" strikingly echoes Brabantio's accusation that Othello has enchanted his daughter:

> Judge me the world if 'tis not gross in sense
> That thou hast practiced on her with foul charms,
> Abused her delicate youth with drugs or minerals
> That weaken motion. I'll have't disputed on;
> 'Tis probable, and palpable to thinking.
>   [I: 2: 71–75]

In Wordsworth, "gross in sense" is transmuted to "grosser sense," and "palpable to thinking" to "scarcely palpable to him who does not think." Fiction, at least fiction of a certain type, involves a kind of witchcraft, and Wordsworth is at pains to exorcize the craving for such stimulation from both his readers and himself.

Wordsworth's contempt for the moving accident reappears in a letter to Coleridge written in Germany:

> I also took courage to devote two days (O Wonder) to the Salisbury Plain. I am resolved to discard Robert Walford and invent a new story for the woman. The poem is finished all but her tale. Now by way of a pretty moving accident and to bind together in palpable knots the story of the piece I have resolved to make her the widow or sister or daughter of the man whom the poor Tar murdered. So much for the vulgar. Further the Poets invention goeth not. This is by way of giving a physical totality to the piece [*EL*, pp. 256–257]

The playful tone masks strong exasperation with the *Salisbury Plain* project. By using "The Female Vagrant" in *Lyrical Ballads* (1798), Wordsworth has obliged himself to substitute a new tale if he wishes to salvage his considerable efforts. The letter to Coleridge suggests two stages in his thinking about the replacement. The reference to Robert Walford, the murderer in "The Somersetshire Tragedy," suggests that Wordsworth had planned to incorporate that poem, or a version of it, in *Adventures on Salisbury Plain*.[14] "The Somersetshire Tragedy" narrated an uncommon incident of common life, the squalid story of a husband who, married to one woman and loving another, had murdered his wife. Presumably the Female Vagrant was to be the woman whom Walford had loved, and, in telling her story, she would have roused the guilt of the Sailor, who had also committed murder. The new story proposed in the letter is still more titillating. By confronting the "poor Tar" with his indirect victim, Wordsworth would be concocting a coincidental meeting which would make the guilt unbearable. Clearly, it is the sort of thing that happens rather more often in books than in life.

Either tale would have given *Adventures on Salisbury Plain* the mere "physical totality" it required to be publishable, but

---

[14]Jonathan Wordsworth, "Startling the Earthworms," *Times Literary Supplement* No. 3899 (3 December 1976), p. 1524 (review of *SPP*).

Wordsworth did not finish the poem in 1799.[15] The shifts in his poetic principles apparently make it impossible for him to work further, even on a project which has cost him much labor. The second *Salisbury Plain* is precisely the sort of poem against which Wordsworth inveighs in 1798–1800. Everything about it is extravagant; the appeal is constantly, as he later said, "to coarse sympathies" (*PW*, I, 334). Its sixty-two stanzas describe two murders, sacrificial wickers at Stonehenge, a storm, a gibbet, the beating of a child, the reunion of the Sailor with his dying wife, and finally the Sailor's own execution. The Sailor's response to the beaten child points up the dilemma Wordsworth faces in reworking the poem in 1799: "Deluge of tender thoughts then rush'd amain / Nor could his aged eyes from very tears abstain" (ll. 647–648). This reaction is precisely that of the soggy audience of whom Wordsworth spoke scornfully to Klopstock. No doubt, the Sailor has good reason to feel a "deluge of tender thoughts," but one also suspects that the reader too is supposed to feel such extremity of sympathetic emotion. The Sailor shows us how to respond to the pathetic spectacle, and the expected response, like the events themselves, is extreme and violent.

Instead of making "a new story for the woman," Wordsworth apparently turned to "Ruth." This poem, "written in Germany 1799" (*PW*, II, 509), is substantially a revision of "The Female Vagrant." It tells much the same story: the girl brought up by her father, her love of nature, a soldier-husband, the lure of America, the woman's isolation and alienation after the loss of her husband, her madness and wandering in the countryside. In returning to the old tale, however, Wordsworth revised it to reflect issues of current interest to him. The resulting poem is a parable of Nature's betrayal of the heart that loves her. Like "She Grew Three Years in Sun and Shower," it expresses an ambivalence not present in the lyrics of spring 1798. But "Ruth" is also about the dangers of the imagination; it warns of the

[15]The start of the tale may be on DC MS. 16, p. 40ʳ (*SPP*, pp. 182–183). The precise date of this interpolation cannot be determined, beyond saying that it is later than the fair copy.

perilous and all-too-human attraction posed by the exotic and extraordinary, by, one might say, the "moving accident."

From the beginning, Ruth is a child of the English countryside:

> And she had made a pipe of straw
> And from that oaten pipe could draw
> All sounds of winds and floods;
> Had built a bower upon the green,
> As if she from her birth had been
> An Infant of the woods.
>
> [ll. 7–12]

To this girl steeped in the natural comes "a Youth from Georgia's shore" (l. 13). He uses descriptions of life in the wilderness to woo her:

> Among the Indians he had fought,
> And with him many tales he brought
> Of pleasure and of fear,
> Such tales as told to any Maid
> By such a Youth in the green shade
> Were perilous to hear.
>
> He told of Girls, a happy rout,
> Who quit their fold with dance and shout
> Their pleasant Indian Town
> To gather strawberries all day long,
> Returning with a choral song
> When day-light is gone down.
>
> He spake of plants divine and strange
> That ev'ry day their blossoms change,
> Ten thousand lovely hues!
> With budding, fading, faded flowers
> They stand the wonder of the bowers
> From morn to evening dews.
>
> [ll. 37–54]

To call tales of American flora and frontier adventures "perilous" is again to take the side of Brabantio against Othello. The problem with such stories and descriptions is their appeal to the thirst for degrading stimulation. The exotic and the strange seduce the imagination and cause Ruth, like Desdemona, to fall disastrously in love.

The Youth from Georgia is a man of words, a type of the Poet.[16] Throughout, his linguistic powers are emphasized: "In finest tales the Youth could speak" (l. 26); "He told of Girls, a happy rout"; "He spake of plants divine and strange"; "He told of the Magnolia" (l. 55); "The Youth of green Savannahs spake" (l. 61). The picture he creates of life in America is idyllic but untrue:

> And then he said "How sweet it were
> A fisher or a hunter there,
> A gardener in the shade,
> Still wandering with an easy mind
> To build a household fire and find
> A home in every glade.
>
> What days and what sweet years! Ah me!
> Our life were life indeed, with thee
> So pass'd in quiet bliss,
> And all the while" said he "to know
> That we were in a world of woe,
> On such an earth as this!
>
> [ll. 67–78]

These palpable fictions cause Ruth to agree to go to America with the stranger; and one feels that the stories and Ruth's susceptibility to them are to blame for what happens to her. As the youth creates his dream-world, he invokes the Lucretian theory of tragic pleasure. Life in the earthly paradise is all the more attractive for the knowledge that "a world of woe" exists outside. The couple will be like the man on shore who watches the foundering ship with complacent pleasure. In "Ruth" this com-

---

[16]Indeed Mary Moorman characterizes him as "Wordsworth's picture of what he himself might have been if he had grown up in a savage society" (I, 427).

monplace is associated with the dangerous pleasures of the imagination. The temptation to believe oneself apart from human suffering is part of the dream that eloquence tempts us to believe. Finally, Ruth is all too aware of the "world of woe," for at the poem's end, she becomes herself an emblem of human misery.

Thus, out of *Salisbury Plain*, with its violence of rhetoric and incident, is written a cautionary tale against the temptation to take pleasure in improper and extravagant stories. "Ruth" is told, if not against itself, against other, similar tales that have not the justification it gains in being a parable against fiction. In warning of the dangers of the moving accident, Wordsworth can use, yet another time, the powerfully moving story of the deserted woman.

IV

One result of Wordsworth's suspicions of the moving accident is his assumption of an elegiac voice in the poetry written at Goslar in 1799. Elegy, particularly as Wordsworth practices it, is suspended between narrative and lyric. It does not choose to tell the story that gives emotional significance to the poem, yet the knowledge of the death informs thoughts or incidents that would be trivial without it. Such episodes as a boy mimicking owls ("There Was a Boy"), the moon dropping behind a house ("Strange Fits of Passion"), or an old man holding a bough ("The Two April Mornings") are valorized by our awareness that these unremarkable events are part of a larger, sadder tale. Such a consciousness of mortality takes the place of the consecutive plot of tragic romance.

The "Lucy" poems, particularly, act as appendices to tragedy. The story they tell by glimpses is familiar both in life and literature, but the remarkable feature of the poems is what is absent from them. After reading the four "Lucy" poems in *Lyrical Ballads* (1800), the reader knows little about such rudimentary facts as who the lovers were, where they lived, who their families were, let alone what specifically their relationship was or what happened to the girl.[17] Our expectations of a conventional love-found-love-lost narrative would be to learn some such details. It is as if Wordsworth set out to write a tragic story without plot or even characters, to achieve the sympathetic response by centering on the bare fact of death and on the survivor's reaction to it. In place of moving accidents, there is the drama of consciousness:[18] for the excitement of the death, we are asked to substitute an uncanny premonition in "Strange Fits of Passion" or the ironically pathetic vulnerability of having been "without human fears" in "A Slumber Did My Spirit Seal."[19]

The direction of Wordsworth's thought about the poetry of human life is suggested in the criticism of Bürger's poetry which he offers Coleridge:

> It seems to me, that in poems descriptive of human nature, how-ever short they may be, character is absolutely necessary, &c.: inci-dents are among the lowest allurements of poetry. Take from Bürger's poems the *incidents*, which are seldom or ever of his own invention, and still much will remain; there will remain a manner of relating which is almost always spirited and lively, and stamped and peculiarized with genius. Still I do not find those higher

[17]For a striking discussion of these poems, see Ferguson, *Language as Counter-Spirit*, pp. 173–194. Ferguson rightly focuses on the mysteriousness of Lucy: "our uncertainty about what the name 'Lucy' refers to". She claims that the poems ultimately call "into question the very possibility of locating an object of representation." I would suggest that the problem in the "Lucy" poems is not so much the possibility of literary discourse as the implications of narrative when the "object of representation" is human. If "the whole movement of the Lucy poems is one of asceticism, . . . the process of learning to do without," the pri-mary things being denied are the "extraordinary incidents" of ordinary litera-ture.

[18]See Hartman, *Wordsworth's Poetry*, pp. 157–162.

[19]The extent to which Wordsworth consciously eradicated elements of plot from his "story" is suggested in the early versions of "Strange Fits of Passion" and "She Dwelt among th' Untrodden Ways" (*EL*, pp. 236–238). The stanzas dropped in revision are those which tell what happened, most notably: "And she was graceful as the broom / That flowers by Carron's side; / But slow distemper checked her bloom, / And on the Heath she died."

beauties which can entitle him to the name of a *great* poet. [*EL*, p. 234][20]

Elements of plot seem palpably artificial to Wordsworth, the daydreams, or more often the nightmares, of the overheated imagination. "Character" apparently offers a more legitimate form of literary pleasure, enabling the poet to achieve "higher beauties."

In opposing character and incident, Wordsworth anticipates the Victorian discrimination between novels of plot and of character;[21] indeed he voices the central principle underlying the novels of Austen, Trollope, James, Woolf, and Forster. The paradox of his theoretical stance is theirs: no doubt, as James points out, "it is an incident for a woman to stand up with her hand resting on a table and look at you,"[22] but why should an author go to the trouble to make such an episode important when more sensational events occur, not only in other books, but in real life as well? In Wordsworth, as in the novelists, the answer to this vexing question has to do with what Thomas McFarland has termed the "fructifying tension" between the "strong urge to creative fantasy" and "the drive to realism."[23] By imagining other people's inner realities, the poet offers a fiction closer to

[20]In expressing such opinions to Coleridge, Wordsworth could be confident of finding a receptive audience. Despite his own practice in "The Rime of the Ancient Mariner" and "Christabel," Coleridge too was suspicious of the arbitrary workings of the imagination in forming mere accidents. About Southey he had written in 1797, "I am fearful that he will begin to rely too much on *story* and *event* in his poems, to the neglect of those *lofty imaginings*, that are peculiar to, and definitive of, the poet. The *story* of Milton might be told in two pages" (*STCL*, I, 320).

[21]E. S. Dallas, *The Gay Science* (London: Chapman & Hall, 1866), II, 288–295. In "The Art of Fiction" (1884), Henry James could speak of the "old-fashioned distinction between the novel of character and the novel of incident." In practice, however, James's effort, as much as Wordsworth's, was to avoid the "moving accident."

[22]Henry James, "The Art of Fiction," in *The Future of the Novel*, ed. Leon Edel (New York: Vintage, 1956), p. 16.

[23]Thomas McFarland, "Creative Fantasy and Matter-of-Fact Reality in Wordsworth's Poetry," *JEGP* 75 (1976), 5.

ordinary experience than the events of such poems as *Lenore* and *Des Pfarrers Tochter*.

Wordsworth's desire to internalize the action of narrative poetry also appears in the "Preface" to *Lyrical Ballads*: "it is proper that I should mention one other circumstance which distinguishes these Poems from the popular Poetry of the day; it is this, that the feeling therein developed gives importance to the action and situation and not the action and situation to the feeling. My meaning will be rendered perfectly intelligible by referring my Reader to the Poems entitled *Poor Susan* and the *Childless Father*, particularly to the last Stanza of the latter Poem" (*Prose*, I, 128). The wish to give priority to feeling is just that, a wish. As James asked, "What is character but the determination of incident? What is incident but the illustration of character?"[24] It is doubtful that the two examples Wordsworth cites in the "Preface" make his meaning "perfectly intelligible," or indeed that character in his or anyone's poetry can have absolute priority over circumstance. How, one might ask, could the narrator of the "Lucy" poems be of interest without the incident of Lucy's death? Nonetheless, a look at "Poor Susan" and "The Childless Father" will suggest what Wordsworth has in mind. First, the three concluding stanzas of "The Childless Father":

> The bason of box-wood, just six months before,
> Had stood on the table at Timothy's door,
> A Coffin through Timothy's threshold had pass'd,
> One Child did it bear and that Child was his last.
>
> Now fast up the dell came the noise and the fray,
> The horse and the horn, and the hark! hark away!
> Old Timothy took up his Staff, and he shut
> With a leisurely motion the door of his hut.
>
> *Perhaps* to himself at that moment he said,
> "The key I must take, for my Ellen is dead"

[24]"The Art of Fiction," pp. 15–16.

But of this in my ears not a word did he speak,
And he went to the chase with a tear on his cheek.

[ll. 9–20; my italics]

The poem's action is an "incident" worthy of James: a man closes his door slowly and goes hunting after shedding a tear. The interest for Wordsworth lies in attempting to read the man's mind. This guesswork is presented only as the deductions of a person informed of the situation, one who knows of the death six months earlier and perhaps of the relationship between Timothy and Ellen. The poem, however, honors the man's privacy and refuses to probe into his sorrow. It brings us to feel with him, even while making us conscious that this sympathy may be based on fiction.

"Poor Susan" is another poem in which nothing external happens. A woman hears the song of a thrush on a London street, and images of rural life come before her mind as she associates the experience with her childhood in the country:

At the corner of Wood-Street, when day-light appears,
There's a Thrush that sings loud, it has sung for three years:
Poor Susan has pass'd by the spot and has heard
In the silence of morning the song of the bird.

'Tis a note of enchantment; what ails her? She sees
A mountain ascending, a vision of trees;
Bright volumes of vapour through Lothbury glide,
And a river flows on through the vale of Cheapside.

[ll. 1–8]

The change in location of the narrative voice is the most notable feature of these stanzas. The point of view shifts from external description to look through the woman's eyes. The perspective changes following the question that expresses the external narrator's puzzlement at the woman's response to the song: "'Tis a note of enchantment; what ails her?" Like old Timothy going unhappily to the hunt, Susan's melancholy in what ought to be a pleasant situation causes the narrator to guess what troubles her. In this case, the surmise is expressed by a shift to the woman's perspective: we see what she sees and presumably identify with her feelings.

"Poor Susan" takes its title from Bürger's *Des armen Suschens Traum*, which Wordsworth worked through while in Germany.[25] The letter to Coleridge criticizing Bürger's reliance on "incidents" suggests that Coleridge had put him in the way of it: "I have read 'Susan's Dream,' and I agree with you that it is the most perfect and Shaksperian of his poems" (*EL*, p. 234–235). In Bürger's poem, poor Susan describes a nightmare from which she awakes to find it truth. In her dream, her lover comes to her bedside, breaks her engagement ring, and commits several other acts of vandalism. On waking, she finds all has happened as in the dream and resigns herself, in the manner of ballad heroines, to an early death: "*Der Traum hat Tod gemeint.*"[26] *Des armen Suschens Traum* is not without charm, but it hardly demands to be taken seriously. Whatever pity we might feel for the girl is absorbed by our pleasure in the supernatural fantasy. The story of the dream coming true, which we recognize as a mere fiction, distracts us from her sorrow. The daydream of Wordsworth's poor Susan is rooted in the laws of the association of ideas. She hears the bird, and the images of her youth pass through her mind. The significance of her vision derives solely from the importance which she as an individual attaches to it emotionally, and, therefore, from the importance the reader attaches to her as a fictional character.

By moving the action of narrative into the thought processes of his characters, Wordsworth can claim to have avoided those "incidents" that are the "lowest allurements of poetry." The center of interest becomes individual psychology, "the manner in which our feelings and ideas are associated in a state of ex-

[25]The relation of "Poor Susan" to the German ballad is emphasized by the revised title Wordsworth gave the poem in *Poems* (1815), "The Reverie of Poor Susan," an exact translation of the title of Bürger's poem.
[26]Gottfried August Bürger, *Werke* (Weimar: Volksverlag, 1962), pp. 59–60.

citement" (*Prose*, I, 126). The scientific pretentions of this stance in some measure protect the poet from the sense of himself manipulating and exploiting the suffering of his fellow human beings. Fiction disguised in the rags of truth seems less the responsibility of a single imagination.

V

In "Ruth" the motif of "driving the flying deer" expresses the aggressiveness of the imagination toward its victim. The youth from Georgia weaves a vision of chasing, hunting, and, left unsaid, killing and eating:

> Sweet Ruth! and could you go with me
> My helpmate in the woods to be,
> Our shed at night to rear;
> Or run, my own adopted bride,
> A sylvan huntress at my side
> And drive the flying deer!
>
> Beloved Ruth!" No more he said
> Sweet Ruth alone at midnight shed
> A solitary tear,
> She thought again—and did agree
> With him to sail across the sea,
> And drive the flying deer.
>
> [ll. 85–96]

Wordsworth leaves uncertain why Ruth sheds the "solitary tear" before agreeing to hunt, but possibly she realizes that in accepting the dream, she will partake of its aggression and destructiveness. The pleasure of being a sylvan huntress lies in having something to pursue and kill.

This pleasure, I would guess, is related to the pleasures of tragedy. The excitement of causing suffering, if only in the imagination, seems connected to the pleasure of contemplating it. Nonetheless, in "Ruth," questions about the poet's relation to suffering are contributory but not central to the more general indictment of imagination. The following year, however,

Wordsworth returns to the image of driving the flying deer, and in "Hart-leap Well" he faces more directly the problem of the imagination's involvement with suffering.

As the opening poem of the new volume of *Lyrical Ballads* (1800), "Hart-leap Well" serves as a preface for the work that follows; it allegorizes Wordsworth's poetic situation even as it presents a manifesto for the kind of poetry he wishes to write. The poem's most striking feature is its bipartite structure. The first part tells of the "remarkable chace" in which Sir Walter kills the hart and decides to construct a pleasure-house upon the spot where it had died. The second part offers "another tale," of the poet's meeting with a shepherd at Hart-leap Well and their mutual ruminations upon the spot's history. The tale of Sir Walter and the deer depicts the aggressive, morally dubious aspects of imaginative activity, and the second part of the poem attempts to open a space for the innocent contemplation of suffering.

The poem's moral suggests the question at issue:

> One lesson, Shepherd, let us two divide,
> Taught both by what she [nature] shews, and what conceals,
> Never to blend our pleasure or our pride
> With sorrow of the meanest thing that feels.
>
> [ll. 177–180]

The temptation to regard this as another version of "He prayeth best who loveth best, / All things both great and small" should be resisted. The main issue is not the morality of hunting but the morality of pathos. Blending pleasure and pride with the sorrow of others is the primary enterprise of sentimental and tragic fiction. In the revised "Preface" (1802), Wordsworth asserts "We have no sympathy but what is propagated by pleasure: I would not be misunderstood; but wherever we sympathise with pain, it will be found that the sympathy is produced and carried on by subtle combinations with pleasure" (*Prose*, I, 140).

In Part One of "Hart-leap Well," Sir Walter, a naturalized version of Bürger's *wilde Jäger*, represents the human mind as it takes pleasure in destruction and suffering.[27] The chase itself is described in terms which make it seem an extraordinary incident: "This race it looks not like an earthly race; / Sir Walter and the Hart are left alone" (ll. 27–28). Wordsworth's phrasing is meant to remind the reader of Bürger, whose hunt indeed becomes unearthly as God himself calls up a "ghastly huntsman" and the "dogs of hell" to hunt the hunter.[28] Wordsworth's glance at the other poet only emphasizes his own difference; the "remarkable chace" he narrates is finally only a hunt, and in the end no "awful voice of thunder" speaks.

The most unusual feature of the hunt, at least as far as Sir Walter is concerned, is that the exhausted deer has covered "Nine roods of sheer ascent" (some two hundred feet) in four leaps to reach the spot where it died; he exclaims, "Till now / Such sight was never seen by living eyes" (ll. 50–54). Given the sorts of things which occur in Bürger and Lewis, this is an intentionally bland "extraordinary incident." Deliberately, Wordsworth stays within the real world, and Sir Walter's wonder is none the less for being directed toward a purely natural phenomenon. Even this muted stimulation is for Wordsworth a doubtful good. As the knight gazes at the "darling place," he feels "too happy for repose or rest" (ll. 45–48). In his thirst for stimulus, he ignores what the poet points out to us, the delicate pathos of the spring "trembling still . . . with the last deep groan" of the hart (ll. 43–44). Wordsworth is at best ambivalent toward the turbulent "overflow of powerful feelings" that opens the mind to the world around it. "There Was a Boy" seemingly exalts the process by which the landscape's "solemn imagery" enters "unawares into his mind," while "Nutting" and "Hart-leap Well" associate such human restlessness with the destruction of natural tranquillity.

[27] See Geoffrey Hartman, "False Themes and Gentle Minds," in *Beyond Formalism* (New Haven: Yale University Press, 1970), pp. 283–297, for a stimulating discussion of the relation of "Hart-leap Well" and *Der wilde Jäger*.

[28] The phrases here are from Walter Scott's translation, "The Wild Huntsman" (Edinburgh, 1797; London, 1798).

"Hart-leap Well" links this aggressiveness to artistic endeavor. It is, after all, Sir Walter who gives the place, and therefore, the poem its name. Having noticed the hart's "miraculous" leaps, he exclaims:

> I'll build a Pleasure-house upon this spot,
> And a small Arbour, made for rural joy;
> 'Twill be the traveller's shed, the pilgrim's cot,
> A place of love for damsels that are coy.
>
> A cunning Artist will I have to frame
> A bason for that fountain in the dell;
> And they, who do make mention of the same,
> From this day forth, shall call it Hart-leap Well.
>
> [ll. 57–64]

This is a domestic version of Coleridge's exotic fantasy, "Kubla Khan." The pleasure-house, arbour, and spring mirror constituent elements of "the new paradise"[29]—the "stately pleasure dome," "gardens bright with sinuous rills," and the "mighty fountain" in the "deep romantic chasm." All is naturalized and toned down in Wordsworth, but the essential willfulness of Sir Walter is little different from Coleridge's insistent "I would build that dome in air, / That sunny dome! those caves of ice!" The imagination-as-Kubla forces itself upon the external world. It decrees that the "cunning Artist" regulate and methodize nature, and in three months' time "A cup of stone" receives "the living well" (l. 82). It calls up "dancers and the minstrel's song" to people the "pleasant bower" of its own creation. It utters hybris: "Till the foundations of the mountains fail / My mansion with its arbour shall endure" (ll. 73–74). At its heart, however, the kind of art represented by Sir Walter is dead. All that it touches petrifies; "the Hart, stone-dead," the "cup of stone" around "the living well," and the "three pillars of rude stone Sir Walter rear'd" emphasize the inadequacy of the imperialistic, visionary

---

[29]Parrish, citing Mary Robinson's ode "To the Poet Coleridge" (1800), suggests that "The New Paradise" may have been the first title of "Kubla Khan" (*Art of the "Lyrical Ballads,"* p. 205).

imagination, the mind that blends its pleasure and its pride with sorrow.

The second part depicts an alternative version of the imagination. The discrimination between good and bad fiction is explicit in the transitional stanza between the two parts:

> The moving accident is not my trade,
> To freeze the blood I have no ready arts;
> 'Tis my delight, alone in summer shade,
> To pipe a simple song to thinking hearts.
>
> [ll. 97–100]

By rejecting the moving accident, Wordsworth makes room for a less aggressive relation of poet to reader. Piping a "simple song to thinking hearts" seems less manipulative and morally suspect than employing "ready arts" to give the reader a cheap thrill. As Part One shows the workings of the imagination in an aggressive mode, Part Two works toward establishing an innocent relation of the imagination and suffering.

The kind of accident Wordsworth would substitute for the arbitrary "moving accident" imitates the accidental element of life:

> As I from Hawes to Richmond did repair,
> It chanc'd that I saw standing in a dell
> Three aspins at three corners of a square,
> And one, not four yards distant, near a well.
>
> What this imported I could ill divine,
> And, pulling now the rein my horse to stop,
> I saw three pillars standing in a line,
> The last stone pillar on a dark hill-top.
>
> The trees were grey, with neither arms nor head;
> Half-wasted the square mound of tawny green;
> So that you just might say, as then I said,
> "Here in old time the hand of man has been."
>
> I look'd upon the hills both far and near;
> More doleful place did never eye survey;

> It seem'd as if the spring-time came not here,
> And Nature here were willing to decay.
>
> [ll. 101–116]

The second "tale" of "Hart-leap Well" thus begins with the poet attempting to read an apparently significant landscape. His careful location of the four aspens, particularly the "one, not four yards distant, near a well," is reminiscent of the narrator's obsessive precision in "The Thorn." In great measure, too, the process of mind is similar. No reason exists why the configuration of four tree trunks in an approximate square should import anything at all. Only the imagination lends them ominous significance—like human torsos they stand "with neither arms nor head." For the poet, as earlier for Sir Walter, the spot represents something "never seen by human eyes": "More doleful place did never eye survey." The mind indulges in fictions: "It seem'd as if" entertains a thought that the poet knows is false. Spring does, after all, come to Hart-leap Well, and there is no permanent decay in nature. In short, it is another instance where Wordsworth stimulates his mind by contemplating forms in their relationship to man. One should not, however, lose sight of the fact that the willfulness, the craving for a story, lies within the poet himself.

The narrator stands "in various thoughts and fancies lost"; he has given himself up to his imagination, but there is no small ambivalence toward being thus "lost." At this point, the old shepherd "chances" along and puts an end to the poet's open-ended speculation:

> Him did I accost,
> And what this place might be I then inquir'd.
> The Shepherd stopp'd, and that same story told
> Which in my former rhyme I have rehears'd.
>
> [ll. 119–122]

Having established the facts, however, the Shepherd wants to account for the apparent dolefulness of the place:

> There's neither dog nor heifer, horse nor sheep,
> Will wet his lips within that cup of stone;
> And, oftentimes, when all are fast asleep,
> This water doth send forth a dolorous groan.
>
> Some say that here a murder has been done,
> And blood cries out for blood: but, for my part,
> I've guess'd, when I've been sitting in the sun,
> That it was all for that unhappy Hart.
>
> [ll. 133–140]

The opposition between "some say" and "I've guess'd" suggests "The Thorn" narrator's blend of neighborhood superstition and individual surmise. The Shepherd's claim that the waters groan when all (including presumably himself) are fast asleep undercuts the seriousness with which one is expected to take the "curse." The important matter is not the superstition itself but the act of guessing. The stanzas that follow are laden with surmise:[30]

> What thoughts must through the creature's brain have pass'd!
> From the stone on the summit of the steep
> Are but three bounds, and look, Sir, at this last!
> O Master! it has been a cruel leap.
>
> For thirteen hours he ran a desperate race;
> And in my simple mind we cannot tell
> What cause the Hart might have to love this place,
> And come and make his death-bed near the well.
>
> Here on the grass perhaps asleep he sank,
> Lull'd by this fountain in the summer-tide;
> This water was perhaps the first he drank
> When he had wander'd from his mother's side.
>
> In April here beneath the scented thorn
> He heard the birds their morning carols sing,

---

[30]In my emphasis on surmise, Wordsworth's impulse toward fiction, and his ambivalence toward it, I am in debt to Hartman's readings in *Wordsworth's Poetry* and elsewhere. See also McFarland, "Creative Fantasy and Matter-of-Fact Reality."

> And he, perhaps, for aught we know, was born
> Not half a furlong from that self-same spring.
>
> [ll. 141–156]

The Shepherd is finally as unable as the poet to divine the import of the place. He pleads ignorance of the cause for the hart's return and fills the void of knowledge with an avalanche of *perhaps*. The pictures drawn in these stanzas are self-avowedly fictions, imaginative responses to the fact of suffering and death. The difference between this operation of imagination and that of Sir Walter is that the Shepherd has sympathy for the object of his contemplation. He makes an effort to imagine the feelings even of a suffering animal: "What thoughts must through the creature's brain have pass'd!" This sympathetic intuition, like Sir Walter's pleasure-house, is the product of creative fiat; but where Sir Walter sees the hart's leap merely as an unusual phenomenon, the Shepherd interjects, "O Master! it has been a cruel leap." The present perfect form of "has been" emphasizes the kind of sympathetic projection Wordsworth is using to redeem for poetry the power of suffering.[31]

The poet's response to the Shepherd's hypotheses is equivocal:

> "Grey-headed Shepherd, thou hast spoken well;
> Small difference lies between thy creed and mine;
> This beast not unobserv'd by Nature fell,
> His death was mourn'd by sympathy divine.
>
> The Being, that is in the clouds and air,
> That is in the green leaves among the groves,
> Maintains a deep and reverential care
> For them the quiet creatures whom he loves.
>
> [ll. 161–168]

The move at the end of "Hart-leap Well" to a higher pantheism is like that in the Alfoxden notebook fragments, where the

---

[31]For discussions of Wordsworth's use of this tense, see John A. Alford, "Wordsworth's Use of the Present Perfect," *Modern Language Quarterly* 33 (1972), 119–129; Julian Boyd and Zelda Boyd, "The Perfect of Experience," *Studies in Romanticism* 16 (1977), 3–13.

pantheistic and pathetic sympathies coalesce. In fact, the sympathetic response to nature ratifies and purifies the sympathetic response to suffering. If nature itself and natural man, that is, the Shepherd, respond with sympathy to projections of suffering, surely it is all right for the poet and the reader to do so.

We are not, however, supposed to take literally the pantheistic speculations of "Hart-leap Well." The extreme claims of such belief are modified and equivocated. That a "small difference" exists between poet and Shepherd reminds one, after all, of the real differences between them. As a member of the educated class, the poet cannot really accept the Shepherd's superstitious belief that the place is cursed. For him, the notion merely provides something for the mind to play with; and, indeed, the end of the poem explicitly rejects the superstition:

> The Pleasure-house is dust:—behind, before,
> This is no common waste, no common gloom;
> But Nature, in due course of time, once more
> Shall here put on her beauty and her bloom.
>
> She leaves these objects to a slow decay
> That what we are, and have been, may be known;
> But, at the coming of the milder day,
> These monuments shall all be overgrown.
>
> [ll. 169–176]

The ruins gain their uncommonness not from magic but from the story connected with them. They tell "what we are, and have been" and remind us that nothing human endures "Till the foundations of the mountains fail."

Thus, "Hart-leap Well" proposes a relation of imagination and suffering where the pleasures (and pains) of sympathy are legitimized by the divine Being's "deep and reverential care."[32]

[32]In *Home at Grasmere*, MS. B, Wordsworth describes the experience at Hart-leap Well in autobiographical terms:

> And when the trance
> Came to us, as we stood by Hart-leap Well—
> The intimation of the milder day
> Which is to come, the fairer world than this—
> And raised us up, dejected as we were

This scheme works as well as it does because the suffering victim is an animal. We do not identify with it, and therefore are content to accept the godlike view of its pain. When the victim is one of us, however, such detachment is more difficult. The solution proposed in "Hart-leap Well" is at best fragile, and the situation of poet and reader in regard to suffering becomes more precarious when, as in "The Brothers," we identify with literature's human victim.

VI

The Fenwick notes closely link "Hart-leap Well" with "The Brothers": "The first eight stanzas were composed extempore one winter evening in the cottage; when, after having tired myself with labouring at an awkward passage in 'The Brothers,' I started with a sudden impulse to this to get rid of the other, and finished it in a day or two" (*PW*, II, 514). That Wordsworth works on one poem after reaching an impasse on the other is suggestive, particularly given that the one is a parable about the imagination's relation to suffering and the other an attempt to turn an instance of local human suffering into a poem.[33] The source of "The Brothers" is well known. In November 1799, Wordsworth, touring the Lakes with Coleridge, heard about a

---

> Among the records of that doleful place
> By sorrow for the hunted beast who there
> Had yielded up his breath, the awful trance—
> The Vision of humanity and of God
> The Mourner, God the Sufferer, when the heart
> Of his poor Creatures suffers wrongfully—
> Both in the sadness and the joy we found
> A promise
>
> > [Beth Darlington, ed., *Home at Grasmere* (Ithaca, N.Y.:
> > Cornell University Press), pp. 50–52]

Here, as in "Hart-leap Well," God's feelings are little different from those of the poet; He is, in fact, the sympathetic author and reader writ large. The sympathy that causes the reader to mourn, and suffer after a sort, is mirrored in the very heavens. The fact that God does it, by definition, makes it all right.

[33]The link between the two poems is further suggested by Wordsworth's tardy attempt to put "The Brothers" at the head of the volume in place of "Hart-leap Well"; *EL*, p. 290.

young man who had fallen from a cliff while sleepwalking. Coleridge describes the incident in his journal:

> Nov. 12 ... A little beyond Scale Force a man, named Jerome Bowman, slipped, broke his leg, & crawled on his hands and knees up & down Hill 3 miles to that Cottage in Sycamores where we met the dirty old Woman with the two Teeth— / All this is in the night— / he died soon after, his Wounds festering—This man's Son broke his neck before this by falling off a Crag—supposed to have layed down & slept—but walked in his sleep, & so came to this crag, & fell off—
>
> This was at Proud Knot on the mountain called Pillar up Ennerdale—his Pike staff stuck midway & stayed there till it rotted away— [*STCNB*, I, 540]

By the time they separated in mid-November,[34] it had evidently been determined that Wordsworth would write a poem using the Bowman material. The next communication with Coleridge, the 24–27 December letter from Grasmere, refers to "The Brothers" in a way that indicates Coleridge's prior knowledge: "I have begun the pastoral of *Bowman*: in my next letter I shall probably be able to send it to you" (*EL*, p. 277).

"The Brothers" retains the general outline of events recorded by Coleridge. Wordsworth judiciously leaves out Jerome Bowman crawling three miles in order to focus on the son's tragedy; the somnambulatory victim and the staff caught on the crag are what raise the story above the ordinary run of rural accidents. Obviously, however, there is more to "The Brothers" than the "pure crude fact"[35] of the Bowman episode. Some fifty lines, of 449 in the poem, suffice to present the story that the old woman told. The remainder, the product of meditation active upon a real-life moving accident, centers on the "character" of a brother who did not figure at all in the Bowman story. Wordsworth is able, at least in this poem, to write about an "extraordinary incident" even while preserving his increasingly fastidious narrative

---

[34]Reed *EY*, p. 281.
[35]Robert Browning, *The Ring and the Book*, I: 35.

principles. The compromise, however, is tenuous, and through-out the poem, the strains that eventually cause him virtually to abandon pathetic poetry are visible.

Instead of presenting the Bowman tragedy directly, Wordsworth chooses once again to construct a dramatic narrative framework. "The Brothers," like *The Ruined Cottage* and "The Thorn," is the story of a man relating a story. The priest of Ennerdale tells of the Ewbank brothers, Leonard and James, to a stranger whom he takes to be a typical Lake-Country tourist. Ironically, the stranger is Leonard himself, who, having returned from twenty years at sea, is ignorant and fearful of his brother's fate; for reasons that remain obscure, Leonard, though "well known" to the priest "in former days" (l. 37), speaks "as to one / Unknown" (ll. 117–118). The dramatic ironies which emanate from this improbable situation are powerful. For example, in one exchange, Leonard attempts to find out by indirection if his brother is yet alive:

> *Leonard:*   It seems, these Brothers have not liv'd to be
> A comfort to each other.—
> *Priest:*   That they might
> Live to that end, is what both old and young
> In this our valley all of us have wish'd,
> And what, for my part, I have often pray'd:
> But Leonard—
> *Leonard:*   Then James still is left among you—
> *Priest*: 'Tis of the elder Brother I am speaking.
>
> [ll. 290–298]

Leonard is desperately concerned about his brother, but the priest is not to be denied his story. He is determined to tell Leonard Ewbank about Leonard Ewbank, and proceeds to do so. Again, in response to the priest's reminiscence that "poor Leonard" promised to return to "grow old among us," Leonard says,

>   If that day
> Should come, 'twould needs be a glad day for him;

> He would himself, no doubt, be happy then
> As any that should meet him—
>
> [ll. 333–336]

It is hardly a cheerful day for Leonard, as he speaks to the only person he will meet in Ennerdale. The effect of the irony is to focus attention on the act of narrative. In "The Brothers," the tale of James Bowman-Ewbank's death becomes secondary to his brother's feelings and situation; the framework itself becomes the center of dramatic tension and the reader's sympathies.

The poem opens with the priest muttering, as one pictures Wordsworth muttering in his old age, against tourists:

> These Tourists, Heaven preserve us! needs must live
> A profitable life: some glance along,
> Rapid and gay, as if the earth were air,
> And they were butterflies to wheel about
> Long as their summer lasted; some, as wise,
> Upon the forehead of a jutting crag
> Sit perch'd with book and pencil on their knee,
> And look and scribble, scribble on and look,
> Until a man might travel twelve stout miles,
> Or reap an acre of his neighbour's corn.
>
> But, for that moping son of Idleness
> Why can he tarry *yonder*?—In our church-yard
> Is neither epitaph nor monument,
> Tomb-stone nor name, only the turf we tread,
> And a few natural graves. To Jane, his Wife,
> Thus spake the homely Priest of Ennerdale.
>
> [ll. 1–16]

An odd way indeed to begin a poem based on an incident one has learned of on a tour of the Lakes! Apparently the tourist is a self to be cast out. He is the man, whether melancholy or joyful, whose relation to the outside world involves only surface frippery and cheap emotion. In his melancholy phase, he frequents graveyards, searching out piquant epitaphs and quaint monuments—his thoughts, no doubt, run to "dreams and fictions pensively compos'd, / Dejection taken up for pleasure's sake, / And gilded sympathies" [*Prel* VI: 481–483].

Later, the priest, barely veiling his contempt for the putative tourist, responds to Leonard's leading question about "changes" in the vale:

> On that tall pike,
> (It is the loneliest place of all these hills)
> There were two Springs which bubbled side by side,
> As if they had been made that they might be
> Companions for each other: ten years back,
> Close to those brother fountains, the huge crag
> Was rent with lightning—one is dead and gone,
> The other, left behind, is flowing still.—
> For accidents and changes such as these,
> Why we have store of them! a water-spout
> Will bring down half a mountain; what a feast
> For folks that wander up and down like you,
> To see an acre's breadth of that wide cliff
> One roaring cataract—a sharp May storm
> Will come with loads of January snow,
> And in one night send twenty score of sheep
> To feed the ravens, or a Shepherd dies
> By some untoward death among the rocks:
> The ice breaks up and sweeps away a bridge
>
> [ll. 139–157]

The priest's criticism is of the craving for the sublime; the tourist he describes is of a type with readers who respond only to "extraordinary incident." That part of the mind stirred by natural power and human disaster is made to seem trivial and not a little ghoulish: "what a feast / For folks . . . like you" might well have been addressed to both poet and reader. The priest's mention of the shepherd dying "some untoward death among the rocks" is most striking, given that "The Brothers" takes such an event for its subject. Thus, within the text of the poem is implicit criticism of the very feelings from which the poem has arisen; Wordsworth borders on admitting that the moving accident is indeed his trade.

In the chatty digression about the "brother fountains,"

Leonard recognizes the projection of his own worst fears; the reader, of course, knows a classical omen when he comes across one. The drying up of the spring is an uncanny reflection of the death of a human being. It has a status similar to the "decay" of nature in "Hart-leap Well"; reader and writer indulge in the pleasant fiction of connection and sympathy between nature and its suffering creature. At the same time, such connection gives a sense of significance lacking in the picturesque landscape a tourist sees. The springs imply the possibility of a relation between man and nature deeper than the feast of curiosity.

It is important, too, that the priest is wrong about Leonard. Because he is not a tourist, Leonard has no problems about a spurious or insincere relation to the story of James Ewbank. He can hardly hold vain dalliance with the misery of his own dead. His position is that of spectator *ab intra*. Wordsworth emphasizes Leonard's dual status as audience and character by having the priest remark on his responses to the narrative. The description of old Walter Ewbank's care for his orphaned grandsons breaks off to say: "If you weep, Sir, / To hear a stranger talking about strangers, / Heaven bless you when you are among your kindred!" (ll. 239-241). The ironies are manifold. As he stands in the churchyard among his only kindred, Heaven is hardly blessing Leonard. The priest, in his ignorance of the situation, makes what he believes is a conciliatory remark to the man whom he has earlier insulted. For the priest, Leonard's sensibility clears him of the imputations of insincerity and shallow curiosity associated with tourism. This distinction is analogous to that which Wordsworth wants to make between the pathos of the moving accident and the pathos of tenderness.

Elsewhere in the narrative, the priest interrupts a description of James's sleepwalking:

> He in his sleep would walk about, and sleeping
> He sought his Brother Leonard—You are mov'd!
> Forgive me, Sir: before I spoke to you,
> I judg'd you most unkindly.
>
> [ll. 362-365]

The priest thus introduces a possible relation of audience to suffering which is neither that of the tourist nor of a person directly involved. In his eyes, the fact that the stranger seems moved by the tale absolves him from mere sublime-mongering; tears become the measure by which one judges the legitimate response to suffering. At the end of "The Brothers," the priest is so impressed by Leonard's supposed sensitivity that he invites the once-scorned stranger to dinner. The effect of this mistaken apprehension is to separate the grounds of his judgement from the particular instance. The reader does not have to judge for himself the rightness or wrongness of the priest's ideas as general principles because the priest is clearly mistaken at a less problematic level. Thus, room is still left for an innocent relation to human suffering; tears may yet be an index of humanity rather than luxurious self-indulgence.

In "The Brothers," Wordsworth has the priest tell two "tales of sorrow" (l. 341). Besides that based on the younger Bowman's accident, there is the story of Leonard Ewbank's misfortunes:

> But, as I said, old Walter was too weak
> To strive with such a torrent; when he died,
> The estate and house were sold, and all their sheep,
> A pretty flock, and which, for aught I know,
> Had clothed the Ewbanks for a thousand years.
> Well—all was gone, and they were destitute.
> And Leonard, chiefly for his brother's sake,
> Resolv'd to try his fortune on the seas.
> 'Tis now twelve years since we had tidings from him.
>
> .   .   .   .   .
>
> When last we heard of him
> He was in slavery among the Moors
> Upon the Barbary Coast—'Twas not a little
> That would bring down his spirit, and, no doubt,
> Before it ended in his death, the Lad
> Was sadly cross'd—Poor Leonard!
>
> [ll. 306–314; 323–328]

This story is entirely the product of Wordsworth's own fictional bent; it has nothing to do with either of the Bowman deaths.

Moreover, within the ironic context of "The Brothers," it is not entirely true. The confident assertion of death in slavery provides a definite ending for the story being told, even while Leonard's presence exposes its fictionality.

Oddly, the tale of James Bowman-Ewbank's death is couched in the same kind of language:

> we all conjectur'd
> That, as the day was warm, he had lain down
> Upon the grass, and, waiting for his comrades
> He there had fallen asleep, that in his sleep
> He to the margin of the precipice
> Had walked, and from the summit had fallen head-long,
> And so no doubt he perished: at the time,
> We guess, that in his hands he must have had
> His Shepherd's staff; for midway in the cliff
> It had been caught, and there for many years
> It hung—and moulder'd there.
>
> [ll. 409–419]

"No doubt" echoes the earlier occasion when the reader had every reason to doubt. The exotic story of Moorish slavery and the domestic tale of a shepherd's "untoward death among the rocks" converge in the area of fiction. In fact, the local tragedy is more a matter of speculation and mystery than the far-away one. The concern with detail, the creation of circumstances by "conjecture" to explain the brute facts, is finally as much an endeavour of imagination as Wordsworth's effort to make the thornbush "prominently an impressive object."

The ending of "The Brothers" bears a notable resemblance to the conclusion of *The Ruined Cottage*:

> The Priest here ended—
> The Stranger would have thank'd him, but he felt
> Tears rushing in; both left the spot in silence,
> And Leonard, when they reach'd the church-yard gate,
> As the Priest lifted up the latch, turn'd round,
> And, looking at the grave, he said, "My Brother."
> The Vicar did not hear the words: and now,
> Pointing toward the Cottage, he entreated

> That Leonard would partake his homely fare:
> The other thank'd him with a fervent voice,
> But added, that, the evening being calm,
> He would pursue his journey. So they parted.
> It was not long ere Leonard reach'd a grove
> That overhung the road: he there stopp'd short,
> And, sitting down beneath the trees, review'd
> All that the Priest had said.
>
> [ll. 420–435]

The narrator of *The Ruined Cottage* similarly "turned aside in weakness" and had no "power / To thank him for the tale which he had told" (ll. 495–496). Once alone, he had "reviewed that Woman's suff'rings" and felt the "impotence of grief" (ll. 498–500). In *The Ruined Cottage*, however, the evening tranquillity is an index of the calm of tragic catharsis; here, as in Wordsworth's memories of Peele Castle in "Elegiac Stanzas," natural serenity serves only as an ironic counterpoint for human anguish. In "The Brothers," there is no "evening resting place"; Leonard Ewbank pointedly refuses to enter the parson's cottage and chooses instead to become a rootless wanderer, "A Seaman, a grey headed Mariner" (l. 449).[36] The implications of such an ending are most apparent in the description of Leonard's renunciation of his childhood vale:

> All press'd on him with such a weight, that now,
> This vale, where he had been so happy, seem'd
> A place in which he could not bear to live.
>
> [ll. 438–440]

One is tempted to read this as something more than a single character's despair. The metaphor of "All press'd on him with such a weight" recalls Wordsworth's references to pressure in the context of contemplating human suffering. The Pedlar, it

---

[36]Ferguson, saying Leonard is "as blasted as Coleridge's Ancient Mariner," acutely suggests: " 'The Brothers' (along with the very different 'Hart-leap Well') represents a poetic alternative or rebuttal to 'The Ancient Mariner' " (*Language as Counter-Spirit*, p. 51).

will be remembered, "had no painful pressure from within / Which made him turn aside from wretchedness / With coward fears"; the Fenwick note to *The Borderers* suggests that it might have been wise "to relieve the mind from the pressure of incidents so mournful" by making the plot "more complex" and adding "a greater variety of characters" (*PW*, I, 342). What Wordsworth saw as "pressure" in his later years, earlier had been "sublime." Thus, in *Prelude* (1805) VII, the heart is "wrought upon by tragic sufferings" (l. 500); in the 1850 version, it is "pressed by tragic sufferings." "Wrought upon" implies creation, "pressed" largely suggests discomfort. "Pressure," of course, is a crucial element in the eighteenth-century theory of the sublime; in Burke and elsewhere, it is only when the terror "does not press too close" that it "produces delight."[37] The pressure of the grief which Leonard feels reflects the pressure that Wordsworth feels increasingly in response to fictional projections of suffering. As the tranquil ending of *The Ruined Cottage* is a metaphor of cathartic response, the conclusion of "The Brothers" is emblematic of pathos acting "beyond the bounds of pleasure." It represents the failure of the spectator *ab intra*; and in a sense, the vale which Leonard leaves is the "vale of tears" which is no longer, after 1800, a common region of Wordsworth's song. At any rate, "The Brothers" is the last of the series of poems which explore the response to pathos within a fictional tale; it is the last poem in which Wordsworth adopts the complicated structure of narrator, audience, and victim, which I have traced from *Salisbury Plain* through *The Ruined Cottage*, "The Thorn," "Simon Lee," "The Idiot Boy," and "Hart-leap Well."

VII

In many ways "Michael" is the simplest of Wordsworth's extended tales of human suffering. It has none of the narrative contortion of *The Ruined Cottage* and "The Brothers." The

[37]Edmund Burke, *An Enquiry into the Sublime and the Beautiful*, ed. J. T. Boulton (New York: Columbia University Press, 1958), p. 46.

reader finds no surrogate for himself, and there is only the shadow of a narrator. The sole remnant of Wordsworth's earlier mannerisms appears in the prefatory lines (1–39), where Wordsworth, speaking as poet of Grasmere, addresses "you" the reader to explain the story that follows. "Michael" is yet another poem, the last of the *Lyrical Ballads* chronologically, centering around a form contemplated in its relation to man:

> Nor should I have made mention of this Dell
> But for one object which you might pass by,
> Might see and notice not. Beside the brook
> There is a straggling heap of unhewn stones!
> And to that place a story appertains,
> Which, though it be ungarnish'd with events,
> Is not unfit, I deem, for the fire-side,
> Or for the summer shade.
>
> [ll. 14–21]

It is again that Wordsworthian (and modern) paradox, the desire for a story without events. As in "Hart-leap Well," the appeal is to thinking hearts in "summer shade." The commonness of the central object and the simplicity of the story make the excitement of pathetic fiction seem less threatening.

Wordsworth further justifies the subsequent story by invoking his childhood feelings about shepherds:

> It was the first,
> The earliest of those tales that spake to me
> Of Shepherds, dwellers in the vallies, men
> Whom I already lov'd, not verily
> For their own sakes, but for the fields and hills
> Where was their occupation and abode.
> And hence this Tale, while I was yet a boy
> Careless of books, yet having felt the power
> Of Nature, by the gentle agency
> Of natural objects led me on to feel
> For passions that were not my own, and think
> At random and imperfectly indeed
> On man; the heart of man and human life.
>
> [ll. 21–33]

The tale of suffering becomes the link between man and nature. In *Prelude* VIII, Wordsworth explores this idea further, but here he is content to assert that "this Tale . . . led me on to feel / For passions that were not my own." Listening to the sufferings of Michael, and presumably those of other shepherds, the child becomes educated toward sympathy. To the poet of *The Recluse*, who aspires to write "On Man, on Nature, and on Human Life," this is a critical development.

Following this polemic apology for a "history / Homely and rude," however, "Michael" proceeds in a straightforward manner. Like *The Ruined Cottage*, the poem is a tragedy of hope, but there is no worrying about dalliance with misery or about the moral effects of pathos. For once Wordsworth is primarily interested in telling the story, in giving the facts without exploring matters of response. His poetic intent is more descriptive than usual; he uses Michael to epitomize the "domestic affections" and character of the 'Statesmen, "a class of men who are now almost confined to the North of England . . . small independent *proprietors* of land . . . men of respectable education who daily labour on their own little properties" (*EL*, p. 314). This mimetic focus draws Wordsworth away from issues of pathetic response: to some degree, the attempt to present things-as-they-are absolves the poet of responsibility for his story. He can think of himself as a kind of historian, one who hardly invents his plot and therefore is morally bound only to hold an honest mirror up to life.

The mimetic theory of fiction embraced in "Michael" is, no doubt, successful, possibly because the practical necessity of producing a replacement for "Christabel" in the 1800 *Lyrical Ballads* hardly permitted agonizing over the propriety of exploiting the 'Statesmen in literature. Nonetheless, "Michael" is the last major attempt at an autonomous narrative on a tragic subject until *The White Doe of Rylstone* (1807–1808). The intervening years see the lyrics of spring 1802, the expansion of the two-part *Prelude* to thirteen books, prolific sonneteering, and the publication of *Poems in Two Volumes*. In comparison with the *Lyrical Ballads*, however, there is little effort to exploit pathetic energies;

"The Sailor's Mother" and "Resolution and Independence" are among the few poems which rely on the "impressive" power of human suffering.[38]

Thus, Wordsworth seems to have abandoned the dream of uniting Tenderness and Imagination. The contradictions implicit in *Lyrical Ballads'* effort "to make the incidents of common life interesting" are never finally overcome, and the poet virtually ceases to exploit tragic materials in his poetry. Nonetheless, questions about tragic response and its significance continue to interest him. It was apparently still necessary to define and domesticate this powerful source of imaginative energies. The revised 1802 "Preface" to *Lyrical Ballads* attempts to reconcile the pain and pleasure of contemplating suffering. The Poet, in considering "an infinite complexity of pain and pleasure," is analogous to the Anatomist who deals with "painful" objects but "feels that his knowledge is pleasure" (*Prose*, I, 140). The greater part of Wordsworth's ongoing attempt to resolve such questions, however, occurs in *The Prelude*. As he was well aware, the growth of at least one poet's mind was entwined with the contemplation of human misery, and one of the primary efforts of his long autobiographical poem is to achieve a satisfactory formulation of the relationship of his imagination to human suffering.

---

[38]In response to Sara Hutchinson's criticism of "The Leech-gatherer," Wordsworth writes, "though I believe God has given me a strong imagination, I cannot conceive a figure more impressive than that of an old Man like this, the survivor of a Wife and ten children, travelling alone among the mountains and all lonely places, carrying with him his own fortitude, and the necessities which an unjust state of society has entailed upon him." (*EL*, pp. 366–367). The old man's human tragedy does not appear in the poem's final text; the death of the family is passed over while the decline of the leech population is given full play. Decline in nature seems to be substituted for human loss. The evolution of "Resolution and Independence" from a tale of character to one of visionary encounter is traced by Jared R. Curtis, *Wordsworth's Experiments with Tradition: The Lyric Poems of 1802* (Ithaca, N.Y.: Cornell University Press, 1971), pp. 97–113.

7   Human Suffering and the
Growth of a Poet's Mind:
The Prelude, 1799–1805

Softly let all true sympathizers come,
Without the inventions of sorrow or the sob
Beyond invention. Within what we permit,
Within the actual, the warm, the near,
So great a unity, that it is bliss,
Ties us to those we love.
— Wallace Stevens, *Esthétique du Mal*, V

I

It is not surprising that Wordsworth's most ambitious autobiographical poem should explore the relation of his imaginative development to the contemplation of human misery. Any
inventory of his mental growth purporting to completeness or
honesty has to consider his profound interest in the wretched of
the earth. The subject is, however, difficult and potentially guilt-
ridden. Viewed skeptically, the dignified and somber engagement with tragedy too easily becomes wanton dalliance with suffering. The recurrent shadow in Wordsworth's analysis of tragic
response is the possibility that there is only momentary pleasure
in the contemplation of a Margaret or a Michael. Nonetheless,
the successive versions of imaginative growth postulated in *The
Pedlar*, "Tintern Abbey," the "Intimations Ode," and, finally,
The Prelude, offer explanations, or rationalizations, of the poet's
fascination with tragic materials. In fact, Wordsworth's first impulse to autobiography emanates from his earliest attempts to
explore the question of tragic pleasure. *The Pedlar*, it will be

remembered, represents an effort to determine what kind of person could "afford to suffer / With those whom he saw suffer." Its transparently autobiographical depiction of a poet originates as an overflowing from *The Ruined Cottage*. The tale of Margaret's suffering and the powerful response it evoked turn Wordsworth's mind back upon itself. An ideal self, the Pedlar becomes "rich in our best experience" and "lives in all things that surround" him because every day enlarges his "sphere of pleasure and of pain."

"Tintern Abbey" is primarily concerned with the problems of loss and alienation and, thus, with human suffering taken philosophically. The poem dramatizes, in Keats' phrase, a mind convincing itself "that the World is full of Misery and Heartbreak, Pain, Sickness and oppression." The compensation for the passing of youthful vision, however, has specifically to do with the imagination's projections of human suffering:

> Not for this
> Faint I, nor mourn nor murmur: other gifts
> Have followed, for such loss, I would believe,
> Abundant recompense. For I have learned
> To look on nature, not as in the hour
> Of thoughtless youth, but hearing oftentimes
> The still, sad music of humanity,
> Not harsh nor grating, though of ample power
> To chasten and subdue.
>
> [ll. 86–94]

The central concern, as in *The Ruined Cottage* and *The Thorn*, is the contemplation of "forms / In the relations which they bear to man." The poet hears in nature the "still, sad music" because he has learned to linger over such objects as the spear-grass and the thorn. He finds, or creates, human associations for them. Although the power of such music is "to chasten and subdue" rather than to stimulate our minds, the triangular relation of mind, nature, and human suffering is much the same as in the "Addendum" to *The Ruined Cottage*. Wordsworth still looks to nature in order to read "some sweet and tender lesson . . . Of human suffering or of human joy." The excitement of sympathetic contemplation thus complements and eventually displaces the transient excitement of the child's immediate, passionate response to nature. The appetite for nature in itself having been sated, the poet seeks "a remoter charm" and "interest" borrowed from something other than the eye ("Tintern Abbey," ll. 82–84). Such charm and interest are provided by consciousness of the human presence. Similarly, in the great "Ode," "years that bring the philosophic mind" discover "soothing thoughts that spring / Out of human suffering." Here, too, tragic response in some measure replaces "the hour / Of splendour in the grass, of glory in the flower."

It is, therefore, almost inevitable that *The Prelude* should discuss, at some length, the imagination's engagement with human misery. The topic was important, and Wordsworth had the courage to investigate the dark premises underlying his interest in suffering. Indeed, he proposes no fewer than three versions of sentimental response in the various *Preludes*. As the poem expands from two to five to thirteen books between 1799 and 1805, a revised formulation of the relation of suffering and imaginative growth accompanies each stage of composition. The central texts are the "spots of time" sequence in the two-part *Prelude*, the abortive final book of the five-book version (MS. W), and *Prelude* (1805) VIII, "Love of Nature Leading to Love of Mankind." In each, exploring his imagination's relation to tragic materials is crucial in Wordsworth's attempt to define and explain himself.

II

With the publication of the two-part *Prelude* of 1799, a "new" Wordsworth poem has become available to the generality of readers.[1] This early version is, for the most part, equivalent to

---

[1]The text of the two-part *Prelude* used here is the "reading text" from *The Prelude, 1798–1799*, ed. Stephen Parrish (Ithaca, N.Y.: Cornell University Press, 1977), pp. 43–67. Parrish's text is substantially equivalent to that of Jonathan Wordsworth and Stephen Gill in *The Norton Anthology of English Literature*, ed. M. H. Abrams et al., 4th ed. (New York: Norton, 1979), II, 232–255.

Prelude (1805) from I:271 ("Was it for this . . . ") to the end of Book II. The major variant is the inclusion of the "spots of time" among the other childhood reminiscences. In 1799, these episodes and the accompanying explanatory materials appear to a purpose radically different from Wordsworth's later use of them. In *Prelude* (1805) XI, they illustrate, somewhat obscurely, how the impaired imagination is restored as the poet finds in his childhood the "hiding places" of his power. The spot of time exists as a moment when "the mind / Is lord and master." The Wordsworth of 1799, however, is not greatly concerned that the "outward sense" be "but the obedient servant" of the will. An interchange between inner and outer is sufficient; the human consciousness, an "agent of the one great mind, / Creates, creator and receiver both" (Two-Part *Prelude* II:302–303). The original concept of the spot of time has to do not with the mind's mastery of external things, but with human suffering and the response of the child's imagination to it.[2]

In the 1799 *Prelude*, the spots of time sequence begins as Wordsworth interrupts a prolonged catalogue of the child's seasonal activities in the Lake Country. After defending his nostalgic listing, he shifts ground radically and breaks into the talky jargon that might be called his self-defining voice:

> All these and more with rival claims demand
> Grateful acknowledgement. It were a song
> Venial, and such as if I rightly judge
> I might protract unblamed; but I perceive
> That much is overlooked, and we should ill
> Attain our object if from delicate fears

[2]In "The Spots of Time in Early Versions of *The Prelude*," *Studies in Romanticism* 12 (1973), 389–405, Sybil Eakin describes the evolutionary character of Wordsworth's concept of the spot of time. Eakin astutely emphasizes that the portrayal of the mind as "lord and master" is a later elaboration and claims that, in 1799, the spots form an integral part of the argument of Part I. I see less unity than Eakin in *Prelude* (1799), Part I, and will argue that, in their earliest form, the spots' primary purpose is not to document the origins of Wordsworth's love for nature but rather to chart the mind's early relation to human suffering. Nonetheless, Eakin's approach to the spots of time is sound: a spot of time in 1799 was not the thing it became in 1804–05.

Of breaking in upon the unity
Of this my argument I should omit
To speak of such effects as cannot here
Be regularly classed, yet tend no less
To the same point, the growth of mental power
And love of Nature's works.

[I:247–258]

Understandably, this passage was dropped during the 1804 revision. One has the impression of a man flailing about to express something he but half-understands. The tortured syntax, serpentine structure, and vague abstractness of the second sentence reflect the difficulty of transition between the seasonal experiences and the subsequent episode of the drowned man. Much of it seems clumsy and confused: Wordsworth has said nothing previously about "our object," nor would have one suspected, from the poem thus far, that this poet had delicate fears about the unity of his argument. Nonetheless, these lines are important, for they represent the first effort to define the spot of time. Wordsworth speaks of "such effects as cannot here / Be regularly classed," implying that the effects previously discussed had been available for "regular" classification. Indeed, the other major sections of *Prelude* (1799), Part I, do lend themselves to categories. "Severer interventions" (l. 79) and "gentle visitation" (l. 73) fit recognizably within eighteenth-century concepts of the sublime and the beautiful; the section on the seasons, like Thomson's poem, ultimately relies on the permanent, cyclical order of the year for its regularity. Only the spots of time seem to resist categorization and orderly definition.

When Wordsworth speaks of irregular effects, a language of moral discrimination enters the poem. As so often, he finds disorder both exciting and morally dubious. A continuation of the seasonal catalogue would be, in Wordsworth's terms, a "venial" song. Normally, one would attach a nonpejorative meaning to this use of venial, something like the "venial discourse" between Adam and Raphael in *Paradise Lost* IX, trivial but enjoyable. However, the lines that follow are loaded with other words

that imply ethical choice: "If I *rightly* judge," "might pro-
tract *unblamed*," "we should *ill* attain our object," "*delicate
fears.*" Taken singly, any of these phrases seems innocent
enough; the primary meanings are divorced from considerations of right and wrong. Together, however, they form a verbal
cluster resonant of guilty action. If the catalogue of the seasons is
venial, does the subsequent section smack of mortal sin? Does a
poet remain unblamed if he judges wrongly in writing of the
mind's dark embrace with human suffering? In attaining his
object, does he do ill? Such questions are implicit in the language
with which Wordsworth introduces the spots of time. The reference to "delicate fears" suggests that there is indeed something
indelicate, unseemly, morally doubtful, about the accounts that
follow. We have seen in *The Ruined Cottage* and "Hart-leap Well"
that poetry which relies on "sorrow" for its "pleasure" and
"pride" makes Wordsworth profoundly uneasy. Here, too, he
seems uncertain that irregular reminiscences are venial, or if
he can present them unblamed. However this may be, Wordsworth's central claim is unambiguous: such irregular effects
foster "the growth of mental power / And love of Nature's
works." Thus, the contemplation of suffering, in the subsequent
episodes of the drowned man and the gibbet, has causative
priority over the love of nature. It is not Love of Nature, Leading to Love of Mankind, but sympathy with man leading to love
of nature. The "world where want and sorrow were," as in "The
Old Cumberland Beggar," is the seedbed of imaginative growth.

In the 1799 *Prelude*, the discussion of effects that "cannot here
be regularly classed" provides the theoretical framework for the
child's discovery of the drowned man:

> Ere I had seen
> Eight summers (and 'twas in the very week
> When I was first transplanted to thy vale,
> Beloved Hawkshead! when thy paths, thy shores
> And brooks were like a dream of novelty
> To my half-infant mind) I chanced to cross
> One of those open fields which, shaped like ears,

Make green peninsulas on Esthwaite's lake.
Twilight was coming on, yet through the gloom
I saw distinctly on the opposite shore
Beneath a tree and close by the lake side
A heap of garments, as if left by one
Who there was bathing: half an hour I watched
And no one owned them: meanwhile the calm lake
Grew dark with all the shadows on its breast,
And now and then a leaping fish disturbed
The breathless stillness. The succeeding day
There came a company, and in their boat
Sounded with iron hooks and with long poles.
At length the dead man 'mid that beauteous scene
Of trees, and hills, and water, bolt upright
Rose with his ghastly face.

[ll. 258–279]

As in "The Old Cumberland Beggar," the emphasis is on the spectator—"I saw distinctly," "half an hour I watched," even "ere I had seen / Eight summers." The child watches the heap of garments even as he has "scanned" the Discharged Soldier "with a mingled sense / Of fear and sorrow." Somehow the experience instills and deepens his love of nature. Anxious expectation and horrible fulfillment only intensify natural tranquillity, the "beauteous scene / Of trees, and hills, and water." The cadence of the phrase suggests the "rocks and stones and trees" with which Lucy is "rolled round" in the contemporaneous "A Slumber Did My Spirit Seal." If indeed the return to nature is equivalent in these poems, it would suggest that the ending of "A Slumber Did My Spirit Seal" is more positive for Wordsworth than a bare reading of the text would indicate, that Lucy's death is important because it endows nature with a remoter charm, the interest of human suffering. At any rate, the geography of Esthwaite provides a metaphor of the contemplation of suffering. On "the opposite shore," the child stands removed from the relics of death-by-water; poet and reader are similarly separate from the suffering that is the subject of their poem.

In the two-part *Prelude*, the episode of the drowned man introduces Wordsworth's most direct statement about the imaginative importance of tragic response:

> I might advert
> To numerous accidents in flood or field,
> Quarry or moor, or 'mid the winter snows,
> Distresses and disasters, tragic facts
> Of rural history that impressed my mind
> With images, to which in following years
> Far other feelings were attached, with forms
> That yet exist with independent life
> And, like their archetypes, know no decay.
>
> [ll. 279–287]

Thus, the effects that cannot be regularly classed have to do with "tragic facts." As in *The Ruined Cottage*, theoretical discussion of pathetic response evokes Othello's account of his courtship. "I might advert / To numerous accidents in flood or field" echoes the Moor speaking "Of moving accidents by flood and field."[3] The accidents that Wordsworth cites are those of his early poetry. *An Evening Walk* describes a family dying of exposure on a moor. The Windy Brow expansion of the same poem tells of a girl who visits a quarry at midnight, "that sad spot . . . / Where crushed by falling rocks her lover fell" (*PW*, I, 18). The frozen family, the chamois hunter of *Descriptive Sketches*, and the forsaken Indian woman all die "'mid the winter snows." In the 1799 *Prelude*, Wordsworth wants to claim a positive effect for such "distresses and disasters." They are not trivial "moving accidents" but significant episodes that impress the mind with images.

The most serious difficulty in the passage lies in the distinction among "images," "forms that yet exist," and "their archetypes." The relevant text is Locke's *Essay concerning Human Understanding*,[4] where the word *archetype* appears often, in a context similar

---

[3] *Othello*, I, 3: 134; noted by Abrams, *Norton Anthology*, II, 239.
[4] Basil Willey's "Wordsworth and the Locke Tradition" is still most useful in describing Wordsworth's ambiguous relation to Locke (in *The Seventeenth-Century Background* [New York: Columbia University Press, 1934], pp. 293–305). See also

to that of the 1799 *Prelude*. Wordsworth follows Locke in using the word in its etymological sense: *archi*, first, plus *typos*, impress, stamp, type (*OED*). For Locke, an archetype may or may not reflect external reality, but the word itself denotes patterns etched on the mental tablet, rather than real "substance." For example, in the discussion of "Adequate and Inadequate Ideas": "*Our complex ideas of modes*, being voluntary collections of simple ideas, which the mind puts together, without reference to any real archetypes, or standing patterns, existing anywhere, are and cannot but be *adequate ideas*. Because they, not being intended for copies of things really existing but for archetypes made by the mind, to rank and denominate things by, cannot want anything."[5] In Locke's epistemology, "simple ideas" are sense impressions; "complex ideas" are combinations of "simple ideas" by the "voluntary" intellect of man. In discussing the "tragic facts of rural history," Wordsworth makes a similar progression from simple to complex. Upon simpler ideas (such as the perceived shapes and colors of the clothes, the corpse, and surrounding scenery), "the mind . . . exercizes an *active* power in making these several combinations." "Once furnished with simple ideas, it can put them together in several compositions, and so make a variety of complex ideas,"[6] or, as Wordsworth says, his mind possesses "images, to which in following years / Far other feelings were attached." In this case, therefore, the "archetype" is the original sensory and emotional experience; the "forms" are the sum of the original "archetype" and the subsequent feelings and experiences associated with it. Both are permanent as they are impressed upon the human mind.

Wordsworth deleted the discussion of rural tragedies from the 1805 *Prelude*. The ideas expressed no longer conformed to his

Arthur Beatty, *Wordsworth: His Doctrine and His Art*, University of Wisconsin Studies in Language and Literature no. 24 (1927); Ben Ross Schneider, *Wordsworth's Cambridge Education* (Cambridge: Cambridge University Press, 1957), pp. 106–111.

[5] John Locke, *An Essay concerning Human Understanding*, ed. Alexander C. Fraser (Oxford: Clarendon, 1894), I, 504.

[6] Locke, *Essay concerning Human Understanding*, I, 382.

views regarding the imagination's relation to suffering; probably they seemed to partake of wanton dalliance with misery. In 1799, however, the contemplation of suffering is directly linked to a central Wordsworthian passage. The "spots of time" declaration follows immediately:

> There are in our existence spots of time
> Which with distinct pre-eminence retain
> A fructifying virtue, whence, depressed
> By trivial occupations and the round
> Of ordinary intercourse, our minds
> (Especially the imaginative power)
> Are nourished, and invisibly repaired.
> Such moments chiefly seem to have their date
> In our first childhood.
>
> [ll. 288–296]

This passage is continuous with the preceding theoretical statements. "Spots of time," like "forms / That yet exist with independent life / And . . . know no decay," describe points of stasis and permanence in the universal flux. "Distinct pre-eminence," with its emphasis on apartness, also recalls the "independent life" of pathetic "forms." "Fructifying virtue," invoking a metaphor of organic energy, says much the same thing as "the growth of mental power." In short, the "spots of time" theory extends the discussion of the "tragic facts"; it describes how the permanent forms "that yet exist" affect everyday life. Apparently they function much like the remembered landscape of "Tintern Abbey."[7] "The round / Of ordinary intercourse" echoes that "dreary intercourse of daily life" upon which nature impresses "quietness and beauty." The scene on the Wye provides "life and food / For future years," feeding the mind "with lofty thoughts," much as "our minds / (Especially the imaginative power) / Are nourished" by the spots of time. For Wordsworth in 1798–99, recollecting a "pastoral landscape" is remarkably like

---

[7]Jonathan Wordsworth and Stephen Gill, "The Two-Part *Prelude* of 1798–99," *JEGP* 72 (1973), 512.

looking back upon past encounters with vestiges of human suffering. Where the one seems obviously innocent, however, the other is not a little ghoulish. In the redistribution of Part I in 1804, therefore, the poet separates the spots of time declaration from the contemplation of suffering. In so doing, he makes the theory seem more mysterious and expansive than it had originally been.[8]

In the two-part version, as in *Prelude* (1805), the boy's discovery of the gibbet place illustrates the general theory of the spots of time. The core of the experience is the encounter with a spot made bloody by association with human guilt and sorrow:

> I led my horse and, stumbling on, at length
> Came to a bottom where in former times
> A man, the murderer of his wife, was hung
> In irons; mouldered was the gibbet mast,
> The bones were gone, the iron and the wood,
> Only a long green ridge of turf remained
> Whose shape was like a grave.
>
> [ll. 307–313]

This description has little to do with what the child finds. Attention is lavished on what is absent, the bones, the iron, the wooden mast. The only thing he actually sees, "a green ridge of turf," might exist anywhere. Given the evidence, how does the

---

[8]A common practice among readers and teachers of Wordsworth, including this one, is to refer to virtually all of the many vivid retrospective epiphanies in *The Prelude* as "spots of time." Thus, Jonathan Bishop, in "Wordsworth and the 'Spots of Time,'" *ELH* 26 (1959), 45, "Using the phrase in a looser sense, the 'spots of time' must include the descriptions of Wordsworth's boyhood exploits as a snarer of woodcocks, a plunderer of bird's nests, a skater, a rider of horses, and such single events as the famous Stolen Boat episode, the Dedication to poetry, the Discharged Soldier, the Dream of the Arab-Quixote," *etc.* Similarly, Geoffrey Hartman, "To these ["Waiting for Horses" and "The Discovery of the Gibbet"] . . . we can add other incidents retained as part of Books I and II: the robbing of bird's nests, the boat-stealing, and similar wanton or willful acts" [*Wordsworth's Poetry* (New Haven: Yale University Press, 1964), p. 214]. In the strict and original sense of the phrase, however, the spots of time include only the three episodes placed around the "spots of time" declaration in the two-part *Prelude*, Part I.

child know he has stumbled upon the spot where the gibbet had been hung? In the 1804 version, he has it in writing:

> on the turf,
> Hard by, soon after that fell deed was wrought
> Some unknown hand had carved the Murderer's name.
> The monumental writing was engraven
> In times long past, and still, from year to year,
> By superstition of the neighbourhood,
> The grass is clear'd away; and to this hour
> The letters are all fresh and visible.
>
> > [*Prel* XI: 292–299]

Everything is pat. The child reads the "fresh and visible" letters, and they tell him where he is. The 1799 *Prelude*, however, discovers no such definite signs. The child must have prior knowledge, some neighborhood gossip or matron's tale; the vestiges in themselves are hardly sufficient to establish a human presence. In fact, it is not even important whether he is where the gibbet has been hung, but only that he thinks he is. He has heard the story of a "man, the murderer of his wife," who had been put to death and hung in a gibbet. With justification or not, he connects the particular place where he stands with the "tragic fact of rural history."

Jonathan Wordsworth has noted that "in a curious way the passage reminds one of 'The Thorn'," and indeed the elements of the poet's memory are remarkably like those of his fiction. In *The Prelude*, the "long green ridge of turf" is shaped "like a grave," while "The Thorn" describes a "heap of earth o'ergrown with moss . . . like an infant's grave in size." In both cases, the speaker advances no certain proof; only similes connect the bulge of earth and the fact of death. A "naked pool" recalls the "little muddy pond of water" where Martha Ray's baby was rumored to have drowned. Even the sudden discovery of the "girl who bore a pitcher on her head" is not unlike the narrator's discovery of Martha Ray in similarly inclement circumstances.[9]

---

[9]Jonathan Wordsworth, "The Growth of a Poet's Mind," *Cornell Library Journal* 11 (Spring 1970), 19–20.

In both poems, the mind invests a spot with the significance of suffering. "The Thorn," however, is grotesque parody, and the experience in the gibbet bottom possesses "fructifying virtue." By setting the experience back in his childhood, Wordsworth puts a safe distance between himself and an exploitative relationship to suffering. Nevertheless, the similarity between "The Thorn" and the gibbet episode indicates the precariousness of Wordsworth's use of suffering as a source of imaginative energy. The distinction between the obsessive old sea-captain and the poet rummaging in his childhood for encounters with suffering is of degree rather than of kind. The constant threat is that the one will slip over into the other, that the poet will become indistinguishable from the sailor.

The spot of time exists apart from the confrontation with suffering which provides its energy. In both the gibbet episode and "Waiting for Horses," tragic facts impress the mind with images. The spot of time is the image, not the tragedy. Thus, as the child leaves the place where he believes a gibbet has been hung, he sees

> A naked pool that lay beneath the hills,
> The beacon on the summit, and more near
> A girl who bore a pitcher on her head
> And seemed with difficult steps to force her way
> Against the blowing wind.
>
> [ll. 315–319]

His recent experience endows this common sight with the power to impress the child's mind. The theoretical distinction between archetypes and forms is reflected as Wordsworth repeats the catalogue of things seen on that long-ago day:

> It was in truth
> An ordinary sight but I should need
> Colours and words that are unknown to man
> To paint the visionary dreariness
> Which, while I looked all round for my lost guide,
> Did, at that time, invest the naked pool,
> The beacon on the lonely eminence,

> The woman and her garments vexed and tossed
> By the strong wind.
>
> [ll. 319–327]

The repetition of images imitates the process by which the mind evokes and broods over the spot of time. One is invited to partake in the poet's experience by the sense of *déjà lu* which Wordsworth's bold redundancy instills. The reader, too, if only in words, possesses the images of the pool, beacon, and girl, to which he has attached his own feelings; thus, when he meets the familiar forms a second time in the text, they recreate in him the kind of experience Wordsworth is describing.

"Waiting for Horses" presents "Another scene which left a kindred power / Implanted in my mind" (ll. 329–330). There are, of course, significant differences between the two spots of time. The primary excitement in "Waiting for Horses" lies in Oedipal guilt of some sort; only secondarily does the imagination's perception of a "world where want and sorrow are" animate the scene. Also, Wordsworth perceives the implanted image before experiencing the grief and guilt that energize it; not until his return home and the death of his father does the expectant waiting on the mountain take on significance:

> The event
> With all the sorrow which it brought appeared
> A chastisement, and when I called to mind
> That day so lately passed when from the crag
> I looked in such anxiety of hope,
> With trite reflections of morality
> Yet with the deepest passion I bowed low
> To God, who thus corrected my desires
>
> [ll. 353–360]

The distance between the child and the present speaker is emphatic. The adult Wordsworth does not believe in divine chastisement of the child's activities; he characterizes the prayerbook diction of "God, who thus corrected my desires" as a "trite reflection of morality." The important thing is not what the child felt, but *that* he felt "deepest passion." The emotional mixture of guilt and sorrow attaches "far other feelings" to the archetypes of

> the wind, and sleety rain,
> And all the business of the elements,
> The single sheep, and the one blasted tree,
> And the bleak music of that old stone wall,
> The noise of wood and water, and the mist
> Which on the line of each of those two roads
> Advanced in such indisputable shapes
>
> [ll. 361–367]

The essential element of the spot of time is the mind's recapitulation of a scene that death has endowed with significance. In 1799, Wordsworth is willing to proclaim that such scenes provide a major source of his imaginative power.

In the two-part *Prelude*, "Waiting for Horses" is followed by a passage transitional to a section describing the "gentle visitation" of nature:

> [Nor sedulous to trace]
> How other pleasures have been mine, and joys
> And by extrinsic passion peopled first
> My mind with forms, or beautiful or grand,
> And made me love them, may I well forget
> How other pleasures have been mine, and joys
> Of subtler origin
>
> [ll. 375–381]

The 1805 *Prelude* strips these lines of their original meaning. They appear immediately after the description of the ice splitting on Esthwaite, and the obscure phrase, "by collateral interest," drops out entirely. As revised, the passage refers generally to the opposition, operant throughout *Prelude* I, of the beautiful and the sublime. In the 1799 *Prelude*, however, the reference is specifically to the immediately preceding "spots of time" and, therefore, to the imaginative effects of pathos. By "collateral interest," Wordsworth evidently means the interest created in objects "placed side by side" (*OED*) with suffering. "Collateral" is not a common word in Wordsworth's poetry, but in the two-part *Prelude* it reappears, in a less obscure context, forty-seven lines later:

> the earth
> And common face of Nature spake to me
> Rememberable things: sometimes, 'tis true,
> By quaint associations, yet not vain
> Nor profitless if haply they impressed
> Collateral objects and appearances,
> Albeit lifeless then, and doomed to sleep
> Until maturer seasons called them forth
> To impregnate and to elevate the mind.
>
> [ll. 418–426]

"Collateral objects" are impressed on the mind by "quaint associations." The psychology is that of the spots of time—in the same sense, the sheep and thorn are "collateral" to the father's death; the pool and girl, to the horrifying discovery of the gibbet.

It is therefore *by means of* "collateral interest" and "by extrinsic passion" that Nature "peoples" the mind with "forms." "Extrinsic passion," too, describes an aspect of the spot-of-time experience, equivalent to the "deepest passion" (l. 359) that the child felt in "Waiting for Horses." The passion is extrinsic because it comes from outside of nature, from the mind's ferment in response to suffering. Passion itself is a word associated with suffering, as Wordsworth's "Essay, Supplementary to the Preface" notes: "Passion, it must be observed, is derived from a word which signifies *suffering*" (*Prose*, III, 81). The sympathetic response to suffering, therefore, provides the passionate energy that implants forms in the mind. That this passion "peopled" the mind with forms suggests the humanization of nature which sympathy produces; there is a like effect at the end of *The Ruined Cottage*: "A thrush sang loud, and other melodies, / At distance heard, peopled the milder air" (ll. 532–533). Notably, in the 1799 *Prelude*, suffering peoples the mind with "forms, or beautiful or grand." Wordsworth is indifferent whether the experience is of the sublime, as in the contemplation of the girl with the pitcher, or of the beautiful, as in the sight of the calm lake that yields the corpse. The important thing is the intensity of experience; and the imagination of suffering is a primary source of the intensity and energy that make experience vivid.

Thus, the 1799 *Prelude* presents a theory of pathetic response that is essentially Lockean in its structure and vocabulary. The emphasis is on the links that strong emotions forge between the mind and the world outside. The original "spots of time" segment is Wordsworth's most straightforward effort to explore the mind's relation to "tragic facts." Perhaps, this very directness caused him to turn away from it and attempt to formulate a more satisfactory, less obviously exploitative theory of pathetic response when he returned to *The Prelude* in 1804–05.

III

"I am now after a long sleep busily engaged in writing a Poem of considerable labour" (*EL*, p. 432), proclaims Wordsworth in a letter of January 1804. The poem is again *The Prelude*, but the concept of a modest tail-piece to *The Recluse* has expanded to five books. Another, roughly contemporary letter states, "At present I am engaged in a Poem on my own earlier life which will take five parts or books to complete, three of which are nearly finished" (*EL*, p. 436). A month later, Wordsworth tells Coleridge, "I finished five or six days ago another Book of my Poem amounting to 650 lines. And now I am positively arrived at the subject I spoke of in my last. When this next book is done which I shall begin in two or three days time, I shall consider the work as finish'd" (*EL*, p. 452). Of course, Wordsworth never did bring the five-book *Prelude* to completion. No fair copy of such a work exists, for, in March 1804, he decided to expand *The Prelude* yet further. Ten days following the letter to Coleridge, he sent *Prelude* (1805) I-V to solace Coleridge in Malta. These five books (MS. M) are clearly intended as part of a longer work, for the conclusion of Book V promises to speak of "an abasement in my mind" and of the "later gifts" of Books.[10]

It is now impossible to reconstruct the "finished" 650-line Book IV of the five-book *Prelude*. The manuscript evidence has been lost, and the book's contents vis-à-vis the 504-line Book IV of the 1805 *Prelude* are uncertain. The beginning of the abortive final book, however, evidently does exist in MS. W (DC MS. 38). The "Climbing of Snowdon" episode, later to open *Prelude* (1805) XIII, appears on three sides of leaves 41 and 42.[11] In this first fair-copy version, the words "5th Book" immediately above the opening line suggest that Wordsworth intended the episode to open the final book of the five-book *Prelude*.[12] On the bottom third of leaf 42^r, there is a space left blank, evidently for the insertion of further material; on 42^v–46^v Wordsworth copies a passage continuous with the Snowdon episode. Apparently these lines, too, were part of the abortive fifth book and, therefore, help clarify what Wordsworth may have meant by "the subject I spoke of in my last."

The original opening of Book V presents the vision from Snowdon as one of several, essentially similar experiences:

in which Nature works
Oft times, upon the outward face of things,

[10]*Prel*, p. 172. For my knowledge of the five-book *Prelude*, I am substantially in debt to de Selincourt's notes, *Prel*, pp. 619–620; J. R. MacGillivray, "The Three Forms of *The Prelude*, 1798–1805," in *Essays in English Literature from the Renaissance to the Victorian Age, Presented to A. S. P. Woodhouse*, ed. M. Maclure and F. W. Watt (Toronto: University of Toronto Press, 1964), pp. 229–244; Reed *MY*, pp. 637–645; Jonathan Wordsworth, "The Five-Book *Prelude* of Early Spring 1804," *JEGP* 76 (1977), 1–25.

[11]I follow Jonathan Wordsworth's hypothetical numbering of the leaves to include leaves that are no longer in MS. W but whose former presence can be posited from stubs and internal evidence ("Five-Book *Prelude*," p. 7).

[12]The possibility exists that, sometime in March 1804, after he had decided to expand *The Prelude*, but before he reconstructed the 1805 Book V which appears in MS. M (copied by 18 March), Wordsworth started a "5th Book" not meant as a final book. This seems less probable than that "two or three days" after the 6 March letter to Coleridge he started on the final "5th Book," only to put it aside after about 140 lines were written. My discussion assumes that the "5th Book" was meant to complete the five-book *Prelude*; if, however, it was a false start on *Prelude* (1805) V, the reading would not be substantially affected.

As if with an imaginative power
I mean so moulds, exalts, indues, combines,
Impregnates, separates, adds, takes away,
And makes one object sway another so
By unhabitual influence or abrupt
That even the grossest minds must see and hear
And cannot chuse but feel. The power which these
Acknowledge, being so mov'd which Nature thus
Thrusts forth upon the senses is in kind
A Brother of the very faculty
Which higher minds bear with them as their own.

[*Prel*, pp. 483–484]

In the 1805 *Prelude*, the experience on Snowdon represents an epiphanic conversion, but MS. W displays the episode as a common kind of occurrence in the poet's life:[13]

Oft tracing this analogy betwixt
The mind of man and nature, doth the scene
Which from the side of Snowden I beheld
Rise up before me, followed too in turn
By sundry others, whence I will select
A portion, living pictures to embody
This pleasing argument.

[*Prel*, p. 623]

Most interesting for my purposes is that the experiences analogous to Snowdon relate to the contemplation of human suffering.

A rainbow above Coniston Lake provides the second "living picture" to advance the "pleasing argument":

It was a day
Upon the edge of Autumn, fierce with storm;

[13]See Richard Schell, "Wordsworth's Revisions of the Ascent of Snowdon," *Philological Quarterly* 54 (1975), 592–603, for a significant discussion of the episode's original context in MS. W. I am in general agreement with Schell's claim that in MS. A, "Wordsworth took what had been a long and somewhat discursive celebration of the powers of Nature, and made from it a 'meditation' dealing almost exclusively with the powers of the mind."

The wind blew through the hills of Coniston
Compress'd as in a tunnel, from the lake
Bodies of foam took flight, and the whole vale
Was wrought into commotion high and low—
Mist flying up and down, bewilder'd showers,
Ten thousand thousand waves, mountains and crags,
And darkness, and the sun's tumultuous light.
Green leaves were rent in handfuls from the trees,
The mountains all seem'd silent, din so near
Pealed in the traveller's ear, the clouds [?]
The horse and rider stagger'd in the blast,
And he who look'd upon the stormy lake
Had fear for boat or vessel where none was.
Meanwhile, by what strange chance I cannot tell,
What combination of the wind and clouds,
A large unmutilate[d] rainbow stood
Immoveable in heav'n, kept standing there
With a colossal stride bridging the vale,
The substance thin as dreams, lovelier than day,—
Amid the deafening uproar stood unmov'd,
Sustain'd itself through many minutes space.

[*Prel*, p. 623–624]

Nature, like the mind of man, creates permanence in a sea of flux. It blends undifferentiable plurality into oneness; the "commotion" of the vale and its "ten thousand thousand waves, mountains, and crags" focus in the "immoveable" rainbow. The resultant picture contains the first suggestion that the contemplation of suffering is linked to the sublime of Snowdon. As the traveler experiences the turbulence of the storm, he creates a fiction of human misery, fearing "for boat or vessel where none was." No one has ventured out in such weather, yet the mind fabricates the occasion for tragic emotion by hypothesizing "*what if* a boat were out on the lake?" This thought looks back to the opening lines of *De rerum natura*, Book II, and the ambiguous pleasure of watching a ship sink from the vantage of safety. In this case, there is not even a shipwreck, but the fancy must create one.

The third illustration of the "analogy betwixt / The mind of man and nature" is yet more closely connected to pathos:

> One evening, walking in the public way,
> A Peasant of the valley where I dwelt
> Being my chance Companion, he stopp'd short
> And pointed to an object full in view
> At a small distance. 'Twas a horse, that stood
> Alone upon a little breast of ground
> With a clear silver moonlight sky behind.
> With one leg from the ground the creature stood
> Insensible and still,—breath, motion gone,
> Hairs, colour, all but shape and substance gone,
> Mane, ears, and tail, as lifeless as the trunk
> That had no stir of breath; we paused awhile
> In pleasure of the sight, and left him there
> With all his functions silently sealed up,
> Like an amphibious work of Nature's hand,
> A Borderer dwelling betwixt life and death,
> A living Statue or a statued Life.
>
> [*Prel,* p. 624]

If the poet did not say as much, one should not have thought a sleeping horse much like the view from Snowdon. In both experiences, however, Wordsworth wants to establish a creative power outside himself. The peasant, who is the poet's "chance companion," ratifies the perception of external creation; he is no poet, but one of those "grossest minds" who "see and hear / And cannot chuse but feel." The peasant's naive sensitivity to nature's art creates a community of feeling. "We," not the usual Wordsworthian "I," take "pleasure of the sight." The nature of the pleasure, however, is rather problematic, deriving from the mind's play upon a body that appears dead but that is known to be alive. The words describing the horse attach to a corpse: "insensible and still,—breath, motion gone," "all but shape and substance gone," "all his functions silently sealed up." Nonetheless, the horse is only a "Borderer dwelling betwixt life and death." The disjunction between appearance and reality makes it an object of interest and pleasure where a dead horse would obviously be neither.

Jonathan Wordsworth has astutely linked the sleeping horse of MS. W with other "borderers" in Wordsworth's poetry, most notably the Old Man Travelling, the Cumberland Beggar, and the Leech-Gatherer.[14] He might well have added the Discharged Soldier. The "pleasure of the sight" afforded by the horse is like the ambiguous pleasure of scanning the suffering veteran. The fact that animal existence, not human decrepitude, provides the energy here reflects the movement of Wordsworth's poetry away from his earlier modes of imagination. This horse functions like the fisherman of "Point Rash-Judgment" or any other of Wordsworth's old men, but its lack of humanity and its apparent health remove the pleasure from suspicions of sympathetic ghoulishness.

The description of the horse occasions a transition from natural scenes to human suffering:

> To these appearances which Nature thrusts
> Upon our notice, her own naked work
> Self-wrought, unaided by the human mind,
> Add others more imperious; those I mean
> Which on our sight she forces, calling man
> To give new grandeur to her ministry,
> Man suffering or enjoying. Meanest minds
> Want not these monuments, though overlook'd
> Or little prized; and books are full of them,—
> Such power,—to pass at once from daily life
> And our inevitable sympathy
> With passions mingled up before our eyes,—
> Such presence is acknowledg'd, when we trace
> The history of Columbus
>
> [pp. 624–625]

The sight of "Man suffering or enjoying" is "more imperious" yet still analogous to the view from Snowdon. The "grandeur" of

---

[14]Jonathan Wordsworth, "William Wordsworth 1770–1969," *Proceedings of the British Academy* 55 (1969), 211–228.

pathos is even more striking than natural sublimity. As in *The Pedlar*, "sympathy with man" makes one alive to all that is enjoyed and all that is endured. In MS. W, however, Wordsworth turns aside from the direct contemplation of suffering—he passes "at once from daily life" and "passions mingled up before our eyes." A painful pressure from within causes him to grasp instances that have come to his knowledge through the medium of print. "Books are full of them," and, we know from Wordsworth's earlier poetry, so is daily life. Yet, in this putative conclusion to *The Prelude*, the instances that call forth the "inevitable sympathy" are all from books.

No longer does the poet's mind circle around personal images of suffering or create stories to fill objects with meaning. The pathos of MS. W is laboriously culled from travel literature. It is suffering in which Wordsworth's imagination has little creative part except that of the involved reader. In passing the pathos of daily life, Wordsworth chooses to present an exotic, and finally unsuccessful, series of anecdotes about famous explorers: Columbus sees the compass needle change its direction, Gilbert drowns in the Arctic, Park wanders the Sahara, and Dampier has a religious conversion while crossing the Indian Ocean. Each episode points to the reader's status as interested observer: "we trace / The history of Columbus," "Like spectacle / Doth that Land Traveller, living yet, appear / To the mind's eye," "Kindred power / Is with us, in the suffering of that time" (pp. 625–627). Nonetheless, the analogy to Snowdon has become diffuse and exists solely in the impressive "power" shared by natural sublimity and human suffering; both are external influences which "even the grossest minds must see."

Of the four episodes, only the death of Gilbert offers a truly pathetic event:

> Such object doth present
> To those who read the story at their ease,
> Sir Humphrey Gilbert, that bold voyager,
> When after one disastrous wreck he took
> His station in the pinnace, for the sake

Of Honour and his Crew's encouragement;
And they who followed in the second ship,
The larger Brigantine which he had left,
Beheld him while amid the storm he sate
Upon the open deck of his small bark
In calmness, with a book upon his knee—
To use the language of the Chronicle,
'A Soldier of Christ Jesus undismay'd,'—
The ship and he a moment afterwards
Engulph'd and seen no more.

[pp. 625–626]

Gilbert sitting "In calmness, with a book upon his knee" provides an admonitory mirror for "those who read the story at their ease." This reflection suggests an equality of reader and victim not to be found earlier in Wordsworth. When he previously brought the reader into the poem, it had been by means of a figure such as the narrator of *The Ruined Cottage* or "you" in *The Thorn*, an observer of, not participant in, the suffering. The Lucretian paradigm of watching the shipwreck from a safe vantage, too, breaks down. Here we see the tragedy from the viewpoint of men in an only slightly less precarious situation. We see only what those in the brigantine had beheld, and for them, there could be no self-congratulation at being free from danger. For Wordsworth, "calmness" no longer describes cathartic response, but the tranquillity of the stoic hero, whose self-control and sense of duty triumph even in extremity. The element of Christian consolation, too, is new in Wordsworthian pathos.

Elsewhere in MS. W, Wordsworth also uses books to mediate between himself and human suffering. "The Drowned Man of Esthwaite" from the two-part *Prelude* appears accompanied by a commentary that replaces the earlier "I might advert / To numerous accidents of flood or field":

At length, the dead Man 'mid that beauteous scene
Of trees & hills & water bolt upright
Rose with his ghastly face; a spectre shape
Of terror even! & yet no vulgar fear

Possess'd me for my inner eye had seen
Such sights before, among the shining streams
Of Fayery Land & forests of romance:
Thence came a spirit hallowing what I saw
With decoration & ideal grace
A dignity & smoothness, like the works
Of Grecian art & purest Poesy.[15]

No longer is it a question of suffering encouraging the "growth of mental power / And love of Nature's works." In 1804 the drowned man has become "a spectre shape / Of terror," and Wordsworth finds it necessary to assert control over the nightmare images of his childhood. In grotesque, if unconscious, parody of the vision of the sleeping horse, he creates a "statued Death" out of the drowned man. The terms used to describe the corpse, "decoration," "ideal grace," "dignity," "smoothness," are those of neoclassical aesthetics. Books of "purest Poesy" and "romance" create a shelter from the horror. It is not the child, however, who needs refuge from the sublime of human suffering, but the adult poet of 1804. In his later years, Wordsworth recoils not so much from the fact of suffering, as from his earlier imaginative reliance upon it. The "spectre shape of terror," in some sense, is the realization of his earlier dalliance with human misery. As we have seen, such a dalliance forms the core of Wordsworth's fictional enterprise; his stories are virtually all concerned with "man suffering."

Thus, in material that was to have closed the five-book *Prelude*, Wordsworth distances imaginative activity based on human suffering; at the same time he retains a place for such activity in his fable of mental growth. It is, clearly, a troubled compromise: the lines on the explorers are quickly discarded, and the poet finds it necessary or desirable to discuss, yet another time, the issues of fictional suffering—in *Prelude* VIII, "Love of Nature Leading to Love of Mankind."

[15]My text here is from *Prelude* MS. W, DC MS. 38.

IV

The primary subject of *Prelude* VIII is the poet's relation to human existence outside himself. How we feel, think, and dream about our fellow man is the central focus of this book whose title only suggests the complexity and peculiarity of Wordsworth's argument. Much of Book VIII is, of course, related only peripherally to the imagination's use of pathos; such sections as those describing Helvellyn fair, childhood memories of shepherds in the mist, Theocritan and Spenserian pastoral, and the homely tasks of Cumbrian shepherds, however, do explore the relationship between observer (poet and reader) and the observed (the human subject of the poem). The Helvellyn fair may serve as a paradigm:

> It is a summer festival, a Fair,
> Such as, on this side now, and now on that,
> Repeated through his tributary Vales,
> Helvellyn, in the silence of his rest,
> Sees annually, if storms be not abroad,
> And mists have left him an unshrouded head.
> Delightful day it is for all who dwell
> In this secluded Glen, and eagerly
> They give it welcome. Long ere heat of noon
> Behold the cattle are driven down; the sheep
> That have for traffic been cull'd out are penn'd
> In cotes that stand together on the Plain
> Ranged side by side; the chaffering is begun.
>
> [*Prel* VIII: 10–22]

An itemization of the populace follows: "a lame Man, or a blind," an "aged woman," "the Showman," a "Mountebank," "some sweet Lass of the Valley" selling fruit, and so forth. The critical transition is that between "Helvellyn . . . sees" and "(you) Behold." The animist fiction turns out to be a disguise for the author and reader peeping down upon the quaintly rustic "summer festival."

This separation between observer and observed, characteristic of Wordsworth's poetry generally, is particularly marked in *Pre-*

lude VIII as Wordsworth attempts to come to terms with human otherness. The central desire is to establish a significant, yet not exploitative, relationship between himself and the human subjects of his poetry. This need springs from the previous book, "Residence in London," where the city's imaginative and spiritual poverty all but engulf the shaping power of imagination. Book VII's concluding image, the freak-show at Bartholomew Fair, is synecdochic of London's "blank confusion":

> a type not false
> Of what the mighty City is itself
> To all except a Straggler here and there,
> To the whole Swarm of its inhabitants;
> An undistinguishable world to men,
> The slaves unrespited of low pursuits,
> Living amid the same perpetual flow
> Of trivial objects, melted and reduced
> To one identity, by differences
> That have no law, no meaning, and no end
> [*Prel* VII: 695–704]

Book VIII struggles against the perception of human insignificance and wretchedness; Wordsworth's revulsion from "those loathesome sights / Of wretchedness and vice" (ll. 65–66) is never far from the surface of the poetry.[16] The effort is to create a human otherness unlike London's uncontrollable plurality, to locate a fixed "point" (VIII: 457) in the perpetual flow of trivial

---

[16]In *The Limits of Mortality* (Middletown: Wesleyan University Press, 1959), David Ferry argues that the misanthropy apparent in *Prelude* VII, "The Gypsies," "Personal Talk," and elsewhere, reflects Wordsworth's impatient disgust with mere humanity: "His genius was his enmity to man, which he mistook for love, and his mistake led him into confusions which he could not bear" (p. 173). Ferry ingeniously links this hatred of man to the mystic's desire for transcendental experience and presents a Wordsworth for whom hatred of nature leads to hatred of man. It seems to me, however, that it is the multiplicity of London that troubles Wordsworth's rage for order rather than any metaphysical anxieties about human limitation. The London of Book VII is the symbol of human activity and suffering on a scale that defies the desire of the poet to comprehend it. Such multiplicity must particularly trouble a poet, like Wordsworth or Whitman, who has taken upon himself to encompass in his work all man, nature, and human life.

objects. Wordsworth claims to find some such appropriate human center in the childhood memories of shepherds. Whatever the merits of the primary argument,[17] the search for a love-worthy humanity leads Wordsworth to reconsider the relation of his imagination to suffering. Radical questions about the human object of imagination, for Wordsworth, necessitate discussion of the poetic exploitation of suffering. In *Prelude* VIII, this discussion presents itself as a progress of the imagination's relation to human misery from early childhood.

The first encounter with the power of suffering occurs as the boy hears stories at Ann Tyson's knees:

> But images of danger and distress,
> And suffering, these took deepest hold of me,
> Man suffering among awful Powers, and Forms;
> Of this I heard and saw enough to make
> The imagination restless; nor was free
> Myself from frequent perils; nor were tales
> Wanting, the tragedies of former times,
> Or hazards and escapes, which in my walks
> I carried with me among crags and woods
> And mountains; and of these may here be told
> One, as recorded by my Household Dame.
>
> [*Prel* VIII: 211–221]

These lines reprise those regarding "the tragic facts of rural history" in the two-part *Prelude*. Significant differences between the two passages, however, reflect the change in Wordsworth's attitude between 1799 and 1804. In the earlier passage, "tragic facts" impress the mind with "images" of suffering, to which the associative faculty attaches "far other feelings" and creates "forms" quite different from the original "archetypes"; these images and forms foster "the growth of mental power / And love of Nature's works." Sympathy with man leads to love of nature.

---

[17]I am inclined to agree with Raymond D. Havens, *The Mind of a Poet* (Baltimore: Johns Hopkins University Press, 1941) that Book VIII is "a conspicuous illustration of Wordsworth's fondness for attributing to the influence of nature qualities with which it has little or nothing to do" (p. 108).

In *Prelude* VIII, Wordsworth makes no such confident assertions about the mind's powers. Nature takes the initiative, leading the child to some ambiguous love of man. "Forms" are not the creation of the child's imagination but segments of external nature pressing in upon him. The effect of such forms is trivial beside the grand claim that "there are in our existence spots of time." The imagination is merely made "restless," and by 1804, Wordsworth feels considerable ambivalence toward such internal turmoil.

The "Matron's Tale," though not among Wordsworth's most successful narratives, tells much about the direction of his thought. Given the introductory remarks about "man suffering" and "the tragedies of former times," we might expect the subsequent story to be unhappy in its outcome. Instead, after the tantalizing reference to the "Brothers-water, named / From those two Brothers that were drown'd therein" (ll. 231–232), Wordsworth describes the search by a shepherd and his son for a lost sheep. In the course of the tale, the child becomes trapped on an island in a rising stream; but all turns out well when the father rescues him. As if the poet realized that his introductory remarks demanded a corpse, the sheep, rather gratuitously, is turned sacrificial lamb, "borne headlong by the roaring flood" (l. 282). In earlier works, "Simon Lee" and "The Idiot Boy," we have seen Wordsworth play upon the reader's expectations of pathos, but evidently in Book VIII the story itself is meant to make the imagination restless. With an explicitness rare in his great poetry, Wordsworth insists, regarding the boy on the island: "The sight was such as no one could have seen / Without distress and fear" (ll. 307–308). Tragic emotions are called forth in the service of tragicomedy. Abbie Potts has speculated that the "Matron's Tale" is a version of man's relation to God the Redeemer, but Lindenberger seems closer to the mark in speaking of Wordsworth's "habit of skirting the tragic."[18] The poet who

---

[18] Abbie Potts, *Wordsworth's "Prelude"* (Ithaca, N.Y.: Cornell University Press, 1953), p. 330; Herbert Lindenberger, *On Wordsworth's "Prelude"* (Princeton: Princeton University Press, 1963), p. 247.

had earlier deemphasized the moving accident eliminates it entirely or, rather, substitutes an equally artificial but optimistic coincidence.

In the first stage of the child's relation to suffering, the tale comes from outside him, and he is in no way responsible for it. In the second, however, he is both creator and audience of pathetic fantasies:

> But when that first poetic Faculty
> Of plain imagination and severe,
> No longer a mute Influence of the soul,
> An Element of the nature's inner self,
> Began to have some promptings to put on
> A visible shape, and to the works of art,
> The notions and the images of books
> Did knowingly conform itself, by these
> Enflamed, and proud of that her new delight,
> There came among those shapes of human life
> A wilfulness of fancy and conceit
> Which gave them new importance to the mind;
> And Nature and her objects beautified
> These fictions, as in some sort in their turn
> They burnish'd her. From touch of this new power
> Nothing was safe: the Elder-tree that grew
> Beside the well-known Charnel-house had then
> A dismal look; the Yew-Tree had its Ghost,
> That took its station there for ornament:
> Then common death was none, common mishap,
> But matter for this humour everywhere,
> The tragic super-tragic, else left short.
> Then, if a Widow, staggering with the blow
> Of her distress, was known to have made her way
> To the cold grave in which her Husband slept,
> One night, or haply more than one, through pain
> Or half-insensate impotence of mind
> The fact was caught at greedily, and there
> She was a Visitant the whole year through,
> Wetting the turf with never-ending tears,
> And all the storms of Heaven must beat on her.
>
> [ll. 511–541]

This passage fulfills Wordsworth's promise, at the end of MS. M, to speak of "an abasement in my mind / Not altogether wrought without the help / Of Books ill-chosen." The "notions and the images of books" here provide the archetypes of suffering which lead the imagination astray. In general, this passage has been taken to represent Wordsworth's rejection of his early poetry. The yew-tree ghost is a figure out of *The Vale of Esthwaite*, and the widow resembles a beggar woman in *The Borderers*, who paces at midnight in a churchyard "upon the self-same spot, . . . round and round" (*PW*, I, 143).[19]

Wordsworth's attack, however, is not solely upon the lurid sentimentalism of his youth. The description of his childish ways calls into question any literary interest in pathetic materials. The fall from imaginative grace occurs simultaneously with the effort to think up stories based on suffering. The "poetic faculty" remains pure only so long as it is "mute" and "inner." The "promptings to put on visible shape," to imagine stories about people, constitute the original artistic sin. The power of pathetic fancy distorts the truth of life. Nothing is safe from it; the mind fastens onto "common mishaps," gives them exaggerated importance by brooding obsessively upon them, and thereby makes the tragic "super-tragic." The model of story-making decried is, in fact, the characteristic form of Wordsworthian pathos. Catching greedily at facts lies at the center of the *Lyrical Ballads*: the "impressive" thorn, James Bowman's staff on the cliff-face, Michael's sheepfold, the four trees at Hart-leap Well are the realities on which imagination feeds and from which tales of human suffering radiate. As Wordsworth renounces the interplay of nature and pathetic fiction, he renounces his own past

[19] In *The Making of Wordsworth's Poetry* (Cambridge: Harvard University Press, 1973), Paul Sheats traces the ghost's previous disincarnation (p. 27). Jonathan Wordsworth and Mary Jacobus have found the sentimental model of the woman in the churchyard in Blair's *The Grave*: "The new-made *Widow* too, I've sometimes spy'd, / Sad sight! slow moving o'er the prostrate Dead"; *The Music of Humanity* (New York: Harper & Row, 1969), pp. 60–61, and *Tradition and Experiment in Wordsworth's "Lyrical Ballads" (1798)* (Oxford: Clarendon, 1976), p. 141.

practice. The guilty art from which he distances himself had provided the exquisite meshing of Margaret and her garden, the drowned man and the calm lake.

As Wordsworth's criticism of pathetic fictions continues, he denies the power of objects to present "some sweet and tender lesson to our minds / Of human suffering." Such stories belong only to the corruption of our wanton imaginations:

> Through wild obliquities could I pursue
> Among all objects of the fields and groves
> These cravings; when the Foxglove, one by one,
> Upwards through every stage of its tall stem,
> Had shed its bells, and stood by the wayside
> Dismantled, with a single one, perhaps,
> Left at the ladder's top, with which the Plant
> Appeared to stoop, as slender blades of grass
> Tipp'd with a bead of rain or dew, behold!
> If such a sight were seen, would Fancy bring
> Some Vagrant thither with her Babes, and seat her
> Upon the turf beneath the stately Flower
> Drooping in sympathy, and making so
> A melancholy Crest above the head
> Of the lorn Creature, while her Little-Ones,
> All unconcerned with her unhappy plight,
> Were sporting with the purple cups that lay
> Scatter'd upon the ground.
>
> [ll. 542–559]

Any object is available to pathetic whimsy if willful fancy so desires. The vagrant family suggested by the flower apparently alludes to the similar family in *An Evening Walk*.[20] In that scene, the pathos had been lurid, the effects unsubtle:

> Oft has she taught them on her lap to play
> Delighted, with the glow-worm's harmless ray
> Toss'd light from hand to hand; while on the ground
> Small circles of green radiance gleam around.
> Oh! when the bitter showers her path assail,

[20]Jacobus, *Tradition and Experiment*, pp. 134–135.

And roars between the hills the torrent gale,
—No more her breath can thaw their fingers cold,
Their frozen arms her neck no more can fold.

[ll. 275–282]

Understandably, Wordsworth wishes to distance himself from such embarrassing crudity. It is, however, not merely gross sentimentalism that he calls into question. The entire enterprise of making up stories about human suffering becomes doubtful. Wordsworth's most understated "tale of silent suffering" began, after all, as a "wild obliquity" from an object transmuted by imaginative craving. "A broken pane which glittered in the moon" (*PW*, I, 314) provides the germ from which the story of Margaret grows.[21] The "sympathy" of man and nature mocked in *Prelude* VIII is a primary theme of the poetry of 1798, particularly *The Ruined Cottage*, where the Pedlar claims to "feel one sadness" with the waters of the spring. In describing the leap from object to pathetic fiction, the poet digresses to include an image recalling the Pedlar's meditation on Margaret's suffering. The "slender blades of grass / Tipp'd with a bead of rain or dew" bring to mind the delicate artistry of "the high spear-grass on that wall, / By mist and silent rain-drops silver'd o'er." The allusion exposes and subverts the visionary moment as mere imaginative wantonness.

Thus, Wordsworth describes the second stage of the imagination's relationship to suffering, in such a way as to place firmly in his past the "adulterate Power" that plays willfully "among the shapes of human life." His tone belongs to one rising on stepping stones of his dead self; his apology for youthful foibles is ingenuous:

> Where the harm,
> If, when the Woodman languish'd with disease
> From sleeping night by night among the woods
> Within his sod-built Cabin, Indian-wise,

---

[21]See Hartman, *Wordsworth's Poetry*, pp. 136–137.

> I call'd the pangs of disappointed love
> And all the long Etcetera of such thought
> To help him to his grave? Meanwhile the Man,
> If not already from the woods retir'd
> To die at home, was haply, as I knew,
> Pining alone among the gentle airs,
> Birds, running Streams, and Hills so beautiful
> On golden evenings, while the charcoal Pile
> Breath'd up its smoke, an image of his ghost
> Or spirit that was soon to take its flight.
>
> [ll. 610-623]

Such "calling," whether of the "pangs of disappointed love" or
other interesting complications, is the essence of fiction. The
maker of stories does not care what the facts are, except insofar
as he exploits them and transmutes them. Wordsworth trivializes
the process and dismisses it contemptuously as the "long Etcet-
era of such thought." Even so, his mind is not content to rest
long with the bare facts. Against the hackneyed fiction of disappointed love, he raises an oddly ambiguous truth. Two possibilities are presented: either the man has "retir'd to die at
home" or he is "pining alone" among the beauties of nature.
"Haply, as I knew" is close to being oxymoronic; one either
knows or does not. "Haply" leaves room for speculation and
fantasy, and indeed, the mind turns quickly to fiction. The ordinary charcoal smoke becomes an "image" of the woodcutter's
ghost.

A third stage in the poet's imagination of human suffering
follows, "a time of greater dignity . . . in which / The pulse of
Being everywhere was felt" (ll. 624-627). In his new condition,
the poet approaches the cities of man, Cambridge and London,
and has "temporal shapes / Of vice and folly thrust" upon his
view (ll. 642-643). The new response to human suffering is a
version of the sublime:

> This notwithstanding, being brought more near
> As I was now, to guilt and wretchedness,
> I trembled, thought of human life at times

> With an indefinite terror and dismay
> Such as the storms and angry elements
> Had bred in me, but gloomier far, a dim
> Analogy to uproar and misrule,
> Disquiet, danger, and obscurity.
>
> [ll. 657–664]

Terror, disquiet, danger, and obscurity are qualities associated with Burkean sublimity. Though the sublime treats of powerful emotions and uncertainties, it at least provides a label or concept to stabilize and domesticate ungovernable multiplicity and the pressure of other people's suffering. By placing the myriad turbulence of human life in a familiar, defined, and therefore less threatening context, Wordsworth makes the City appear less overwhelming than in Book VII. He now can say, "London! to thee I willingly return" (l. 679).

Wordsworth chooses the moment of his first entry into London to define his relations with the human sublime:

> At length I did unto myself first seem
> To enter the great City. On the roof
> Of an itinerant Vehicle I sate
> With vulgar Men about me, vulgar forms
> Of houses, pavements, streets, of men and things,
> Mean shapes on every side: but, at the time,
> When to myself it fairly might be said,
> The very moment that I seem'd to know
> The threshold now is overpass'd, Great God!
> That aught *external* to the living mind
> Should have such mighty sway! yet so it was
> A weight of Ages did at once descend
> Upon my heart; no thought embodied, no
> Distinct remembrances; but weight and power,
> Power growing with the weight: alas! I feel
> That I am trifling: 'twas a moment's pause.
> All that took place within me, came and went
> As in a moment, and I only now
> Remember that it was a thing divine.
>
> [ll. 692–710]

The superfluity of exclamation, the awkward admission that "I feel / That I am trifling," the repetitive emphasis on "the very moment" suggest a man laboring for structure and meaning. Wordsworth knows his first encounter with the city ought to have had the significance of a spot of time. Looking back, however, he barely can distinguish when he "seemed to know" that he had entered the city, much less recall any substantial images. Despite his attempt to draw something from the well of memory, he can find "no thought embodied, no / Distinct remembrances" among the "vulgar forms" of the city. The only possible assertion is that he felt "weight and power," a phrase which ambivalently invokes both the negative and positive effects of sublimity, oppression as well as that power whose "hiding places" *The Prelude* seeks to discover.

Having reached a dead end of assertion unparticularized by distinct images, Wordsworth inserts an epic simile:

> As when a Traveller hath from open day
> With torches pass'd into some Vault of Earth,
> The Grotto of Antiparos, or the Den
> Of Yordas among Craven's mountain tracts;
> He looks and sees the cavern spread and grow,
> Widening itself on all sides, sees, or thinks
> He sees, erelong, the roof above his head,
> Which instantly unsettles and recedes
> Substance and shadow, light and darkness, all
> Commingled, making up a Canopy
> Of Shapes and Forms and Tendencies to Shape
> That shift and vanish, change and interchange
> Like Spectres, ferment quiet and sublime;
> Which, after a short space, works less and less,
> Till every effort, every motion gone,
> The scene before him lies in perfect view,
> Exposed and lifeless, as a written book.

[ll. 711–727]

According to Reed, in *Prelude* MS. WW the earliest drafts toward this passage are enmeshed in "Simplon Pass" material.[22]

[22]Reed *MY*, pp. 641–642.

The simile of the traveler entering the cave appears between "*we had crossed the Alps*" (*Prel* VI: 524) and "Imagination! lifting up itself" (525). Thus, in the original context, the "shapes . . . that shift and vanish" describe a response to natural sublimity equivalent, or alternative, to the "Power" that comes athwart the poet's song in *Prelude* VI. The dislocation brought on by London is apparently analogous to losing one's way in the Alps, and "a ferment quiet and sublime" takes place in the mind as it attempts to reconstitute a world of meaningful images.

In this context, "blank confusion" becomes positive. The cavern "spreads and grows," light and dark "commingle," ferment "works." Wordsworth characteristically links such verbs to poetic power. Only when things are in focus, "in perfect view," is the scene "Exposed and lifeless, as a written book." Imaginative process is preferred to its product. The cave simile emphasizes the extent to which things of the mind do not stay put:

> But let him pause awhile, and look again
> And a new quickening shall succeed, at first
> Beginning timidly, then creeping fast
> Through all which he beholds; the senseless mass,
> In its projections, wrinkles, cavities,
> Through all its surface, with all colours streaming,
> Like a magician's airy pageant, parts,
> Unites, embodying everywhere some pressure
> Or image, recognis'd or new, some type
> Or picture of the world; forests and lakes,
> Ships, Rivers, Towers, the Warrior clad in Mail,
> The prancing Steed, the Pilgrim with his Staff,
> The mitred Bishop and the throned King,
> A Spectacle to which there is no end.
>
> [ll. 728–741]

All of this activity is located in the observer. Reality, despite its various shapes and colors, is "senseless." The imagination "parts" and "unites" the mass of things, just as in Coleridge it "dissolves, diffuses, dissipates, in order to recreate" (*BL*, I, 202). And, again, the direction of imagination is toward fictions. From the uncertainty of the cave's twilight, it creates a "type / Or picture of the world" and allows itself to embody "A Spectacle to which there is no end." The process of mind is not unlike the child's indulgence in fantasies of suffering: turning a foxglove into "some Vagrant" with her babes is perhaps less different from transforming a stalagmite into a mitred bishop than Wordsworth would believe. The cave simile, however, allows him to be temporarily comfortable with fiction. That the spectacle is only a dream, for the moment, hardly matters.

The concept of sublimity provides structure for what had been only confusion and horror in Book VII:

> With strong Sensations, teeming as it did
> Of past and present, such a place must needs
> Have pleas'd me, in those times; I sought not then
> Knowledge; but craved for power, and power I found
> In all things; nothing had a circumscribed
> And narrow influence; but all objects, being
> Themselves capacious, also found in me
> Capaciousness and amplitude of mind
>
> [*Prel* VIII: 752-759]

The appetite for power is less worthy than the search for knowledge, and Wordsworth distances his present self from what he had been "in those times." One would hardly have imputed such a craving to the poet in *Prelude* VII, however; there the problem was simply one of being overwhelmed. By ingenuously acknowledging his past cravings for power, Wordsworth asserts the possibility that he had, and therefore may still have, "capaciousness and amplitude of mind." Thus, he can find in London, not confusion and meaninglessness, but a sublimity like that of nature:

>   a sense
> Of what had been here done, and suffer'd here
> Through ages, and was doing, suffering, still
> Weigh'd with me, could support the test of thought,
> Was like the enduring majesty and power
> Of independent nature; and not seldom

Even individual remembrances,
By working on the Shapes before my eyes,
Became like vital functions of the soul;
And out of what had been, what was, the place
Was throng'd with impregnations, like those wilds
In which my early feelings had been nurs'd,
And naked valleys, full of caverns, rocks,
And audible seclusions, dashing lakes,
Echoes and Waterfalls, and pointed crags
That into music touch the passing wind.

[ll. 781–796]

Earlier the poet had found "no thought embodied, no / Distinct remembrances" (ll. 704–705); he now claims, however, to possess "individual remembrances" and a "sense" that can "support the test of thought." The weight of suffering is unambiguously the source of power. It is noteworthy how the language of the two-part *Prelude* has once again been usurped. There, "forms which yet exist with independent life" had tended to "the growth of mental power / And love of Nature"; the spots of time, the mind's encounter with suffering, possessed a "fructifying virtue." In *Prelude* VIII, reproduction and re-creation are also suggested, by the "impregnations" available from both nature and human suffering; nature is primary, however, providing the analogy that grounds the contemplation of suffering. The experience of natural sublimity makes the sublimity of suffering comprehensible, bearable, and morally innocent. "Individual remembrances" working on present "shapes" describe a process opposite to that of the mind attaching present "feelings" to, and creating new "forms" upon, the "archetype" of original experience. In 1799, the mind works with the power of suffering; in 1804, power works on the mind.

The description of the London experience becomes, finally, indistinguishable from the natural sublime:

When from that awful prospect overcast
And in eclipse, my meditations turn'd,
Lo! Everything that was indeed divine

> Retain'd its purity inviolate
> And unencroach'd upon, nay seem'd brighter far
> For this deep shade in counterview, that gloom
> Of opposition . . .
>
> [ll. 811–817]

The crucial moment, as always in Wordsworth, is when the mind "turns." The word describing the dislocation of experience is the biblical "Lo!" In this case, however, the poet looks up to see, not a moon "naked in the Heavens" (*Prel* XIII:41), but the "purity inviolate" of human nature. As in "The Climbing of Snowdon" and "Crossing the Alps," there is a play between "the darkness and the light" (*Prel* VI: 567), the "brighter" purity and "the gloom of opposition." An exalted vision of humanity is, therefore, held equivalent as a sublime object to the Alpine gorge or the moon standing over a sea of mist. In order to illustrate further his sense of human sublimity, Wordsworth refers to a moment in *Paradise Lost* which partakes both of natural sublimity and of the knowledge of suffering:

> . . . that gloom
> Of opposition, such as shew'd itself
> To the eyes of Adam, yet in Paradise,
> Though fallen from bliss, when in the East he saw
> Darkness ere day's mid course, and morning light
> More orient in the western cloud, that drew
> "O'er the blue firmament a radiant white,
> Descending slow with something heavenly fraught."
>
> [*Prel* VIII: 816–823]

Wordsworth's quotation from Milton is, in fact, longer than the text indicates. Lines 820–823 are virtually identical to *Paradise Lost* XI: 204–207.[23] The moment that Wordsworth cites, in Mil-

---

[23]The only differences, besides those of tense and typography, are "the" substituted for "yon" (l. 821), and "Descending slow" for "And slow descends" (l. 823). In "Wordsworth's Marginalia on *Paradise Lost*," *Bulletin of the New York Public Library* 73 (1969), 177, Bishop C. Hunt presents Wordsworth's comment on the passage from Milton: "It may however be observed that Gray in making his bards vanish in a bright track instead of a murky cloud has given his picture

ton's version of history, is man's original experience of sublime dislocation in terrestrial nature. The lines spoken by Adam describe the approach of the Archangel Michael on his errand to expel man from the garden. For Adam, the morning brightness in the west represents an ominous disjunction of nature. The apparent subversion of natural order, as we have seen, is at the heart of the Wordsworthian sublime; time and again, whether in a striding mountain, wheeling heavens and earth, or woods decaying, never to be decayed, the suspension of belief in ordinary nature brings a sense of the power and mystery of life. In *Paradise Lost*, this original sublime experience is connected to the fall of man and subsequent human suffering. Michael is coming to show Adam the sorrowful future of fallen man. The vision he brings to Adam, in fact, while darker, is much like that universal "misery forced upon my sight" in *Prelude* VII and VIII. London is Wordsworth's version of the "Cities of Man." In a sense, too, Wordsworth, fresh from his childhood experiences, is like Adam, "yet in Paradise, though fallen from bliss."

The human sublime, like the natural, reaches consummation with "the extinction of the comparing power of the mind, & in intense unity" (*Prose*, II, 356):

> Add also, that among the multitudes
> Of that great City, oftentimes was seen
> Affectingly set forth, more than elsewhere
> Is possible, the unity of man,
> One spirit over ignorance and vice
> Predominant, in good and evil hearts
> One sense for moral judgements, as one eye
> For the sun's light.
>
> [ll. 824–831]

---

too much sameness and lost that contrast which is so striking in Milton's." For Wordsworth, Gray's description of bards disappearing "In yon bright track, that fires the western skies," is not sublime because the passage possesses neither distinct "individual forms" nor "that state of opposition & yet reconcilement" which forms "the highest state of sublimity" (*Prose*, II, 351, 357).

The many collapses into the one, as Wordsworth finds in London the image of mankind's unity. The ambivalence of his attitude toward the sublime unity of human masses is evident when we compare this assertion to the passage that opened my discussion of Book VIII:

> An undistinguishable world to men,
> The slaves unrespited of low pursuits,
> Living amid the same perpetual flow
> Of trivial objects, melted and reduced
> To one identity, by differences
> That have no law, no meaning, and no end
>
> [*Prel* VII: 699–704]

In one passage the "unity of man" is expansive and positive, in the other, "one identity" results in a world without law, meaning, or purpose. The first attitude, however, slides easily into the other, according to whether "oneness" seems good or bad.

Thus, the progress of the imagination's relation with suffering described in *Prelude* VIII is tenuous at best. The conclusions are precariously close to the starting point. Wordsworth's determined optimism places a positive construction on the final sense of unity, but the asserted progress looks distinctly like a dilemma. In the face of paradox, however, the poet stands his ground. The final reference to the pleasures of tragedy in *The Prelude* still asserts the positive nature of the contemplation of suffering, but places the possibility of such radical innocence safely in the future:

> thus haply shall I teach,
> Inspire, through unadulterated ears
> Pour rapture, tenderness, and hope, my theme
> No other than the very heart of man
> As found among the best of those who live
> Not unexalted by religious hope,
> Nor uninformed by books, good books though few,
> In Nature's presence: thence may I select
> Sorrow that is not sorrow, but delight,
> And miserable love that is not pain

To hear of, for the glory that redounds
Therefrom to human kind and what we are.
Be mine to follow with no timid step
Where knowledge leads me

[*Prel* XII: 237–250]

The project that is going to accomplish these things is *The Recluse*. In that unwriteable poem, the problems of imaginative dependence on pathos will be resolved. There, Wordsworth will find "good books though few" which will not enflame the "wilfulness of fancy and conceit." There, soothing thoughts will indeed spring out of human suffering.

Epilogue

> We will grieve not, rather find
> Strength in what remains behind;
> In the primal sympathy
> Which having been must ever be;
> In the soothing thoughts that spring
> Out of human suffering;
> In the faith that looks through death,
> In years that bring the philosophic mind.
>> —"Ode: Intimations of Immortality"

In its later books, *The Prelude* makes little inquiry into the imagination's response to suffering. The philosophical and social problems of suffering—"Why is there evil in the world?" and "What causes suffering in the present constitution of society?"—largely replace literary and psychological speculations emanating from "What is the nature of my relation to the suffering in my poetry?" In Books IX and X, "Residence in France," human misery serves primarily as a pretext for the poet "to lament / What man has made of man." Beaupuis, pointing dramatically to the "hunger-bitten girl," says " 'Tis against *that* / Which we are fighting" (*Prel* IX: 518–519). "Vaudracour and Julia," despite its autobiographical elements, primarily depicts the tyranny of the *ancien régime*. In his reimagination of the September Massacres, Wordsworth conjures "up from tragic fictions" a nightmare vision out of *Macbeth*:

> And in such way I wrought upon myself,
> Until I seem'd to hear a voice that cried,
> To the whole City, "Sleep no more.'
>> [*Prel* X: 75–77]

Caught between the guillotine and the cannons of the British fleet at Wight, Wordsworth finds an appropriate image for human life, modern and ancient, in the sacrificial altar of the Druids, "fed with living men."

Faced by such a universe of death, Wordsworth follows his great forebears and attempts to justify and vindicate the ways, if not of God, of life, to Man. As M. H. Abrams notes, *The Prelude*, Book XIII particularly, presents "a theodicy transacted between mind and nature."[1] "Pain" is "Evil" only to "those / Who know not what they say" (XIII: 148–149), and *The Prelude* becomes

> this Song, which like a lark
> I have protracted, in the unwearied Heavens
> Singing, and often with more plaintive voice
> Attemper'd to the sorrows of the earth;
> Yet centring all in love, and in the end
> All gratulant if rightly understood.
>
> [*Prel* XIII: 380–385]

It is only natural that, as a would-be philosophical poet, Wordsworth would turn to the problem of evil. *Unde malum?* is the central question for the man who wants to believe in the benevolence of God and nature. Further, the drowning of his brother John in February 1805 gave the question personal urgency. A month after the event, he writes to George Beaumont:

As I have said, your last letter affected me much: a thousand times have I asked myself, as your tender sympathy led me to do, "why was he taken away?" and I have answered the question as you have done. In fact, there is no other answer which can satisfy and lay the mind at rest. Why have we a choice and a will, and a notion of justice and injustice, enabling us to be moral agents? Why have we sympathies that make the best of us so afraid of inflicting pain and sorrow, which yet we see dealt about so lavishly by the supreme governor? Why should our notions of right toward each other, and

[1] *Natural Supernaturalism* (New York: Norton, 1971). p. 112.

to all sentient beings within our influence differ so widely from what appears to be his notion and rule, if every thing were to end here? Would it be blasphemy to say that upon the supposition of the thinking principle being destroyed by death, however inferior we may be to the great Cause and ruler of things, we have *more of love* in our Nature than he has? The thought is monstrous; and yet how to get rid of it except upon the supposition of *another* and a *better world* I do not see. [*EL*, p. 556]

When suffering becomes a religious and philosophical problem, such considerations crowd out the issues of literary and psychological response that I have been raising. Human misery, taken as a reflection of man's fate, is far too serious for less significant questions to hold the field against it.

The primary example of this tendency is *The Excursion*, where the Wanderer and the Pastor unsuccessfully attempt to correct the pessimism and despondency of the Solitary.[2] The poem begins with the story of Margaret, but questions about the emotional response to pathos end with the text of *The Ruined Cottage*. *The Excursion*'s eight subsequent books explore the "choice of life" in a world full of evil and suffering. The story of Margaret in this context becomes less a story about a man telling a sad tale to another than an exemplum of the human condition.

Home at Grasmere (MS. B) tells three tales of husbands and wives uncoupled by death. The stories, two of which were later transferred to *Excursion* VI, are presented as proof that in his "happy valley" the poet's "heart" may

> Breathe in the air of fellow-suffering
> Dreadless, as in a kind of fresher breeze
> Of her own native element
>
> [ll. 449–451][3]

[2]Aside from the rather unsympathetic, prosecutorial tone used toward Wordsworth's failure to be a twentieth-century liberal existentialist, E. E. Bostetter's reading of *The Excursion* as an ultimately unsuccessful attempt to solve the problem of human suffering seems accurate. See *The Romantic Ventriloquists* (Seattle: University of Washington Press, 1963), pp. 66–81.

[3]The text used here is that of Beth Darlington, ed., *Home at Grasmere* (Ithaca, N.Y.: Cornell University Press, 1977), pp. 38–106.

The primary effort is to fulfill the wish of *The Prelude* for the poem that shall select "Sorrow that is not sorrow, but delight . . . / To hear of." Throughout, however, Wordsworth seems on the defensive; the *Recluse* fragment is pervaded by a profound sense that the suffering of the world defies optimistic, or at least human, interpretation. There is, no doubt, an attempt to justify human loss by a vague law of compensation; the poet finds in the family life of the widower and his six daughters evidence of divine benevolence:

> There Thou shalt have proof
> That He who takes away, yet takes not half
> Of what he seems to take, or gives it back
> Not to our prayer, but far beyond our prayer,
> He gives it the boon-produce of a soil
> Which Hope hath never watered.
>
> [ll. 547–552]

Seeing the "delightful family," he can claim to "feel— / Though in the midst of sadness, as might seem— / No sadness" (ll. 540–542). Here, as elsewhere in *Home at Grasmere*, one senses the fragility of the peace Wordsworth finds; continually, the "painful pressure from without" threatens to overwhelm the formulation of an earthly paradise.

Nowhere is the problem clearer or more poignant than in the uncertain questions Wordsworth poses as he interrupts the widow's tale:

> She then began
> In fond obedience to her private thoughts
> To speak of her dead Husband. Is there not
> An art, a music, and a stream of words
> That shall be life, the acknowledged voice of life?
> Shall speak of what is done among the fields,
> Done truly there, or felt, of solid good
> And real evil, yet be sweet withal,
> More grateful, more harmonious than the breath,
> The idle breath of sweetest pipe attuned
> To pastoral fancies? Is there such a stream,

Pure and unsullied, flowing from the heart
With motions of true dignity and grace,
Or must we seek these things where man is not?

[ll. 618–631]

The qualities Wordsworth now wants in poetry—purity, dignity, grace—are, he fears, not to be found in descriptions of human life. The "art" or "music" or "stream of words" he postulates is described only by questions, and the burden of those questions is that poetry can satisfy his demands only in celebrating "things where man is not." The difference between this and earlier discussions of the poetry of human suffering is striking. In *The Ruined Cottage* and the two-part *Prelude*, the focus is on the morality of pathos—the relationship of poet and reader to victim. The problem here has become the very different one of making the discordant voice of life sound sweet to human ears. One senses no great confidence in Wordsworth that such an art is within his reach.

Though in a sense it is the last lyrical ballad, *The White Doe of Rylstone*, too, shows concern with the metaphysical problem of suffering. Emily Norton is the final, perfect incarnation of Margaret: she learns what Margaret never quite does, to bury "torturing hope" and surrender herself to that peculiarly passive suffering that "has the nature of infinity." In *The White Doe*, philosophical ideas, particularly those of stoicism and quietism, are explicitly at issue in a way they rarely are in the *Lyrical Ballads*. Emily becomes for Wordsworth an exemplary figure:

This tragic Story cheered us; for it speaks
Of female patience winning firm repose;
And, of the recompense that conscience seeks,
A bright, encouraging, example shows;
Needful when o'er wide realms the tempest breaks,
Needful amid life's ordinary woes;—
Hence, not for them unfitted who would bless
A happy hour with holier happiness.

[*PW*, III, 282]

Everyone who tries to accomplish anything in *The White Doe*, the father in rebellion, the son Francis in his attempts to help his family, fails. Action is futile, and it is humanity's lot to suffer.

The general trend in Wordsworth's poetry after 1805 is toward suffering taken as a philosophical question and away from it as a problem of literary response and imaginative pleasure. With *The Prelude* ends Wordsworth's self-conscious investigation of his own fictions. In his later work, the philosophical problem of suffering proves a less fruitful center of speculation than the literary problems of suffering had earlier been. The frightful importance of the question and the overpowering burden of earthly evil lead first to the ungainly pontificating of *The Excursion* and then to the evasive triviality of many of the late poems. The play of mind, perhaps Wordsworth's greatest strength as a poet, is stifled; the willingness to experiment and to remain in suspension between ideas is lost. Nonetheless, Wordsworth's effort to discover the premises of his imaginative involvement with suffering had been admirable while he could sustain it, and it is remarkable that he was willing to look so long and deeply into the dark sources of his power.

Index

Wordsworth and the
Poetry of Human Suffering

Designed by Richard E. Rosenbaum.
Composed by The Composing Room of Michigan, Inc.
in 10 point Baskerville V.I.P., 3 points leaded,
with display lines in Baskerville.
Printed offset by Thomson/Shore, Inc. on
Warren's Number 66 Antique Offset, 50 pound basis.
Bound by John H. Dekker & Sons, Inc.
in Holliston book cloth.

Library of Congress Cataloging in Publication Data

Averill, James H   1947–
   Wordsworth and the poetry of human suffering.

   Includes index.
   1. Wordsworth, William, 1770–1850—Criticism and interpretation. 2. Suffering in literature. I. Title.
   PR5892.S93A94   821'.7   79-21783
      ISBN 0-8014-1249-8